Cov

His Bird Dogs
His Field Trials

by
John B. Criswell

Cass Hill
Stigler, Oklahoma

Library of Congress
Catalog Card No. 94-70859

ISBN 0-9633790-0-3 (Hardcover)

Printed in United States of America

PINE HILL PRESS, INC.
Freeman, S. Dak. 57029

Table of Contents

iv

Preface

The prairies.

Impelling vastness seems to roll on and on. Wolfwillow, buck brush, bluffs, grasses and purple sage brave the glorious and burning sun. Acres of summer fallow, in preparation for next year's grain planting, fade into slate-blue as they lift up the rolling hills to one side, or, far, far ahead. Skies are clear, but ominous gray-black clouds suddenly darken the day. Winds and rain follow, then the sun appears – and, lo, a rainbow, magnificent with both ends deep set in the horizon . . . the land of open spaces. The pinnacle of field trials is here.

George Rogers
The American Field
Saskatchewan, 1941

Foreword

I was really just a youngster when my father was diagnosed with Cancer, and had to stop riding a horse. The Southwest Championship was on his schedule, and I went to Booneville to handle the dogs.

Dad told me the best thing I could do was hire Cov and his scout, Roger. I followed his advise.

We were running Polaris Pete. He had a great find, and we were watering him. The front had moved on far ahead of us. As we were getting on our horses, Cov said:

"Walk that horse, boy. Heel this dog back slow. They'll get over the hill, and when you get there he'll just have enough time to cover that big bottom. He will go, won't he? You got this won if he does."

He confirmed what my Dad had already tried to teach me: Save the dog; know where you are, and, more importantly, know where you need to be.

Cov was one of the best dog men there ever was. He knew everything to do.

John Rex Gates
Gates-Eaton Plantation
Midway, Alabama

Introduction

Cov was Cov. A comedian with the timing of a Las Vegas big room star. Warm of spirit. Careful not to let it be noticed. Cantankerous when he thought it would help or teach. He was a field trial dog man for more than 50 of his years. For bird dogs and field trials and people who participated in them were his very life. In his youth he wanted to be a baseball star, and played in the minor leagues for a time. But, in a dispute over a teammate being moved from his position, he quit. Minor issue to some. Major to Cov.

Leon Covington was born near the Red River to an Oklahoma farm family. He trained bird dogs at McAlester – where he met and married a Spanish beauty, Lois Alasandro – near Poteau in Oklahoma, Booneville in Arkansas, Calhoun in Alabama, Caddo in Oklahoma, and on the Saskatchewan prairie. At all, he left friends – and tales in abundance.

He had an understanding of his craft that allowed him to win most of the major trials of his day, and to manage one of the major trials of his later years – the Saskatchewan Open Championship.

He did it all his way.

He was especially careful with a dollar, or even a quarter. He was generous with his stories, and each had the solid truth at its core. Cov needed little embroidery. His special language, and his husky, gravel voice made them live with humor. At his telling, a commonplace event turned to something hilarious, worth remembering, and telling times over. Except as recorded and transcribed, they can not be retold with the high degree of entertainment the original so generously provided. There is the loss of inflection, the timing and timbre of his voice.

Cov had a sense for recognizing extraordinary grounds for training or trials. Part of this remembrance of the man will include an accounting of the Saskatchewan Championship which he brought back to life in 1967, and superintended through 1982, his last season in Canada. It also includes his Oklahoma Puppy Classic, a Cov invention that worked.

Through his humor, his sense of purpose, his love for bird dogs and field trials, he inspired. He educated through his recollections.

He once said of Ches Harris, with whom he traveled as friend and partner, "I never knew how much I'd miss that old man."

Many never knew how much they would miss Cov. John Seawright, Thom Brower, Gary Parker, Freddie Epp, John Rex Gates, Perry Mikles III, Kendrick Doran, Tony Terrell, Bill Allen, Don Hickman, Al Kern.

This book is far from complete. For all who knew him have stories special to their relationship. It is dedicated to the memories of three of his special friends, and mine, Arlin Nolen, Dr. M. E. Gordon and Raymond Rucker.

This is but a reminder for those who were privileged to keep Cov's company, and a partial recollection for those who would have liked to.

John B. Criswell
Whileaway Farm
Stigler, Oklahoma 1994

Book I
Leon Covington
Bird Dog Man

Chapter 1

Lone Survivor

It is fitting that Cov's recollections of Lone Survivor be a starting point, for the liver-headed Pointer was a love of his life. It was a happy Leon Covington who learned that the dog had been elected to the Field Trial Hall of Fame—an honor the handler never concerned himself about for himself, though he richly deserves to join him.

The text of this chapter is from a recording. It was made in the summer of 1982. Cov came by the little house in Mortlach where I was staying. The language, if x-rated in a spot or two, and not politically correct in all ways, was the language of his time. Don Hickman was there, and Don was a new audience. He had not heard the story of Little Jack, and no situation pleased Cov more.

The story of his champion as he remembered it:

So I WAS telling Doc one day, I said, "Doc, the way ol' Jake is beatin' us, he's just pointin' more birds than Lone Survivor" . . . and he did.

He said, "Well, I'll tell you why that is. You drive by a hamburger joint goin' 50 or 60 miles an hour, you might not smell anything. But if you go by there about 15 or 20, you'll smell them hamburgers good. That's the way he's doin' it."

Jack was so fast, you see.

We'd get back in a second series, Jake'd point some birds and they'd order 'em up. I wouldn't even have Jack. He was fast as lightnin'. Every thing he done was fast. You never knew he pointed 'til he pointed. There wasn't no smellin' and messin' around. He'd just be running fast as he could, and just point. I couldn't tell it. Nobody else could.

Jake would foot scent around. If birds had been there, he'd mess around 'til he found 'em. Jack'd be on a quarter ahead. Jake had a loping gait. But he'd just dig up so many birds they'd have to place him. And he run big enough at times.

Take him in close country, woody country, he looked a hellu'va lot better. You could see him. Put Lone Survivor in a thick place, and you might not see him for 20 minutes. Lots of time he'd be gone too long and they'd count him out. You sent him a direction, he went that way. He didn't go out there and go somewhere else, or turn around and come back. He went on. I could send him anywhere.

I couldn't to start with. You know, I didn't get him until he was grown. He run loose on a farm. Didn't know nothin', including his name.

Slept on that farmer's front porch, winter and summer. The farmer got to tellin' Doc how that dog would run. Doc went out there one Sunday. He got a kick out of tellin' this. He went up there one Sunday to see the dog. You see, he thought the dog had died. They killed the whole litter, except him. Give too strong a worm pill. Jack happened to live.

Jack was layin' there on the front porch. The farmer had gone to church. Whistled to him and said, "Come on, Jack." He just looked at him and wouldn't move. Couldn't get him to follow him. Couldn't even get him off the porch. Wouldn't go a'tall. Said he fooled around there about an hour. The farmer come home.

"I thought you said that dog would run and hunt."

"He will."

"Well, I can't get him off the porch."

"I can. Whsssss, come here."

There was a big valley through the farm. He jumped off the porch and went down through the country and went out of sight.

Farmer said, "Just might as well wait, he'll be back."

Doc said, "Believe I'll take him home. Get him wormed."

He was poor. Full of worms.

"I'll get him cleaned up and send him to some dog trainer." He picked me to send him to. I didn't know Dr. Calame, and he didn't know me. He sent him over to Booneville.

4

You talk about wild. He'd be gone. You'd run him down and he'd lay down. Whistle, and he'd go on. He was just as liable to start running backwards. Any way. He hadn't ever gone with anybody. Just hunted by hisself all his life.

He didn't know what the hell you was doin', what you was out there for. We messed with him and messed with him.

I remember one day, it was during the field trial season, and we didn't have much time. We just worked on him when we got a chance. So, one mornin' Spot Settle, he worked for me then, said, "What do you want to put on the wagon this morning?" I had a dog wagon then that was pulled by two mules.

I said, "Put that little Jack dog on there."

He said, "What else?"

"That's all."

"We're gonna work him and quit."

We worked him 'til noon. Lost him half the time. We'd dig him up. He'd run rabbits. We'd hear him barking after a rabbit and we'd know where to go get him. He'd be after one. We'd make him quit.

About noon – I'd say we started about seven – we run him all mornin'. He was still running just as god damn fast as he could run. He got where he'd go with us just a little. Kinda learned what a horse was, and you up there on him. He'd kindly pay a little attention. At least we could see him a little more often.

I lived on one end of the grounds, and my kennel and wagon were at the other end. My mother and father lived over there. Kept dogs at both places. So, we got through eatin' lunch, Spot said, "What do you wanta work this evenin'?"

I said, "Put that little dog back on. We won't take the wagon. We'll just start from the kennel. We'll work that son of a bitch 'til he trots."

We worked him 'til dark – and he ain't trotted yet.

But he was doin' a little better about handlin'.

He was over at the other house when we turned him loose. I had two kennels, about a mile apart. In the evening we'd leave two dogs over there and the next morning we'd run two fresh ones back and then load the wagon at the main kennel.

I heard Spot call point down in a field. Jack had gone through a corn field just knocking stalks. There was a thicket down there about a city block square. Briars an' stuff. He went in

5

there. You couldn't ride a horse in it. Too damn thick. I heard Spot call point again. I thought, "awh, shit, he ain't in there." But I went anyhow.

I asked Spot, "Where's he at?"

"Awh, shit, he's done gone now."

I said, "What was he pointin'?"

"He pointed a rabbit. Listen. Can't you hear him runnin' it." He'd bark, you know. "Well, go get him. See if we can get him back."

I said, "By the way, how'd he look pointin'?"

"He's the prettiest son of a bitch you ever seen.

"Pointed with his tail stickin' straight up as he could stick it. Ain't a crook in it anywhere. Straight as a die."

I thought, hell, I've got a diamond in the rough here.

This Fall, I'll break him. We brought him up here to Canada. We got him fairly well broke. I wouldn't guarantee that he'd stand there very long.

I took him down to the field trial. They used to have a junior all age. That was for three-year-old dogs. I run him in the junior all age and won it. Old man Ed Farrior said it was the greatest prairie race he ever seen. I run him back in the all age and placed him second. I didn't run him in the championship because I was scared of the hour. He was gonna make a mistake in an hour. That's too long. You could get by with 30 minutes.

Got home and to working him on quail. He got better broke and better broke. But he was hell to handle. You just had to watch after him all the time. You know, don't take your eye off the dog and look back, he'd be gone and you wouldn't know where the hell he went.

I won about five or six field trials in a row with him. As fast as I could get to 'em he'd win 'em. He got a name. Everybody was talking about him.

Next year I brought him up here and he went plumb crazy. Couldn't do nothin' with him. Knocked chickens. Chased 'em off. Done everything. Well, I got back home with him. He was still knockin' quail. I was running him in trials and he was making mistakes. He'd have a bird pointed and jump in on it. Break shot. Do something wrong. They'd throw him out.

He was four years old, but it'd be like a three-year-old, you see. It'd be about like a Derby to him.

I told doctor, "Doctor, this dog has got off. What do you say, let's just lay him off. Don't run him any more. I'll keep working him. I'll get him back right again. Might take a little time."

"Hell, no. I got the money and you've got the time. Keep running him."

I won the National with him when he was nine years old. I could run him through the eye-hole of a needle then.

The year before I won, they had run us back in a second series with Stanton's Bud, that was another one of Ed Mack's dogs. We run and run and run. They run us 2 hours and 50 minutes in the second series. I couldn't point a bird at all. Ed Mack couldn't either. Dr. King, and, I think, Cecil (Proctor) was judging, and that guy from Memphis that judged a lot and wrote books on wildlife.

In a second series they can run you anywhere they want to. Backwards. Forwards. You don't have to run the right course. Stanton's Bud pointed in a little briar patch. Had to cross a little creek to get over there and he was standing right over there. I looked in them briars when I went by and I didn't believe they were there.

Clyde Morton said if I'd backed the other dog I'd won it. Lone Survivor was gone. They told me to go get him and bring him back, they wanted to see him back. I went and got him and when I got back, Ed Mack was standing there holding Stanton's Bud by the collar. Just standin' there. Just like a dog'd be standin'. He wasn't pointing or nothin'. Just standin'. I was watching my dog at heel. When I got up there as close as here to that house, I said whsst, and there was Ed Mack with the dog by the collar.

Well, he didn't even want to back. I could make him back if I was around there and got him in a cramp. But he wouldn't back no dog way over yonder by himself. He wouldn't knock 'em. He'd just ease up and get ahead. Steal a point. I knew he'd done it all the time. Long as they didn't catch him, I didn't give a damn.

The next year come around.

I told everybody that I wasn't going back with him no more. I said, "I've been messed around up there and I ain't gonna take this dog up there no more. They don't want to place him. There's something about him they don't like. To hell with 'em."

Lige, an old nigger that worked for Ches Harris for 35 years worked for me then. Good old fella. He'd worked dogs all his life. He was old then. He asked me that morning, said, "Mr. Cov, do you want me to load your saddle and stuff?"

I had a pickup truck there. Imbesi's. He kept one down there all the time. I knew I wouldn't have to take a horse cause Spot would be there with the Garnier's and they had a barn full of them old clumsy walkin' horses that Mrs. Garnier rode. He had good saddle horses. Course, he'd help me, too. Fact, he'd helped me break him, then he went to work for Mrs. Garnier.

So I didn't have to take a scout or a horse.

It was about 10 o'clock, I guess. They'd say something, them niggers would – I had four – about goin' up there. I said, "Just shut up talkin' about it. I told you I wasn't going and I'm not going. I don't want to hear any more about it."

I went on. In about 30 or 40 minutes, Lige walked up to me and said, "Mr. Cov, I helped Mr. Ches Harris win all of his National Championships, and I believe I know what it takes to win. That little dog will win it. I know they pushed you around, throwed you out and done things they shouldn't a done. This just might be your year. If he was mine, I'd walk from here to Grand Junction and lead him to get to run him. That's how much I think it."

He really had more experience than I had. He was up about 60 or 65 then. I guess I was about 30 or 35. Somewhere along in there. I got to thinking about it. Well, that old nigger might know what he's talking about. I started to walk off. I walked off a little piece, and turned around and looked back at him. He was standing there watching me.

I said, "Throw a saddle on there and load some dog food and load the dog. I'll go get me some clothes. I believe I'll go. Take your advise."

I drove in Grand Junction about dark. Them dog trainers were all around there, "Aw, we knew you was comin', shit."

I thought, "You don't know how close I come to not comin'."

I got lucky and drew him in the first day. Believe had eight finds, run a dog race that wouldn't quit. Course I went on back home. It lasted two weeks.

I'd get the Commercial Appeal every morning. One morning old Frank that used to write for 'em, had headlines. Said: "Lone

8

Survivor is laying in his kennel at Calhoun, Alabama, sayin' 'Boys, just try to beat me.'"

Well, I knew damn well nobody beat me up to that time. Nobody never did beat me either.

They'd been talking about he wouldn't back. I say now, he wouldn't when he was over yonder by hisself, but he'd back a dog if he knew I was around there somewhere.

So they decided to run him a second series and see if he'd back. Well, they went up there and got one of them old shootin' dogs that belonged to the Ames Plantation, an old yella-headed dog that looked like he was 10 or 15 years old.

A nigger was runnin' him, Charlie. He'd worked there all his life.

Dr. King said to me, "Mr. Covington we just want to see your dog back."

"I know what you want, doctor."

Clyde Morton had been shittin' me all evening . . . "You know what they're gonna do to you? They're gonna put one of them old shootin' dogs out there and he'll jump on old Jack and trail him and run him plumb out of the country."

I said, "That's what you think. I've got a different idea." I wasn't gonna let him run out of the country. I had him then where I could hollar at him and make him come back. He was flyin' across there. That old yella-headed dog hadn't gone nowhere til he started trailin' and barkin', but he stopped to shit and Jack got away from him. That plantation dog just pulled right here in some sage grass and pointed. Well, that's what I wanted him to do.

Charlie said, "I don't know if he's got any birds or not."

"That don't make any difference. I don't care. Can you make him just stay there, I don't give a damn if he's got birds. I'll get my dog and bring him in here and we'll get this over right here."

They hadn't been loose three minutes.

Well, I got back. Instead of riding plumb up there, I got off my horse, I'll bet as far from here to the corner. I could make him heel. I said "heel" and he walked right along beside me.

First he looked and seen the dog and backed him. Truly backed him. He actually backed that dog.

Somebody made a film of it and showed it to me one time.

9

Dr. King wasn't satisfied with that. He said, "Move him up a little closer, Mr. Covington. I don't believe he sees that dog."

I looked around and the old yella-headed son of a bitch was crawling in that sage grass and I could hardly see him and Jack couldn't. Doc told me again to move him up, he didn't believe he'd seen him.

I just walked a few steps. I said "whhhp." He started in there and stopped. He didn't any more see that dog than I did. I couldn't see him, and I know he couldn't, me standin' up and him on the ground.

He was standing there. He lost his style. He was more or less just standing there then, after he got to where he couldn't see the dog.

Dr. King tapped his leg. "Move him up just a little bit further."

I said, "Doctor, this dog has done seen that dog twice. He's backed him twice, now he's in there layin' down somewhere. I can't see the dog and neither can this 'en. I'm not going to move him any more."

He was a dog that'd get a little mad if you messed with him.

He was liable to run in there and knock 'em. I knew, that, too.

I thought, "god damn it, if you're gonna throw me out and this dog out, you're gonna do it with me and this dog standin' right here in our tracks. I ain't screwin with him no more."

They turned around and said something to each other. I never did hear 'em announce it. Bill Brown rode out of the gallery and congratulated me.

So I just took the dog, and Spot rode up on his horse and rode up the birds. The old shootin' dog had done gone by 'em.

People will tell you Jack pointed the birds himself.

He didn't point the birds. He didn't no more smell them than I did. They was far as here to them trees and off to the side. That old dog had crawled by and missed 'em."

Chapter 2

A Canadian Conference

*ONE EVENING DURING the running of the 1975 Saskat-
chewan Championship, Cov came to my room, as was his usual
habit, at the Midland Motel. It was actually two rooms. The
Moens had remodeled, but left the kitchen in the back of this
one, and I had it during the summer. Marshall Loftin came
by. Bill Allen was already there. Garland Priddy stopped in.
Canadian was available and as the conversation got going, Collier Smith opened the door: "I believe this is better than televi-
sion." I turned on a tape recorder and placed it on the floor
near the edge of the bed where Cov was propped up. The opening subject was Cecil Proctor. The transcript:*

Loftin: You'd see a bunch of dog trainers saddle their horses
and be holding them sons-a-bitches and alookin'. He didn't never
drive up on the grounds 'till about 5 minutes to 8. And when
he did that chauffeur took the horse and he stepped up on
it. It was at the startin' line. There wasn't none of that at-the-
barn business. He was at the startin' line. He had his book.
He squared himself in that saddle, looked at the book and looked
down at the dog. You'd better not say, "I'm comin." Cause it
was your ass. When he squared himself in the saddle, you'd
better have the dog right there.

Cov: When he rode up, you'd better be ready. If it was 7:30,
or 8, or whatever he had said, he'd just say, "Turn 'em loose,
gentlemen."

I'll tell you what he done to me one time. He was such
a great judge I got to love him. But then I hated his guts
sometimes, too.

At Stillwater there was a shortcut you could take and go across a neck of the lake. Well, it rained all night. I didn't know the lake was up. They was just right over there, but you had to drive one mile this way and one mile back to get there. I was in just a little distance but I didn't want to wade that damn creek. I could have lead him over there but I didn't. I said, "Just a minute, I can't get across the creek. I'll be there in just a minute."

Eight o'clock come and they turned the damn dogs aloose. I got there and there they rode off, down through yonder. I don't remember what dog it was, but I told whoever was helping me, "Jump the son of a bitch out here. Let's go. We'll catch up."

Hell, I'll guarantee you they hadn't gone no further than from here to that highway, the other highway over there. I rode up, and he said, 'Mr. Covington, your dog is not running under judgment.' "

I sez, "What?"

"No, you got here late."

I said, "I'll just spot you the five minutes."

"No. You can't do that. Your dog wouldn't run the full hour."

I said, "Hell with the full hour."

"No, he won't be in judgment. You weren't here on time, you'd just be running 55 minutes."

"Well, I'll just run the son of a bitch anyhow."

You know I was about half mean then, too. I wasn't really scared of anybody.

He said, "Ok, Mr. Covington, but your dog won't be under judgment in this trial."

Loftin: Never raised his voice at nobody in his life.

Cov: I run him there about 20 minutes, then I thought, "Aw, hell, this is useless," and I just quit. He ain't gonna look at him. So I took him up.

Loftin: I'd a loved for Hoyle Eaton to have to run under him.

Cov: I would, too. I'd like a lot of these damn boys to have to run under him. I'll tell you that. When they took off across the prairie in front of him, just rode off, he'd just start lookin' down at the ground and never look up another lick. That was the end of you. You was through. You might as well go get that dog, if you could get 'em. He wasn't gonna put up with it.

Loftin: You know, on so many things, he was pretty smart.

Cov: Pretty smart. He was smart as hell.

Loftin: Let me tell you what happened to me one time. You might have had it happen some time or 'nother. I was running a Setter, a Derby. Had him broke. Dog went up a fence row and we were fixin to cross a road. There was a high bank there. He run up to the edge of it and pointed a covey or birds, or, was pointin'. Mr. Proctor was judgin'.

Jack Harper was braced with me. He was running a damn little old dog, runnin' around there, and he run up and smelled him and he got up on my dog and went to screwin' him standing right there. That son of a bitch didn't know what was takin' place. He jumped off and run up and down the fence row. Jack was trying to get him to stop. Finally my dog just laid down. Finally, when Jack caught his dog, my dog stood right up.

The birds had to be right there in front of him, or none, I figured. I climbed the fence and no birds. Bank was high as that door. Mr. Proctor had gone around and come up the road where he could see the birds.

I said, "Mr. Proctor, I don't know, them birds must be across the road. Would it be all right if I just put my dog across the road by hand?"

He said, "Go ahead . . . " or somethin' like that. I just reached over the fence and picked my dog up under my arm . . . a little 'ol bitty Derby. I jumped off this bank and landed right in Mr. Proctor's lap; hit the road, whop. The big covey of birds settin' just across the road went everywhere, me with the dog under my arm. I looked at Mr. Proctor and said, "What would like for me to do now?"

He said, "Put your dog on the ground, shoot your gun and let's go."

I put him down. Loaded. Shot my gun, and we went on. Won the stake, too.

Cov: Tell 'em about how you beat me out of that $10 over there at Booneville. I was runnin' Goober, (Wholesaler) wasn't I?

Loftin: Yea, it was him.

Cov: It was a qualifyin' thing, you know. I run old Goober just before noon. They brought him back in the two hours right after noon. I told 'em it was against the rule of that trial. I'd made the rules for the Southwest. Couldn't run a dog back in a second series the same day. But it didn't make any difference, they run him back just after lunch, first brace. Ole'

Goober was a little tired, maybe. They run him with Storm Trooper. Frank Dempsey broke him. John (Gates) didn't break 'im. I argued like hell. I told 'em, hell, he just got thru running an hour, why didn't you just run him three hours he coulda made it then.

Storm Trooper blinked a covey of birds right off. No question about that. Cold blinked 'em. Mr. Proctor liked Marshall. He'd tell Marshall a little bit. But he wouldn't tell nobody else.

Storm Trooper had seven or eight finds. One or two was rabbits and one was a house chicken. Ole' Goober was doin' pretty good. He was still a knockin'.

Loftin: He was goin' right on, it looked like, through the two hours.

Cov: Damn sure was. Wasn't pointin' many birds. We got on down there in the bottom, over there on the left. We had about a half hour to go and Goober got to pointin' hell out of them birds. Mr. Proctor was wantin' to get rid of him anyhow, I think. He kept pointin' them birds. Pow. I'd shoot and we'd go to the next ones. Pow. I kept on shootin'. Scotty Burgess was judgin' with him. Mr. Proctor came over there to see what was goin' on.

Loftin: And Tom Woodside, all three of 'em.

Cov: Yea, he was. Mr. Proctor came over there to see what was goin' on. He wasn't goin' to come over there and look at the dog till all that started. Well, about ten minutes to go and ole' Goober run outa gas. He did.

Loftin: We started back to the club house.

Cov: Yea, and he liked you. I don't know why, but he did.

Marshall was in the car with him. Didn't he tell you, "Son, you've seen a great dog race today." I don't know what you said. I guess nothin'.

Loftin: I didn't say a damn word.

Cov: Great dog race, hell. He blinked a covey of birds to start with. I'll tell you what he done. He went in there and pointed them birds to start with. The birds got up, and that sob ducked his tail and left there. "Excuse me. I'm sorry I found these." Well, I was lookin' right at him. So was Mr. Proctor. I knew that there couldn't be no way that a man could place a god damn dog running off and leavin' a covey of birds.

Loftin: I come over there where you were, and you said: "I know who won this stake." I said: "I'll bet you ten dollars I have."

14

Cov: I'll call that.

What dog you got? Marshall said, "That dog that run with you." I said, "Hell, they can't place him. He blinked a covey of birds sure as hell and Mr. Proctor seen him. I know he won't place a dog like that.

Damn if he didn't win it.

Loftin: Yes. And I collected, too.

But now let me tell you somethin'. I don't like to be wrong.

Cov: I don't either.

Loftin: I want to go back and correct you You told that wrong. You run that dog just before dinner.

Cov: That's right.

Loftin: They called back six dogs in a second series. In the first brace was Tiny Wahoo and John Gates had a dog called LaBaron. Ok. They called Goober back and they called Storm Trooper back. Then they called, to run the next mornin', Susan Peters and, I can't think . . . What you got so mad about was they called ole' Goober back the same day he run. And it wudn't right. They coulda waited and run the next mornin'. They had one left to run then. But they didn't run him back right after dinner, cause we turned loose right behind the barn toward Henscratch. Tiny Wahoo went to that mountain to the right and they didn't see him no more. LaBaron didn't do nothin. Just quit.

John Gates went on, and I thought he was a fool. I was just young, and I thought "why don't he pick the sob up." He just rode that old white horse and kept goin'. Never picked him up. Went all the way up Henscratch, all the way up Cox' valley. Came back outa that thicket, crossed the valley. When we got over in that open country just after you come back over the mountain, he said, "Mr. Proctor, this dog is sick. I believe I'll pick him up."

He just got to that good country. He turned loose Storm Troop and you come through there with Wholesaler right down behind where you used to live. Come behind the club house and down on the mornin' course.

Cov: I remember comin' through there. You're right.

Loftin: See, John run a little over an hour. What John done, he got through that old bad course, got out there in that good country. Boy, he was tough.

Cov: Now I didn't know Mr. Avant. He was before my time, really. Mr. Ed (Farrior) told me this story.

They was runnin' some trial somewhere. Mr. Avant led this little setter bitch out there. wasn't as big as a piss ant. Turned her loose. She just walked out there about as far as that car and started eating grass. He said, "Gentlemen, somebody has pisoned my little dog. I've got to take her up."

Loftin: Bill Cosner told one about him that I thought was pretty good. Somebody had a stud dog they was pushin'. A guy come to Mr. Avant and said, "Have you had any puppies off'a that dog?" He answered real slow, "Yeah."

"Have you had many of 'em?"

"Yeah. A whole well full."

Cov: Mr. Avant had a dog called "Ringo" that followed him ever where he went. Field trial and all. Just followed him. He'd lose a dog and he'd put ole Ring on him. He'd pick up the track. He'd run him, you see. Bark, too. Just like a fox hound. When he found the dog pointin', he'd just up and set down. Just set there.

Well, Mack Pritchett, Ed Farrior and those boys got it out that they was gonna kill Ringo. Well, Mr. Avant found out about it. He was gonna turn a dog loose to run in a trial. He rode out in front of the gallery, and said, "Gentlemen, I understand that some of these dogs trainers is gonna kill ole' Ringo.

"I suggest they not do that."

I'll tell you, Ches Harris was a good 'en. He could pull more stuff. I seen him up here one time, when Clyde was winnin' everything. He was tough to beat, don't think he wudn't. They was runnin' together out there, right up here on these prairies.

Clyde was kinda a fast handler. Ches called it "dancin' around out there on a horse." Back and forth. "There he goes, judges. You see him over yonder goin' around that bush?" Chess growled his dog'd done been around that bush.

Loftin: Collier, you're Daddy would tell you the same thing if he was settin' here. This man right here, has put the monkey on more judges' back than anybody in the world. I've seen his dogs mess up, and him even make the judge think it was his fault. Dog be over there pointin', the birds get up and leave or somethin' or other, he'd hollar "you're ridin so damn slow the birds have done gone. Get up here where you can see somethin'." He was runnin' out here. Found his bitch and she laid down. When the judge got there. Oh, he was givin' 'em hell for ridin' so slow. Said "she just got tired waitin' on you."

Smith: Yeah, and I was the scout. He had that huntin' coat stickin' out in back coming down through there. Believe he was riding that big horse he got from Bud Epperson.

Loftin: It was always somethin'. He could get 'em feelin' sorry for him.

One time he didn't have Clyde feelin' so sorry. I'd take hounds over there and sell 'em to him in the spring of the year. Mr. Clyde and I were riding along together. Cov running Rampaging over at Selma. Everybody said he wouldn't be running at the end of three hours, and somebody said he wouldn't be alive at the end of three hours, much less runnin'. Clyde come along there. He had run that old orange dog and he had run out of gas. He thought that was the best they had.

Cov: It was.

Loftin: I'll tell you right where we were. Comin across the bridge there onto the mornin course at dinner time, where you come down the road a little ways turn up toward the bee hives. "It sure is remarkable. I'd a never thought he'd a done it. You know, I didn't think Cov was that smart. You know, he's done a great job of handlin' here today. Do you realize that he has never let that dog go in no bad footing all mornin'. Every time he's sent that dog away, he's sent him the easy footing. Pointed some birds, too. Hasn't let him get in a bit of cover. Look at him. Goin' on pretty good, ain't he?"

Went right on past the beehives. Cov rode over there.

"Point over here." Flushed them birds.

"Pick him up."

"I'd never thought he'd a done that."

Criswell: Did you help him run Paladin?

Cov: Yeah. In the National.

I don't think I had over one dog. I ran mine the first day. I knew he didn't do anything.

Clyde said, "What you gonna do tomorrow?"

"I'm going home."

"Oh, Cov," you know how he could whine. "Oh, Cov, will you stay over here and help me? If Freddie's right in the mornin' we can win this."

17

I said, "Well, Clyde, I'll stay and help you. I can get home in a half a day."

"Now I don't want you to leave the gallery. Man and I'll take care of it. You just ride in front of the gallery and take care of him if he gets up there."

"All right, I'll do what you say."

Well, we turned the damn dog aloose. He ran about as perfect a dog race as I ever seen. What he was doin' was runnin' them horse tracks.

We lived not far from each other and I'd be up there in the evenings. He'd go on about what a great dog race Freddie'd run. I got tired listnin' to it.

"Hell, he didn't do a damn thing but run them horse tracks and point the birds that was alongside 'em"

He looked up kinda shocked.

"I didn't know anybody noticed that. You know, they need to do that to stay in front up there."

You know, John Gates hardly ever said anything to a judge. When he did, he was usually right, and got on 'em good.

He told me one time, "You know, Cov, if we were in the room where we could hear these judges discussing these stakes before they announce the winners, hell, we'd quit running."

One time Mr. Proctor got on me about scoutin'. You boys wouldn't scout under him like you do out there now. When you got level with him, that's as far as you went. You could ride all over the country, but when your scout got in front, he'd say, "Whose boy is that out there?"

He knew everybody's scout. Seemed like he looked back as much as he looked forward. He knew your scout, and if he was gone, he'd ask you where he was. "Where's that boy of yours?"

I always said, "I don't know."

"You'd better know. Get him in here."

I kept telling Bill to quit slippin' out of the gallery. That's when he called me a little black-headed sob.

He'd been telling me all day not to do that. Took the dogs up. He was settin on a horse and I was on the ground, pointin' right down at me: "Now, you keep that boy in the gallery."

"Mr. Proctor, I'm not tellin' that boy to go out."

"I didn't say a thing about that. I said keep him in this gallery.

18

"I'm trying the best I can."

"I don't want no more of that."

I was about half pissed off by then.

"Now look. Damit, I'm looking forward. I can't look backwards and forwards all at the same time."

He said, "You god damn little black-headed sob, you've been doin' that all your life. I want you to quit. I ought to throw all your dogs out."

I did get a little hot.

He said, "I'll get down off this horse." That really got to me. I was 26 or 27 years old. I could fight like hell.

"I'll tell you what you do. You just get down."

He grunted and rode off.

I still say he's the greatest judge I ever seen in my life.

Loftin: Sure he was.

I'll tell you what he'd do. He had a body guard for a chauffeur.

Cov: You see, he was in the gamblin business.

Loftin: When he stepped down off that horse out yonder, you wasn't about to walk up and ask him about anything. You was scared to. We respected him.

That body guard held the horse and helped him off. He opened the door of that Cadillac automobile, and Mr. Proctor got in. Here he come to his motel room. You didn't go to that room. He didn't go out of that room, except when he left to eat. Him and that guy would eat, and sometimes whoever was judging with him would eat with 'em. But I'll tell you what, you wouldn't dare walk in there and set at the table with him.

Cov: No, sir, you wouldn't.

When he was judgin' he had nothing to do with no dog trainers, handlers, or owners, either.

Loftin: No, sir. No owner could no more carry him out and buy his supper than nothin' in the world.

Cov: Marshall, were you over there at Booneville the time the cook burned the restaurant?

Loftin: Yeah, I was there. Sure was.

Cov: Well, he and this fella was settin' there eating. They were in the dining room.

Loftin: Tom Woodside was eatin with 'em.

Cov: Same time you screwed me out of that ten bucks.

He had his back to the kitchen. Eating a steak.

Loftin: Nobody would be goin up talking to him either

19

Cov: He didn't want you to talk to him.

The cook set the kitchen afire.

Loftin: He run next door and got some stuff and come back and squirted it on the fire. It really went then.

Cov: Somebody said, "The buildin's afire. It's gonna burn up."

He said to this fella settin with him, "You say the buildin's afire?"

"Yes, sir, Mr. Proctor. It's afire. Looks like it's gonna burn up."

He got up. Layed a ten-dollar bill on the table. Never looked back. Walked right down the street to his motel.

Never did look back. Burned up a whole city block.

He never commented. Never looked back to what the fire was doin. No nothin. Just went to the motel.

He was a wonderful man. But he was the hardest son of a bitch you ever seen to talk to.

Loftin: At one time it looked like dog trainers were gonna run out of business. There wasn't gonna be no trainers. Every trainer in the business was gettin' old. When I started it was me and Roy Jines and Gene Lunsford. Looked like the only ones left. Looked like Mr. Proctor could see what was happening, and he took a likin' to me. Believe it or not. You'd never know it.

Cov: He'd let Marshall ride with him once in awhile. You know, in the evenin' when they were goin' in, to the club house.

Loftin: I'd never say nothin. But every once in awhile he'd say somethin to me.

One time Bob Lee run a dog and he was comin backwards, this way. Dog was on a pretty good cast, comin around a woods line. Bob was pointin' him out.

"Yonder he comes. Right around there."

"Son, son. I can see good out there. But I got a bad neck and can't see nothin' back yonder."

Cov: He didn't want to look back there.

Loftin: Hell, no. Dog wasn't supposed to be back there.

He said one time, "You know, lots of folks don't like to judge with me because I don't like to wait back.

"You know why?

"I like to see the winner."

Cov: He wouldn't wait back long, either. He figured if you was back there you wudn't winnin.

20

Loftin: A dog'd be standing there pointin' a covey of birds. Mr. Proctor 'd look at the dog. You got down and went and flushed. He'd watch the dog. You flushed them. If you was out yonder at them trucks when the birds got up and shot your gun. He'd look at the dog.

That dog could lay down and turn summersets, roll over and play dead. He didn't care.

Cov: He left there.

He'd tell you, every time, when you shot that gun, if the dog didn't drop or do somethin' wrong, he'd wheel that horse and say, "Gentleman," or Mr. Covington, or whoever, "bring your dog on to the front." He'd ride off and leave you.

If you had a find on the way up there, he wouldn't come back and see it.

Loftin: What I'm sayin', Cov, is that so many of these people are putting so much emphasis on when you're goin back to your dog his tail drops or he wiggles around. Mr. Proctor didn't even see the dog then.

Cov: He said your work was over when you shot your gun. And that is right. I think that's right today. It was up to you to get him to the front – and you'd better get him up there, too. If you wanted to win anything.

Ain't no telling how many times I've run under him. Thousands, I guess. He'd tell you to do something. If you couldn't get it done like he told you . . . in other words, he'd say, "Get your dog up there," and you couldn't do it, he'd just drop his head and ride off. You was out.

I still say he was the smartest judge I ever run a dog under – and I could hate his guts.

Loftin: There was only one thing wrong that I could see. When he seen a dog, a dog he liked and wanted to place, and the other judge didn't want to place him, he was smart enough to crook the other guy and get the dog he wanted placed. He'd just outsmart the other judge.

Smith: They tell a story on him being down in Texas somewhere. He and the other judge was locked up on a decision. The other man's dog had about five minutes to go and his got lost. He went in, and they announced the decision before the other judge got back.

Loftin: I was there. It was the Texas Championship. They were all runnin' around there gettin' ready to go home when the other judge come back.

Mr. Proctor was on his way to Oklahoma City.

Cov: He never carried a pencil. Never wrote anything down in his life time.

Loftin: When he and the other judge got crossed up on a pair of dogs, say me and Garland there was running a couple of dogs, one was a short-runnin' dog and the other was a big runnin' dog . . .

Criswell: Which did he like?

Cov: Big running dog. Oh, he liked 'em to run.

Loftin: . . . which ever one he wanted to place, if he thought yours was a runaway dog and he wanted to place the other, he'd get around the field marshal and say they were gonna run a second series. "We want to start over here in these woods."

Cov: He'd put you in a thicket.

Loftin: If it was the other way, and he wanted to place that big-running dog, he'd pick the openest course there.

Cov: Course in a second series you could run on any course the judges said.

He didn't want his judgment beat.

He'd prove to you that his judgment was right all the time. He'd usually be so much smarter that the other one wouldn't know what was happening.

Criswell: When you had Jack and Ed Mack had Jake, how many second series do you suppose you ran in?

Cov: Oh, good lord, I don't know. I don't have no idea.

But he liked Lone Survivor the best.

Loftin: He loved that little dog.

Cov: I'd drive a thousand miles to run under him. Lone Survivor was his kinda dog. He liked a real, shore-nuf running dog, but he wanted him to handle, though.

Loftin: He liked a snappy dog.

Cov: Fast.

Loftin: Jake was lopey; kinda heavy footed.

Cov: He beat me in a second series on three legs one time. Like to have killed Mr. Proctor.

We was over in Arkansas. They didn't run on Sunday. We got through Saturday afternoon. Mr. Proctor wanted to give it to me. They had three judges. One of the sobs didn't want

22

to give it to me. He wanted to give it to Jake. The other fella, so I found out later, it didn't make much difference to him.

I'll tell you how it was. Little Jack was just eatin' that country up and pointin' the shit outa birds. Come up to a feed patch up there by the church, you know exactly where it is. He'd been gone. I didn't know where. Oh, we knew he was ahead of us. Just didn't know where.

I rode around and there he stood. There was a whole bunch of gallery, cars in the road. Spot Settle, who used to work for me, but worked for the Garnier brothers then, said, "Old man, the birds left that dog." Hollered loud. The Judge and everybody could hear him.

I said, "where'd they go, Spot?"

"Lit right in that thicket right up there ahead of you."

I didn't even try to flush. I just jumped off, had to crawl through the fence, and just touched him on the head and that son of a bitch flew outa there like you'd shot him in the ass with a cannon. Before I could get back on my horse, they said, "He's pointin' up here."

Well, hell, I got up there and had to crawl over the fence again. Flushed a single bird right under his nose. Shot. Well, he had a habit, and I don't mind tellin' this, he didn't break shot or nothin like that, but he just wanted to go so bad he didn't want you getting ahold of him.

Loftin: Walk a little bit on you wouldn't he.

Cov: Yeah, once in awhile he would. I knew all this. When I reached, he ducked his head just like that. I grabbed right quick. Well I missed him. He just went on hunting. This other judge said he broke shot. Mr. Proctor said he didn't.

Mr. Proctor got off the horse and he had crossed that fence. He said, "Wait just a minute here." Well, he was standing just as close as that chair. He knew exactly what went on. Dog didn't break shot. He just ducked me when I went to grab for his collar.

Well, they argued and argued there all the night I guess. Called it off til the next morning, which was Sunday and they couldn't run anyway.

They said have Lone Survivor and Warhoop Jake on the first mornin' course Monday morning.

I lost mine on the god damn breakaway. Ed Mack out smarted me. He wouldn't let old Jake go nowhere, didn't go

23

nowhere anyway. He kept him right with him and he pointed five coveys of birds while I was tryin' to find mine. ♦

I'd thought "I'm gonna take the bridle offa mine. Let him roll." I can see that little son of a bitch goin down that draw right now. He was mortally flyin'. We made that turn in that bottom and I didn't have no dog.

But what I wanted to tell you, Mr. Proctor stayed with me. We'd made the turn and lost him. We was hunting him. Mr. Proctor was mad at me cause I couldn't find him. He wanted to place him. He was right to start with, so help me, he was. He waited there on me. We started hunting him. I went way over there, and come back by. Mr. Proctor was right there.

"You got him?"

"No, sir, I ain't got him."

He said, "Well, get him. Hurry up."

We hunted again. I knew that country like a book. I'd trained on it for seven years. I knew every path. Every gate. Everything in there. We just couldn't find him. I went back by him again.

He said, "You got him?"

"No, sir."

"Well, god damn it, get him."

But we couldn't.

They say he waited 48 minutes on me. He was wantin' me to find that dog.

I told that boy that was helpin' we'd might as well quit, I guessed they'd counted us out anyhow. I heard a dog pantin', look around and there he come. Just too late.

Note: In Cov's story about Lone Survivor and Warhoop Jake at the Southwestern, the year was 1951. The judges were Proctor, S. F. Mitchell, Frank C. See. Jack Downs reported the championship, which drew 31 entries. There had been a first series of an hour, a second series of two hours, and Downs described the controversial last find as he "surged forward a pace at shot."

The third series was on a Friday morning described as:

"The sun was out on Friday morning, but cold, crisp day. Temperatures hovered around 18 degrees early. Ice sealed the shallow pools and ponds, the ground was frozen, and high, cutting winds prevailed. We were ahorse at 8:34." He quoted Judge Proctor on the announcement of the final series:

"We'll let them fight it out under identical weather and running conditions." Of the event:

"After casting to a wooded creek, the former (Lone Survivor) vanished and that was the last we saw of him." It was the second consecutive win of the title for Warhoop Jake. The year before, Lone Survivor was runner-up.

Chapter 3

The Canada File

COV HAD A love affair with Canada. He learned it was the place to be with bird dogs in the summer, and he never wavered.

In the early trips, he had the best of help. Usually two black scouts signed on, licensed as assistants.

Lois kept a file of the correspondence she exchanged each year with whoever was in charge at the Department of Natural Resources in Regina. The file was among the field trial things she left to me.

The first is a yellowed sheet, a carbon of the letter she wrote for Cov to Mr. W. A. Hartwell, district superintendent, August. 16, 1954:

"I am returning herewith my Non-Resident Dog Trainer's License No. 29 for 1954. I have changed my training grounds to Mortlach, Sask. Below is a description of the location of my grounds:

"All of Township 18, Range 1, West 3rd.

"I would appreciate your either changing the description in the attached license or making me a new license and forwarding it to me at Mortlach, Sask."

License No. 29 is attached to Mr. Hartwell's reply, the description at Aylesbury, Sask., crossed over. The license was a formal document, provided under the provisions of "The Game Act" and the authorization was to "train or run bird dogs" on the specified land "after July 15th, 1954."

The Covingtons lived at Calhoun, Alabama., in the winter, and, for the summer of '55, got licenses – at $5 each – for two assistant trainers, Lonnie C. Key of Ft. Deposit, Alabama., and Bill Loy of Calhoun. They had sent the government $63 in license fees, and Mr. Hartwell's letter said that "upon checking foreign exchange we find an over remittance of $1.82 which will be forwarded to you in due course." Lois had sent an added $3 to cover rate of exchange. "This is figured at 5%."

There were to be many differences between the Canadian government and the Covingtons, usually of the denomination of a dollar or so.

In May of '55, Hartwell had written a form letter addressed "To All Dog Trainers." It went to those who had trained dogs in the province before and asked that the fees be paid by June 30, and in Canadian currency.

"The Department insists that all Assistant Dog Trainers be properly licensed. We define an Assistant Dog Trainer as any person who assists a Dog Trainer either in handling, caring for or feeding the dogs, anyone who assists in or about the camp of a Dog Trainer."

In '56, Earnest Harris and Leman MacSwain were the assistants. The next year, it was Roosevelt McCall and Mac-Swain. But McCall obviously backed out, and the license was changed to Roger Reed, who was to become a long-time scout, and who exchanged .410 rounds with Cov after the '68 championship. In 1959, Uriah Reed and Glenn Stallworth were the assistants. The next summer Reed and Stallworth were along, with the addition of Henry Givan.

Arnold Gamble of Moose Jaw, owned the house they occupied in '57, and Lois wrote Sept. 12, "I am enclosing one key to the new lock on the door. I will leave your old lock on the kitchen cabinet on the inside of the house.

"We decided to leave tomorrow and also decided not to move our things over until we get here next summer. That will give you more time to move whatever things you want. I certainly would appreciate it if you would leave the coal cooking range, the coal heater and the kitchen cabinet there. We can make some deal on them next summer."

Next May, the deal was struck by Cov writing Mr. Gamble about the house and fixtures. He answered on the back that the stove, heater and cabinet were there, plus a cabinet with a sink.

She made a hand-written list called "Fees to be paid at Canada customs:

"$2 ea bond on dogs (value $800) Typewriter $15 Saddles and bridles $15 410 shotgun $2 Brownie camera $5

"Value of truck, car. papers on both. value low. Date of return — Oct 1"

But 1958 at Mortlach was not a good year for game. July 26, Cov wrote Mr. Hartwell:

"I was wondering if you knew of any training grounds anywhere. I thought perhaps you might know of some grounds that a trainer is not using this year.

"We are just not finding any birds at all, maybe one or two old birds a day — some days not any. I just can't understand it. Last year there were plenty of birds here and the farmers say there were plenty of birds here in the early spring, but they sprayed all of this hay land country and all of the crops for grasshoppers and the farmers tell me that it ran all of the birds off or killed them, because they noticed that right after the spray, they did not see any more birds. So I believe that the spray either killed them or they all left on account of it."

Hartwell replied that he couldn't help with new grounds, but they would look into the spraying.

In '60, "Since there was so much land fenced up at Mortlach last year, I used the little bit of land around Aylesbury which I had been on six years ago, however, at Mr. W. B. Hyshka's suggestion, I filed on both pieces. I will not know until I get there where I will be, but will advise you. If you know of any grounds available, I would appreciate very much your advising me."

Hyshka was the conservation officer at Moose Jaw, and he had helped referee a dispute over some chickens killed the summer before. Cov didn't want to pay the farmer's price and wound up with the Mounties involved. As the story goes, the arbitration went Cov's way and he wrote the farmer a check, which he promptly threw on the ground. Cov referred to it in a letter:

"We have not heard any more from our friend Mr. Spearman, however, he never has cashed the check. No doubt he will file a suit against us when we get there."

For those who have gone to the Mortlach grounds, Mr. Spearman lived east of what came to be known as chicken row, near Pelican Lake. Remnants of the old house and barn remained for years.

Their camp was moved back to Mortlach in late July of '60, and '61 seemed uncertain as to location:

"I am planning on moving south of Valjean on the grounds that Barney Moseley used three or four years ago. I wonder if it would be possible to hold the grounds open until I can get up there and see if I can find a house to live in on these grounds. I am leaving for Canada on June 25th, and should be there June 30th."

On July 7:

"Please change my Canadian residence address from Mortlach to Aylesbury . . ."

By 1967 he had established what was to be a long-term summer residency at Mortlach, and struck up an arrangement with friends in Moose Jaw and Victor Eastmond, who owned the farm center to Cov's grounds, to renew the Saskatchewan Championship.

In '71, the Canadian government, in one of its many periods of change, wrote the trainers, "There seems to be an increasing demand each year for the available training grounds in Saskatchewan and we would ask that you complete the attached form and return it with your remittance not later than June 15, 1971, to ensure your grounds will be available for you . . . If we have not heard from you by June 15, we will assume you will not be returning to Saskatchewan . . . "

In April, Cov replied:

"I want my same grounds that I have had for many years north of Mortlach, Sask. In this small town I have no way of obtaining Canadian currency, therefore I always file on my grounds and remit as soon as I get to Canada, which is the first part of July. However, I want it recorded that I want my same grounds. Also at this time I do not have the names of my helpers."

The small town was Caddo, where he had recently moved to the Stuart Ranch, several thousand acres of ideal quail country in southeastern Oklahoma. His friend, Mr. Hartwell had retired or changed jobs, and a D. G. Wyllie had replaced him.

Records for the '50s are complete. Correspondence kept up. That changed as the years went by until in the early '70s there was an apparent lack of attention to detail. Lois had found a bottle of bourbon to be a good friend while living in Alabama, and the move to Caddo brought on a virtually constant bout with liquor that lasted until she became ill at the end of the decade.

Cov was drinking more during those years, and age helped make it difficult to perform as he had in the past. Patrons dwindled, and he was more irritable over details – and the hovering threat he felt about the possibility of not being able to go to Canada. It would be the greatest loss he could imagine.

When he received a letter in early '73 covering the Canadian requirements, including the need for $100,000 in liability insurance, he wrote the regional superintendent, G. J. Fladager:

"As to the $5 you stated we would have to put up on a dog to Canada, will this money be returned when we come back out? The reason I am asking this – some years back we used to put up $1.50 a dog and it was returned when we came out. During that time we paid $10 for a bond and naturally we did not get that back. I thought that is what you might mean to do this year.

"I have been training dogs in Canada I think about 39 years, and I think you can look in my file and you will see that I have not any mistakes against me, and I think I have been going to Mortlach on the same grounds about 18 years.

"I do not go to Canada just for pleasure. I go because this is my only source of making a living in the summertime.

"I am sure that you understand that you cannot train a bird dog as far south as I live because the average temperature is from 100 degrees to 105 a day.

"It is almost impossible to get my license in by the 15th of June because I do not know how many dogs I will bring. Sometimes I will get dogs just two or three days before I leave and sometimes I pick up a dog or two on the way up there."

The next two summers had their administrative problems. Cov didn't agree with the dog fee, or the insurance policy, and it wasn't until the government wrote about the '74 dog population – which included a number of mine – that the fees were paid. Cov also said it wouldn't matter if we went through the formality of asking authorization for the trial.

"I am terribly sorry that I did not write in for a permit for permission to run a field trial in Canada. I knew that we had to have one as we have always done in the past – I just forgot to do it. When I did think of it, I wasn't at camp and did not think of it when I was there . . . There are some Canadian people that help me put this trial on, and people around Mortlach love it. The trials don't make any money but the people around Mortlach and Caron do. We are always happy to break even."

That last was not quite so.

The days when the camp was filled with dogs, and there was plenty of help — scouts, boys to feed, a woman to help Lois with the cooking — had faded away. It wound down to a half dozen dogs or less and one helper, often another trainer who'd made an arrangement to use the grounds for the summer.

There was a succession of summer "assistants", Don Bodiford, Bill Risinger, Bud Keesee, Marc Appleton. But the most welcome was Rod Cowan, about Cov's age and a veteran of the business who had moved from California back to his native Tennessee. Dan Becker of Jonesboro, Ark., fit with Cov and Rod, a quiet young man eager to learn what he could and to do what the aging trainers asked.

In 1980, Cov got a hand-delivered letter which said the wildlife officer had checked the camp, and that there were 60 dogs, 32 more than licensed, and:

" — a 410 shotgun containing a empty shell in the chamber and 3 full shells in the magazine (found in saddle sheath).

" — A 20 gauge shotgun and part box of #8 shells"

The letter cited the regulation:

"No person shall: (a) 'carry or have in his possession in the field or fire or discharge or cause to be fired or discharged while training a bird dog, any firearm or live ammunition, other than a training firearm using blank cartridges, except during an open bird season and under game bird license.' "

The guns weren't Cov's. He may have shot a bird or so through the years, but never would he have had a gun in a scabbard. For all the arguments over a dollar he may have had with his Canadian neighbors, he respected their land and game.

During the '76 season Cov and his "assistants" had problems with a man who leased some of the "Queen's Land," as the government-owned property is known. He had 80 acres in the middle of the running grounds, unfenced, and dared man or dog to cross — at the point of a gun. Rod Cowan was a victim of his wrath, and so was Cov's Canadian friend, Maj. Mel Babcock, who later retired from the Canadian Air Force and moved to Alabama.

Cov checked the agriculture department's records and wrote Gary Anderson of Boharm:

"The Department of Tourism and Renewable Resources also informs me that this is a multi-purpose leased land, that is, several people may have the same land leased for various purposes, and when one man has his purpose completed, the other man's lease can then be exercised.

"Now you have your hay made and I didn't interfere with you. I don't want you to interfere with me when I run my dogs across that land."

The lessee, a year or so later, was accused in one of the province's most sensational murder-for-hire cases.

Cov's swings of emotion about the Canadian government were in direct relation to the latest infringement on what he saw as his right to go north unfettered. The file which Lois kept illustrates the continual changing of Canadian policy toward dog trainers, and reassures that the hand-wringing heard each spring, "This will be the last . . . it's all over up there . . ." is nothing but renewal of old paranoia.

Summers in Canada go on.

Chapter 4

His Places, His Friends

COV DIDN'T OWN a hammer. Or paint brush. He was a dog man. Exclusively.

Regrettably that didn't always set well with land owners. He knew exactly what was ideal in land to work dogs, and to run field trials. But he wasn't into keeping up such incidental things as barns and fences.

He had been spending summers at Mortlach off and on several seasons when he finally made arrangements with Vic Eastmond to move to the old homestead some three miles north of town, and a mile west. There was a two-story house with porch around two sides. Three out buildings, also old and frame, were a few yards to the north. One was used as a saddle house. Another housed part of the help in the days of plenty. Later it became a feed room. There was an outdoor privy near the two broken strands of old barbed wire called a lot fence.

The out buildings fell down for lack of attention. The privy burned one Sunday morning.

It was 1973. Tommy Long and I had been there since late July. Cov picked up a young man hitch-hiking along Highway 69 through Caddo, put him to work. Jody had a new wife by summer, and she went north with them.

Jody knew precious little about dogs, and made real the old saying about dangers of a little knowledge. He wore a large earring, mod as the times demanded.

I had driven to Melita for the weekend at the Gates camp, and, as Sunday mornings went, Lois and Cov, Jody, Judy and Tommy were relaxing on the porch, Tommy and Cov in a big discussion.

It was dry in August, the prairie grass like kindling. Jody took some trash to the barrel, started a fire and came back to the porch.

"He was afraid we'd say something and he wouldn't hear it," Cov reflected.

In minutes, Tommy looked toward the still-standing saddle house. The grass was flaming. A prairie fire at that time of year could blacken sections of land.

The well, some 20 yards from the porch, had long been regarded as the best around. Cov's crew had used it for seasons, a dug well with hand pump. Handlers carried water from it during the trial for dogs, and for themselves.

When Tommy called fire, Cov jumped off the porch and started pumping, Jody, Tommy and Judy carrying the buckets as fast as they could be filled.

Lois was standing on the edge of the porch screaming for Judy to put the bucket down. She had suffered a miscarriage a week earlier.

"Shut up, mother, and get one yourself," Cov bellowed.

Just then the out-house caught. Poof. In seconds there was nothing left. Wood seems never to rot, just get older and drier. By some miracle, the fire burned to the dusty center of the lot and to a strip that had been mowed around the house and dogs, and it stopped. Fortunately for the house and its meager contents, there was no wind.

But when it was over, there was no toilet. A hay crew had been working across the prairie. They had a trailer for sleeping and a well-built outdoor toilet, complete with official symbol of the Queen's government on the door. The crew seemed to be finished with their work, but hadn't moved camp.

A couple of days later, Bill Allen and Raymond Rucker arrived. After lunch break, Cov announced that he wanted to take his two-ton truck with the closed box and go after the Queen's outhouse.

He told Bill, "Yeah, I saw those boys over there the other day."

"I'll bet you saw 'em. But did you say anything about the outhouse?" Cov replied with a chuckle.

He had a hand-written note which he and Bill tacked to the door of the trailer as we secreted the outhouse into the truck where horses usually stood.

"My toilet burned, and I have women in camp. You're not using yours. Besides I need it worse. If you have to get it back, I'm four miles west."

Nothing was heard about the borrowed toilet. But it was heavy on Lois' mind. One afternoon the following summer, a car with an official emblem on the door drove into the yard. Lois came out on the porch, having already been to her stach, and asked what the man wanted.

"Is this where Leon Covington lives?"

The reply was quick:

"Yes. But he's not here. And we didn't steal that outhouse."

He was from the game department and didn't know or care that one might be missing. Apparently the agriculture people didn't care either. It was still in use the last summer Cov and Lois spent at Vic's.

One chilly morning that summer of '73 the horses were saddled and the little group was about ready to leave the yard when Jody decided he needed to go back inside to get his coat.

"Now he's just going back in there to see his little wife. He knew how cold it was when he got up – there ain't no panes in them windows."

Cov had natural athletic ability, especially at golf, or shooting a .410 from the hip, never aiming. One summer he won the Saskatchewan amateur golf championship at the Moose Jaw Country Club, where he was a summer member.

For the last 15 years of his life, his hands shook, sometimes so that water was easier to drink from a straw than a glass. When he moved to Caddo and went to the Durant Country Club to play golf it was easy to get the first game going for money. He didn't play just for fun. When he picked up a golf club – or a shotgun – the shaking stopped. He cleaned the boys, and was under great suspicion as some sort of set-up.

During his early years, Cov was a most fashionable trainer. He had dogs for the likes of Tony Imbesi, the wealthy New Jersey setter fancier. He had a dozen dogs with Cov, and furnished pickups. He remained a customer and sent dogs to Canada with Cov well into the 1970s. The legendary Montgomery sportsman Sellers Vredenburgh put his dogs with Cov one summer – including Medallion – and made the trip north himself. Unlike John Gates, who was especially fond of Medallion, Cov didn't care for him, and was relieved when he went back to Gates. "He didn't point a chicken all summer."

Vredenburg went to Canada the summer Cov had his dogs, and Cov was playing golf on the Saturday afternoon. For money. Vredenburg and his friends walked up just as Cov was putting, and made a loud noise. Cov continued as if they weren't there, and made it. He had dollars involved.

Cov was featured in major outdoor magazines. His was the popular camp, the in place.

As years took the toll on his physical abilities, he kept plugging away, though there were fewer dog and fewer helpers. Renewal of the Saskatchewan put him into the limelight anew, and introduced him to a generation that never fully appreciated that they were dealing with a man who enjoyed expensive sports coats, and French cuisine. By then he was keeping things together in his own way. Always solvent. Good at collecting what was due him; always promptly paying what he owed.

He decided he'd sell Cokes at the dog wagon during the Saskatchewan. He went to Moose Jaw and bought several cases wholesale, put a few each day in an ice chest that rested in a wooden compartment below the bed of his truck on the driver's side.

He had supplied a cup for quarters, and when scouts come to get a cold drink, without getting out of the seat or looking down, he would admonish them:

"Let's hear something drop there."

Something did. Mostly pennies.

He went out of the Coke business.

Cov enjoyed the close friendship of a few Canadians. One was Ken Forester of Regina, an educator in the city's school system by winter and announcer of the horse races in summer. Ken was an avid bird hunter. When he and Cov first discovered each other, Ken had a shorthair he called "Lady." Ken went to Pointers, and loved to spend free time riding the walking horses and helping work the field trial dogs that Cov or his guests had. Most of all, he knew every inch of the running grounds and always knew where the best check cord bushes were. He developed superior gun dogs for himself, a gentleman of great humor, delightful to be with.

The Forester family knew Cov and Lois, and understood this couple growing old with their very individual ways.

It was amazing that Lois could feed whatever the crew would be in the side-room kitchen with the leaky roof and cabinets that would have been sparse in the '20s, she who in her earlier days dressed in jodhpurs and was the envy at making fancy party dishes. But she and Cov didn't require much, and when Rod Cowan was there he didn't either. It was the young helpers who suffered.

Cowan had an illustrious career as a dog trainer on the west coast, one of the all-time leading handlers of championship winners. He had difficulties with the bottle, a small man in stature, even frail by the time he came north with Cov. He was devoted to yard working his dogs, a nervous man who would walk and lead his young dogs endlessly, all during the lunch breaks, in the late afternoons.

Rod was quiet, pleasant to be with. He carried water from the well for Lois' kitchen needs.

The evening before Cov, Lois and Rod were to leave for home, Canadian friends came by with a bottle of rye, which Cov and Lois helped them consume. After they went to bed, Lois fell. She complained next morning about her arm, but Cov was headed home, and nothing would turn his attention.

They loaded the few utensils, the dogs, and Lois. They were driving a station wagon, Dan and Rod in the big truck with the silver box, warped to right.

Lois was strongly complaining about the pain. When they got through the border and stopped at Minot. Cov got aspirin, liquor and they continued south.

Two days later, when they were at Caddo, the arm was swollen – so bad that doctors at Durant first thought she might lose it. It had been broken.

Cov would explain, "Why we gave her the best care she could get, plenty of whisky and aspirin."

At the hospital a doctor said they would have to cut off a ring. Cov asked how much that would cost, and was told about $20. He turned to Rod and told him to "get the pliers out of the station wagon." He saved that $20.

One summer at the turn of the '80s, Cov made a friend of a doctor in Arkansas who was to send a couple of dogs North. Then the doctor asked about sending his teen-age son. And Cov arranged to borrow a horse. It seemed a perfect set-up. He would get the pay for two dogs, the use of a horse, and a free helper. The young man had a friend he wanted to bring along, and that sounded even better. More help.

The young men had heard only the romanticized side of this Canadian adventure. They had no idea about the living conditions on the upper floor of the old frame house, most of the windows gone, and that their rations were to be those of older folks who relied a lot on a drink of rye. After a couple of weeks of one glass of milk in the morning, and the lack of Lois' understanding that growing boys needed more to eat than did an 80-pound woman near 70, it was really tough going.

Mel Babcock was out to work his dogs and be around the camp. He told his wife about this year's helpers and their plight, and she tucked away a batch of cookies when Mel went to Mortlach.

One morning when Mel arrived, he asked about the boys, and Cov told him they were gone. "Left me up here with all these dogs and no help." He was in a rage about being so wronged by "them spoiled kids."

As the story unfolded, it seems one of the boys took a fall on one of the rough Canadian horses left there, and complained something was broken. Cov told him to get back on the horse and come on, that they didn't have time for that sort of thing.

Several days later, Lois thought better of the matter and took the lad to a doctor in Moose Jaw. It was a shoulder separation, and was appropriately bandaged.

When the boys, awake in their loft, heard Lois loudly telling Cov to "turn off the TV" in the night, that was it. For they well knew the closest electricity was on the main road more than a mile away.

They got to the telephone at the Midland Motel and called home for rescue. The doctor's wife contacted Cov and asked if he'd drive the boys to Regina to the airport, but the answer was a clear "no." He'd taken them on for the summer and needed the help, and didn't have time to be "trapsing all over the country because some kid's whining."

She drove from Arkansas after them, and Cov's great economic coup went sour. He had to employ Dan Becker to fly from Jonesboro to help him the remaining weeks, with the trial, and to drive on the trip home.

Alex Grant lived in Alberta, and drove over early in the season. Two years in the early '70s he bought Derbies which

I had taken north, and, a year or so later, I got to Mortlach later than usual. Grant was there, with his grandson. It was announced that this year Cov was going to sell Grant a dog — Maverick's Hedgerow Jack. He was a white Pointer with orange on his head. Jack didn't like to go with anyone but Cov, and had a habit of laying down when he pointed quail. It seems Grant had watched the dog on Saturday and was satisfied with his ability to find and handle prairie chickens. But he wanted to "see if he'd handle." This was really the least of Jack's problems.

Cov didn't work on Sunday. Period. So Grant stayed over to see the dog again Monday morning.

But Sunday night there was a session at the Midland. Cov was having a few drinks, during which he told his prospective customer, "That grandson of yours can ask more questions than anybody I ever seen."

"That's the only way he'll learn, Cov."

"Well, let him learn from somebody else."

The session went on and Cov was not in good shape next morning. There was a large crew riding, Rucker, Forster, Rod, Dan, Grant and I.

"Jack'll handle for anybody. I'll show you how much I trust him. I won't even ride." The big truck seat was about the extent he could really manage that morning.

Jack hunted ahead of Grant and Dan out across the field south of camp, to the corner. He had been right out front at ideal range. But Grant wanted to see him a little more. That was one cast too many. Jack topped the ridge. Gone.

Cov was on a high spot along the prairie trail, we were fanned out, and it dawned that something was wrong. Here he came, dust flying. I was first.

"Where's the dog?"

"He went over that rise and I guess down in the bottom."

"What you mean is you've lost him. Five grown men. Lose a dog a child can run."

He put the truck in gear and threw sand. Rucker was next, and he got the same treatment. The truck disappeared across the prairie. We put another dog on the ground and in about a half hour Cov came to where we had stopped at a bluff near the lake.

"Has he come back?"

"Yeah."

"Where'd he come from?"

"Down toward the lake."

"Just what I thought. He just went down there to get a little drink."

But Grant didn't buy. For the wrong reason.

For all his rough and bluff exterior, Cov was the first to sense when a handler was heading home with dogs, horses, a family and no money. He volunteered more than one such loan, an act he would never allow to be mentioned.

The summer of 1973 was Cov, Jody, Tommy and me at Mortlach. A grand time. Ken would come out to ride. In the late afternoon Tommy mixed the feed. He soaked dry feed, worked in canned Canadian meat, a portion of shredded wheat, and a can or two of spinach. It squished through his fingers, and had the aroma of something that would be good to eat. The dogs loved it. We'd put the tub on the back of the pickup, Cov on the tailgate, his legs dangling, a can of beer in his hand.

As we carried pans, he give counsel. Usually he'd tell a story about a dog he once had, a situation he'd handled in years gone by. Often the stories would parallel something he'd observed with us that day. It would be something he thought we ought to know, and the use of an illustrative story was the way he conveyed his message. He understood everything about training a dog. He wasn't physically able to do it. He knew grounds, evaluated them at a glance, and planned field trial courses better than any man I've known. He knew the small things about handling dogs which can add up to winning, or not. And he understood human nature, especially those judging his dogs.

In his late years the ability as a professional dog trainer were camouflaged by the stories. The resonence of his voice never waned. It made laughter ring.

In Cov's younger years, Imbessi, heard the stories at Cov's kennel in Alabama regularly. He was there early, in the big league days with up to 20 dogs in Cov's charge. He was also there in the last years, sending dogs north when there was no hope of success.

John Seawright of Little Rock, took special pains to watch about Cov and Lois during their years between Caddo and moving finally back to Booneville. Seawright had first become well acquainted with Cov at Caddo. He took a pointer to him to work.

Seawright's eyes brighten at memory's recall of the stories he heard the couple "discuss." That usually meant one of them told the story, and the other loudly corrected as it unfolded, often to the result that Lois was right on particulars, Cov better on the big setting.

One afternoon on the porch in Arkansas, there was such a session. Imbessi was the subject.

"He'd come over there and stay several days at a time. Kept a pickup there all the time. We were out there feedin' one evening, and he just stood in the front of one little Setter's pen. She was in season. He didn't move. Just stood there. I walked by with some pans after 15 or 20 minutes and he said, 'What'd you breed her to?'

" 'That pointer in the next pen,' and kept on walking. Guess he didn't care for that, but he did move out of the way."

Under the brashness, there was a humanity, even a soft side.

"We run one of his setters one morning and when we got in, he had the dog by the collar and put him in the pen.

" 'Kill that dog,' he told me.

" 'He's your dog. Kill him yourself if you want him killed. I don't kill dogs.' And that was all that was ever said about that."

Cov had one of the Imbessi dogs at the National Championship. Before the start, the crowd congregated and Imbessi leaned against a wood-paneled station wagon. He asked Cov, "You're going to try to win this, aren't you? If you do, I'll give you this car."

Cov bridled, "You gawd damn right I'm gonna try," turned his horse and rode off a little way, turned again and came back.

"And I'll take the car if I do."

One of the last years Cov went to Canada, Imbessi had his son send two dogs north, and it was not a good year. His young helpers had gone home, there was quite a bit of expense, including $660 damage to the truck. He had mentioned this to his New Jersey friend just after they got home and were getting the few dogs distributed.

A few days later Seawright drove up. Cov was in a chair under a shade. He had a letter in his hand. It fell and Seawright picked it up.

"That round-headed WOP sent me $660."

The note said, "I never forget a friend."

41

He protected his independence always, and was not about to "go private." Early in his career he became friends with the famed retriever trainer Cotton Pursell, who was employed by John Olin of Nilo and other plantations.

Olin sent word to Cov that he'd like to hire him at his Georgia place, the message coming from Pursell. They decided to drive over one Saturday and at least look over the situation.

As they turned into the grounds, a white employee was supervising a group of blacks tasslin' corn. Cov stopped and talked to the man who was spending some time "workin' hands."

Pursell showed him all the facilities. They went to lunch. He never saw Olin, but thanked his friend for the invitation and the tour, and said nothing about the job.

Some time later he drove over to a retriever trial, a bit hung over. Olin saw him and sent Pursell over to ask why he had decided not to go to work for him.

"Just tell him I go to Canada every summer. You all don't do that. I go to Canada to train dogs. I don't work blacks in corn fields."

Chapter 5

Flirt, Scouts, Judges

IF ALL THINGS were equal, Cov would pick a black female Pointer every time, and Flirt, or, High Heels, was one of his favorites – and last. She belonged to Herb Holmes, who would go to Caddo and work dogs on Cov's grounds, and he would leave a dog or two with him.

Flirt was one of the last daughters of Gunsmoke, and a dog of quality. Conditioned, she was a true running dog. She found her share of game, but, occasionally, if things didn't go just right, she would settle.

Run, she would.

Cov brought her to Ardmore, to the Oklahoma Amateur's open all-age hour. Bill Allen had come from Georgia to judge. Cov had the flu and didn't feel up to riding. So he turned Flirt over to Bill Risinger. The courses ran, as always, around the lake edge, but the last one cut through the woods near the oil well, crossed the blacktop and finished the last half hour behind the dog kennels. Flirt drew that course.

She hung to the far front, Bill raising his hand to point her out at good intervals until shortly before the oil well. She disappeared. Cov's old truck, which listed as the result of being laid over in a Carbondale ditch, was silver, and the top of the box could be seen going through the woods, down the blacktop, stopping ahead on a dirt road. Bill looked for the dog and finally went to the truck. Cov motioned him on and, miraculously, there she was, right in front. Judge Allen had observed the action.

Cov wasn't one to hand out bouquets, but in the lodge room that evening he went on and on about what a great job Bill and "that boy" had done with Flirt.

"Couldn't nobody have done better. I just appreciate it so much. You just saved me. I want to get that bitch so I can run her at Grand Junction, and I think you got that done.

"You helped her just as much as anybody could."

There was a pause, and Bill Allen spoke:

"Not as much as you did."

"Shit. You caught me."

He ran her in the Saskatchewan in '72 and she found game. When chicken left her, she dropped. Cov was calling point, and as the judges got there they were met with a barrage:

"Why in hell didn't you come on when I called point. Now look here, you've been so gawd damn long that bitch's got tired and laid down. Well, I'm damn sure gonna run her on anyhow."

But he didn't run long.

"You know, Herb keeps a little card up on the kennel gate. Needs a damn secretary. Puts down every time the dog points birds. Don't put down when he does wrong. Guess he don't need a secretary, she'd probably put it all down."

Cov at his fiercest was in a spat at Inola. I went to a room to meet John Rex Gates to go to dinner, and it turned out to be Dr. Hawthorne's room. Cov was standing, waving and talking at the top of his considerable voice. It seems that an extra brace had been added that afternoon, including Cov and Flirt.

"You ran me out there in the dark when you knew nobody could win. You just threw me and this dog away. You knew you could get by with it and it put these other dogs on the courses you wanted 'em on."

He put the drawing on the bed and showed in detail which dogs would be where. John Rex intervened, but he was quickly shut up, and Hawthorne made no defense. Perhaps because he knew Cov was right.

Cov loved to ride in front of a good scout, especially Tommy Long. They worked Flirt almost every morning for about two weeks of her last summer. All three of them enjoyed it. She would run all over the prairie and would have three to four finds before they got to the corner west of camp. She had been ill, but home remedies seemed to have her doing better.

They got her off the chain and started in front of the camp, made a big loop toward Mortlach and had six finds. But when Tommy caught her on the hillside in front of Vic's she wasn't

44

breathing right. Pneumonia had taken its toll and she died a day later in a Moose Jaw clinic. I speculate still what a brood matron she would have been.

It was a summer or so later that I had two young dogs in which Cov took a special interest. He was just driving the dog wagon for us that year. Usually he didn't have enough interest to do more than stop at the right place so we could get the dogs out. While we ran, a trail of dust would lead down the road to Mortlach where there was always a bottle in the motel room.

But he took a shine to these two, a black bitch we called Specialist and a liver male, Special Agent. When we ran them, and especially the female, he drove the roads and helped watch for them, and would even get out and water them when their paths crossed.

Penny made a good showing in the Derby stake, and some of us – especially Risinger – thought she had a piece of it, but not the judges.

The trial was over. "If you had any sense, you'd stay up here another week or 10 days and just work those two pups. Then you'd have two good ones. Lois and I are leaving day after tomorrow, but you ought to stay.

I didn't take his advise. Both dogs placed, but were never up to the promise, Specialist becoming the dam of Ch. Hawk's Nimrod, granddam of Ch. Barshoe Brute.

The next season, Collier Smith thought Tommy was bluffing when he pointed Agent out in the Derby at Stoughton, but then he caught a glimpse of him far enough that he couldn't have got back in the time remaining. But he didn't come back on his own too often.

Judges, that is, their expenses, were a bane of Cov's existence. In Canada the motel was inexpensive enough, $10 to $12, but he considered the cost of booze and food would "add up." Late in a mid-'70s Championship, fog rolled in on the first brace. You simply couldn't see beyond the horse's ears. The dogs had to be picked up. We sat around Vic's and decided to call it off until noon. Cov exploded. The very idea. It might cost another night of judges' expenses.

The last morning of the trial was miserable. Rain. Cold. Strong winds. But we ran. Risinger had Harvest Moon, which wasn't likely to win, and John Rex had Texas Silver Spur, which might well have. But it was impossible and they were taken up. Collier had a dog, and he ran it to the bitter end.

Cov and Raymond Rucker were in the same age category. They both loved bird dogs, Canada in summer, a drink of rye, and Caddo. We ran the Bryan County trial there. And those trials were quite the fun events. All sorts of stakes. Lots of dogs, and good times.

One day at noon, Rucker, who was judging, felt the symptoms of a heart attack. The word spread. Drs. Gordon and Doran were there, and as the two physicians were getting into the matter, Cov came up, fearful that he was about to lose a judge.

"Raymond. What's the matter? Say you got a pain in your chest?

"Have you had a little drink, don't you think that might work?"

Cov's suggestion ignored, Rucker was to be taken to the Durant hospital. In the ensuing confusion, Doran asked Cov for directions. Cov told him, but Lois was listening,

"No, Cov. They want the people hospital. Not the vet."

Later that evening, Rucker was in the hospital's version of intensive care. Tommy Long got in, identified as a son.

After one of the first Bryan County trials was over, I did the book work and there were a few dollars left to go in Cov's trial account. I was loading up, and he came out of the house with a package.

"Here. Mrs. Riley gave 'em to me. I never wore 'em. Might fit you."

Inside was a pair of heavy wool britches, a tweed, lined, obviously tailor made, and covered on the front with soft leather.

The Canadian liquor store employees went on strike one summer. It continued for a time, and provisions were getting low. Actually we were down to one 40-ounce bottle of Windsor, a little of that gone. Rucker was in charge of protecting it, and he had chosen a coat sleeve as the hiding place. Not that we were selfish, just rationing. We drove up in front of the motel, anxious to get pineapple or apple juice, ice — a Rooker.

Raymond opened the truck door, picked up the coat, and the bottle hit the concrete slab.

Cov was punctual about writing letters concerning the dogs he took north. There was a practice among trainers of his time to send a snapshot of the dogs pointing. Picture taking was usually an afternoon taken off from checking cording, frought with mishaps. That evening he would come to the motel and dictate the few letters he had to write and I would type them. Lois had performed this function for years, but she was impaired a few seasons.

I always wrote exactly what he said. To one owner:

"She's doing as well as could be expected. You ought to send me the rest of that money. This bitch needs to eat, and so do I."

—When Hope Evans, who cared for both Cov and Lois at Booneville during their last years, went through the boxes and possessions left behind, gathering up the field trial things for me, one box contained a fragile glass cocktail shaker and six matching glasses, clear with rings of gold.

The top was engraved, a trophy for the Derby at the McAlester (Oklahoma) Club's 1938 trial.

The Field Dog Stud Book reported:

McAlester Club
McAlester OK March 27, 1938
Derby—8 Pointers 2 Setters
1st—STYLISH LADDIE BOY, 271378, Pointer dog, by Stylish Touchstone Jim—Stylish Dottie. E. H. Hughes, owner; Leon Covington, handler.

Hope and I were astonished that such fragile pieces could have survived without a chip through such a lifetime.

In the same trial there was another entry. Cov had told he that he had the setter Kid Crockett, the start of the Soph Setters, and that Mr. Soph had bought him after he "ran out of dogs and borrowed him to hunt in Arkansas."

In the same report:

All-Age—8 Pointers 8 Setters
3rd—KID CROCKET, 246045, Setter dog, by Hummer Lee—Crockett's Alamo Queen. Dow Smalley, owner; Leon Covington, handler.

As I thumbed on through the book, I found that it was on March 20, at the Out-Our Way Club trial near Independence, Kansas that Jack Harper first placed The Texas Ranger, in

47

the Open Senior Puppy with 13 pointers, 2 setters. The great Lester's Enjoy's Wahoo, champion and sire for a young John S. Gates, was a Derby, a category in which he won, plus Runner-up in the National Derby and an Illinois all-age.

1938. Quite a year, for Covington and Harper and Gates, youngsters of the sport.

When Lois and Cov lived in Alabama, Jack Payne and Jimmy Hinton paid a part of his training lease, if not all, and the Clyde Mortons were nearby.

Lois and Mrs. Morton became especially close friends. They spent time visiting, and having a drink.

Cov saw a lot of Morton, but never seemed to tell a complimentary or endearing story about him. He did of Payne and Hinton. He was fond of both.

But of Morton he most often told of the fabled trainer shooting a female Pointer as she stood on a covey of birds. As he would tell it:

"I asked him, 'What the hell did you do that for?'

"He just said, in that high, whine, 'Cov, she can't go three hours.'

"Hell, there are a lot of us that could win with a dog like that."

Cov said that they would go up to the Mortons and sit on the back porch lots of evenings, and after Paladin's last win of the National "he would go on and on about what a great race ole' Fred had. He named him the same as his favorite hound. Always thought he liked the hound best."

Among the things which Lois preserved and packed away in her files were letters which Sybil Morton wrote to her, long, meandering thoughts of a lonely woman, perhaps with alcohol problems and certainly with difficulties dealing with relatives after her husband's death.

Chapter 6

Vic's Place

IN 1982 I WAS at Mortlach for the summer, staying through the trial to judge. Cov talked a lot about past years and mentioned not coming back. It was prophetic for it would be his last summer. The Christmas Edition of the FIELD that winter carried an article I wrote about Vic Eastmond and Cov and Mortlach, illustrated with photos taken in earlier years of a young Tommy Davis, Fred Arant at Mrs. Eastmond's lunch table with Don Ryan and Joe Davis, Cov and Bill Allen behind the old camp house. They are all reproduced again in this volume. The text:

Vic Eastmond's dad held all of the hope that the new West could give a man.

There was the promise of great harvests on the lush, unplowed prairies of Saskatchewan, limitless in horizon, stretching dreams to the end of man's imagination.

It was 1908.

He drove the wagon with his wife and one son from Moose Jaw westward to the 160 acres of land he was to homestead, a piece of Canada that drained to the east toward Pelican Lake, four miles north of the new community of Mortlach.

That year he bought a nearby "place off D. M. Metcalf. It was just a shack and he added the rooms where we eat," Vic remembers.

The first years were good.

In 1912 Vic was born. By 1915 Mr. Eastmond had started a barn. He bought the lumber back east and had it shipped went on the train. The half for the teams of Percherons was built the first summer, and in '16 the cattle half was finished.

An imposing structure, a landmark that stands today . . . leaning to the southeast from the pounding of the northern winter storms.

"In 1917 it started to blow, and on through '18, '19 and '20. I started to school in '18 and I could walk barefoot to the Dobson school and never get a thistle the ground was so bare."

Vic has since bought the school corner, a tree sheltered corner on the southwest edge of the farm as it is today.

"It began to get good again – through '28. That year was a good crop, but in '29 we were dried out – really until about 1940. There was about eight years we didn't grow hardly a damn thing. She was drifting all the time.

"The government came in and tested alfalfa, and started leveling the blow holes and putting the prairie back again."

In '16 or '17 the senior Mr. Eastmond planned to build a home near the farm, the stones were carried from Pelican Lake and stacked for the project. But the winds came and the lack of moisture left devastation.

The stones are still there. The house was never built.

The Eastmonds are still there, too. The third generation – Les and his wife – farm the land. Rotation is used now and wheat and oats are in smaller fields against the day it may be dry again.

It was in the 1940s – neither Vic nor Leon Covington can remember precisely, but they guess 35 or so ago – Cov decided to move from Ailsbury, and he discovered the grounds that were the Eastmond's and the Queen's – vast hay lands planted to alfalfa and crested wheat. He saw the place one afternoon and remembers he moved the next.

Thus, the Eastmond Ranch and Mortlach became a part of field trial history.

Cov has summered there since, until the past two years in the house he rented from Vic, built in 1913 by the Rummell family. The Dodson school was next door.

"Cov's house" has been moved, the porch gone, to the Eastmond homesite and the new breed of Canadians who field trial are mending it for a club house.

The original Eastmond house is plain and small. The kitchen is a sort of side room and entry. There is a dining room and living room with a big table. A bedroom where Vic was born is on the west. 50

Several years ago Vic and Mrs. Eastmond moved to Moose Jaw and a new home, leaving the homestead for use during the harvest, for Vic when he feeds in winters – and for field trial time.

Mrs. Eastmond comes out a few days early, and, morning and noon, meals are cooked for handler, helper, judge and those who come to enjoy the Saskatchewan Championship.

Many a story has been told around the table.

And the finest field trial dogs of an era have been tied on stake chains under the Eastmond shelter trees.

While it had been a training operation for many years, the Mortlach grounds did not become trial grounds until 1967. Early, Cov had many dogs and lots of help. Years took a toll on both.

The Saskatchewan has been a lightning rod – the first trial of the major circuit's year. Most of those who compete have been north for several weeks and satisfied with their handiwork.

It is at Cov's that they meet competition and only a few can be placed from among the many. More judges have caught more flak there than most any other place. Some deserved on merit if not on sportsmanship. Most not at all.

It is a grueling and totally thankless job. Judges on the prairie, for years, rode what the handler on the grounds had in the way of horse stock. And it wasn't much. Consistently rough.

The days are long, eight hours. And virtually nobody else rides it all. Handlers can stay in the car gallery until time to run. In most years it takes a week and more.

The rowdy times and the rough horses have given way to more reasonableness and judges usually trailer their own horses.

The list of winning dogs and winning handlers reflects the place the Eastmond homestead has earned. Flaming Star was the first champion, for Herman Smith.

It has been "Cov's trial;" but it was Vic's place. He has kept the pens usable for horses and hauls the water for them to drink since the place has no well or pump. And he has hay and grain.

The Saskatchewan group which arranged for Vic to move "Cov's house" has set about picking up and mowing the area used by trainers. When they run their amateur trials on the grounds they bring tents and campers and stay the weekend.

They saved the old house from the torch, for when Les decided to move to his family's ranch he started cleaning up Cov's camp area, burning what was left of an outbuilding or two and thought the house should have the same fate.

But the Canadian trialers thought otherwise and preserved it as what might be called an historic monument.

Cov had brought two old horse-drawn dog wagons to the camp. One he had got when Jack Harper quit coming north. The other he said he brought from Ed Mack Farrier's.

The Farrior wagon was pulled to Vic's and sits in front of the old house, a part of Canadian field trial history. No doubt Warhoop Jake and his kennelmates rode many times on the wooden, rubber-tired vehicle behind a pair of horses.

Mortlach – Cov's and Vic's – is far from just the past. It is very much now. It is still the Grade I grounds with plentiful coveys of chickens and Huns placed by nature.

It is still the place the week before Labor Day where the major league Derbies get their first chance at a career . . .

It is still the place where there is reason to believe one will see the sort of performance that Homerun Jim or Flush's Country Squire or Oklahoma Flush could give. There is land enough. Game enough.

Perhaps this coming August.

If not, then next.

For around Mr. Eastmond's homestead there is still a limitless horizon of dreams.

Mr. Eastmond died of a heart attack in Las Vegas in 1985.

Cov protected his grounds – especially against amateurs. One time he agreed to an amateur "invitational" as a part of the Saskatchewan club's program, but nothing more.

Mr. and Mrs. Frank Thompson of Milledgeville, Georgia, went to Canada in the late 60s, and Frank, ever careful about laws and regulations, had inquired about what an amateur was allowed to do. They pitched their tent at Vics, and there was a confrontation of sorts with Cov, who insisted "no amateurs." But Frank knew that he had the exceptions on his side, convinced Cov, and was made welcome.

With Cov gone, the amateur championships moved to Mortlach. With Vic gone, the grounds changed. More land in crops, more fences. The landmark barn was torn down, along with some of the outbuildings around the old homeplace. Cov's summer camp house was pulled across the prairie, but the porch where so many summer hours were whiled away, so many tales told, is gone.

Chapter 7

A Matter of Priorities

THE TEXAS Championship was one of the few titles awarded bird dogs in Cov's days. The entries were as large as any in the country, a AAA event. Cov never missed.

In the early '50s, he was running Lone Survivor and his helper called point a good distance away and across a wide creek. He started to the find with a Judge from Shawnee, Oklahoma, following close behind.

He went down the near bank, and, when he started up the other side, he looked over his shoulder and the judge was still on the rise far back, off his horse, stretched out on the ground.

Cov went back.

"What's wrong"

The judge said he thought he was having a heart attack.

"You go on. Flush the birds and go tell the other judge."

"Oh, are you sure? Don't you think you could get back on the horse if I'd help you."

Cov kept on talking, knowing full well his report of the find wouldn't carry any water. He was persuasive, and the judge got up. Cov helped him on the horse, and led him down the bank, up the other side.

But the judge got off again.

He stretched out on the ground, and said he just couldn't go on.

"Cov, go ahead and flush the birds."

The pleas continued.

"I put a makinaw, you know, those heavy coats we wore then, under his head.

"Can you see him? Right over there. He's standing so pretty. Can you see him now?"

"Yes, just go ahead and flush."

Cov realized he'd got the judge as far as he could.

So he put up the covey. And shot a bird, picked it up and took it back to where the ailing judge lay.

"Did you see the birds? Here's one of 'em."

"That's fine, Cov, just go on back and tell the other judge about it."

"Well, judge," he said, pulling a pencil and scrap of paper, "would you write that down?"

* * *

William J. (Bill) Allen of Georgia was Cov's friend. He was a member of the Bona Allen family, and a newspaperman, writer for the Atlanta Constitution in his young days. He and Bet had homes in the mountains of North Georgia, on Jekyll Island.

Bill, the Constitution outdoor columnist, took up writing for the American Field, and in the days when he traveled the circuit, his were the colorful accounts, vivid, intense. Canada was his favorite. The Continental a close second.

He made the prairie experience ring, and with a single article he could make a hero or heel. He was intrigued by each year's young crop, the Derbies which he followed with such intensity that breeders flocked to the sires of dogs he wrote about, and galleries filled to see them when they went south in winter. Bill's intellect is a marvel, a mind so crammed with information so diverse, recall so quick and accurate. When Bill Allen left the prairies in 1975, the Canadian trials wasted in attention and value to the sport. Breeders and owners were deprived of the color, the romance and glamour of native ground and native game described so as to inspire.

And handlers were deprived of their greatest spokesman. He could also be their greatest antagonist. For what he thought was right or wrong he wrote about. Judges he evaluated. Or deplored. Handlers' antics he reported.

Bill Allen, a wonderful kind, of Cov:

Do you remember the story about when Goober won the Crab Orchard Open All-Age (bigger than most championships at that time) and we were heading for Paris, Texas, for the Texas Championship?

55

We were crossing the Red River on that old iron bridge at Denison, and I said:

"You know who was born here, Cov?"

"Yeah," he announced emphatically, "Me, by God!"

"Oh," I murmured, "I was thinking of President Eisenhower..."

"Hmpf...yeah," he trailed off, unanimated, "him, too...I guess..."

* * *

Stephen Harwood was a bird hunter well before he started his accomplishments with field trial dogs. He and friend, Butch Bond, had been shooting birds on Choate Webster's ranch in northern Oklahoma and were on the way home. They stopped at the Sinclair station in Caddo.

"I had the FIELD, and I told Butch I was going to call a guy who lived there and see about buying some dogs. I dialed Leon Covington, who I had never met and only heard of. It was about 10 on a Saturday night.

"I've been reading that you train dogs, and I'm interested in buying a hunting dog, maybe two.

"He came back with a quick, 'Do what?' "

"I mistakenly thought he hadn't understood, 'I want to buy a hunting dog.'

" 'What you callin' here for, boy?'

"Well, it had your name in the FIELD; said you trained dogs.'

" 'I don't train huntin' dogs. I train field trial dogs.' "

" 'Did he have anything,' Butch wanted to know.

"I don't think so."

* * *

He traveled with Ches Harris one winter, dividing their winnings. The season wound down at the Texas Champinship, and Cov felt as if he had made the biggest contribution in winnings.

They ran the Derby, in which Cov placed. They were into the championship, Cov having run all his dogs, Harris with one not thought too highly of left.

Cov explained that he'd just go on to his sister's place near Denison. They agreed that Harris could get his dog around okay with the help he had. Cov left, never mentioning the Derby money.

Next day, Cov and a couple of friends were partaking of the homemade wine offered at a spot on the Oklahoma side of the Red River near the bridge. Harris saw Cov's truck, and pulled in.

"Well, I was sure I'd have to come up the money. Ches sat down, had a drink with us, got up and said he'd see us down the road. The Derby wasn't mentioned.

"Next morning I was reading the sports page of the newspaper, and there was a little item that said, 'Ches Harris wins Texas Champinship with Norias Kremlin's Joe.'"

Chapter 8

The Last Weekend

COV CALLED EARLY in the week to see if the Oklahoma dog of the year program was going to be at Ardmore on a Sunday morning, 1983. He said he might drive over.

I suggested that he come Saturday and attend a cookout at Tipps' Point. He said he'd think about it, and wanted to know where I was staying. I told him the Lake Murray Lodge, which had been home to field trialers for years before the state bureaucrats made it impossible to use the facility.

He showed up Saturday afternoon, ate and told stories. He was ready to leave fairly early. He had not had a drink of whisky all summer, and didn't then. Next morning he was up early, entertaining a small group clustered around him in the dining room at breakfast.

Jake Kirkland of Kansas, brought along a video recorder, and he set it up in the meeting room. He started taping while Don Powell, Dr. Harold Haston, Fred Oliver and I fed him the key lines of his stories.

Glenn Stalworth and his wife worked for Cov and Lois, and they had a young son called "Dudie". He was Cov's buddy. They were together constantly. The youngster learned the dog trainer's adult language, and sensed that he had little to fear, even from his parents, when Cov was around.

He became a mascot for the dog trainers around the Saskatchewan trial in Canada. When it was time for him to go to school, his parents were told by the officials in the little community of Caddo that it would be best if he went to the Durant school by bus. Otherwise Dudie would be the first black child in Caddo schools. It is likely that under any other circumstance,

Cov would have agreed that the black child should be bussed. Not Dudie. Cov was ready for the battle. To avoid it, and to regain some control over their son, Glen quit and moved south.

That Sunday morning at Ardmore, Cov told about a time in Canada:

"Herman (Smith) was running a setter, and he run out of gas. Dudie knew all the dogs and handlers. He was out on the ground when Herman took him up, and asked, 'Mr. Herman, how'd your dog do?'

" 'Aw, he did pretty good.'

"Dudie walked off, put his hands behind his back and said, 'Didn't look to me like he did a god damn thing.'

"We were in the big truck on that narrow back road going by my old camp. We needed to go over on the prairie to change dogs. Hoyle was up in front of me. Had the road blocked. I hollered for him to go on and get out of the way.

"Nothin happened. I hollered at him again to go on and get out of the way. He didn't move. Dudie was in the truck with me. I stuck my head out the window and hollered. I said 'either go on or get out of the damn way. I've got to get these dogs over yonder.'

"He drove on. While we were driving over there Dudie said to me, 'Mr. Cov, you'd better be careful how you're talking to them white folks, they don't care nothin' about us.' Guess he thought I was black, too."

When the program started, Cov took a seat in the audience. Andy Daugherty and I were to be the program, but the first question was about judges, and we deferred to Cov and what he had been saying to his audience at breakfast.

"Forgot what I said. Oh, I remember. I said when pickin' a judge the first thing you got to think about is whether the fella's got time, whether he can take off from his business and not be in any hurry to get through. I like to get a fella that's been brought up going huntin', foot huntin'. He learns a lot about dogs when he does . . . what he's supposed to do and what he's not supposed to do.

"Next I like to get a fella that's had good dogs, owned good dogs . . . and won with 'em. Usually when you get someone like that, you get someone that's experienced and knows how to judge a dog.

"These fellas that learned how to judge from readin' a book, I haven't had too good a luck with them kind. They make too many mistakes. There ain't nobody that can write a book to tell you how to judge field trials . . . that's been tried . . . simply 'cause a dog don't do the same thing every day. It doesn't happen the same way every time, so you've got to have sense enough to know what causes a dog to do certain things. I don't care who he is. Another main thing is to be able to ride and not give out and get tired and want to quit 'fore he's through."

Cov came to the stage and joined the program. He became the program. Andy did get in an early story:

"The second field trial I helped dad at, I was just 16. At the first, on the breakaway he sent me, and I went three miles through there and when I got back he said, 'Well, we won.' It was news to me, 'cause I hadn't ever seen the dog.

"We were in another all-age stake and we were running Kansas Wind. He had a find. Good. Right out front. On the next one everything was right again. When Dad come leading him out, I was on the ground, and he mumbled to me, 'Now don't call point no more.'

"I didn't pay much attention. We didn't have but 10 minutes to go. He went out of sight to the right and I went over the hill. There he stood. I couldn't let that go. I called point.

"Dad was riding along with the judges, and the judge said, 'Your boy's callin' point over there.' 'No, it's not my scout.' 'Funny, here's the other dog.'

"Here they come. He flushed the birds and turned and made the awfullest face at me, and said, 'I told you not to be callin' point no more.'

"We went on. Right at pickup time he sent me and I went out of sight. There Jack stood again. I just couldn't let him stand there. I went to calling point.

"The judge told Dad again, 'Your scout's callin' point.' 'No he ain't. I'll just go get him, it's pickup.' 'No he's callin' point.'

"I don't think that I'd ever been this tall if Jack hadn't had them chickens."

It was Cov's turn to take the floor:

"I was running a dog called Marvelous Jack and had nine finds with him. He was a good running dog, and I didn't think they could beat him. I looked at my watch after the last one.

I was still on the ground. Had a minute to go and checked. The judges said one minute.

"'My time says it's up right now. He said, 'Turn him loose.'

"There was a bluff over there about a quarter. I was talking to the boy that was helping me. 'You see that bluff over there?' I was taking up all the time I could. He said 'Yeah.' 'That'll just give him enough time to have another find and we don't want that.' He went straight to it.

"The judge said, 'You can take him up.' The boy went around that bluff and stuck his hat up. I went to motionin' no, but they'd seen him. I run hard as I could. Don't need no more, and there might not be no birds there. I got down, some were there shore enough. But when you're clean you want to stay clean."

Cov kept on, story after story:

"One time I was braced with Ed Mack Farrior. On the breakaway the two dogs went off together, and they didn't come back. We sent the boys over there, and they didn't come back. We decided to go see what they was doin'. It was hot as the devil and the bird had got up and flew just a little ways to the next bush.

"My boy got my dog and went to that bush. The bird got up and went back to the first bush. He kept cat walkin' and tried to point it, but it flew back. The other boy tried to get Ed Mack's dog to point and it got up again and flew back to where my dog boys was. It just went back and forth.

"Scotty Burgess was judgin'. I turned around. He was there on the hill with his arms folded just lookin' at us. He said, 'When you fellas get through, you can bring them dogs and come on.'

I said, "We might as well put a lead on 'em.'

— — —

"A dog's supposed to come back once in awhile. I've heard folks say this dog or that runs too big. In my opinion, a dog don't run too big, if he'll come back in the length of time you're supposed to come back once in awhile.

— — —

"I also believe, like Mr. Proctor said, how can you judge a dog with somebody going after him when every time he goes over a hill ahead.

— — —

"When you pointed a covey of birds, and Mr. Proctor said 'heel that dog back to the front,' you'd better heel it—if you wanted to win anything.

"Mr. Proctor and I weren't in love with one another, but I do think he was the greatest judge I ever run a dog under. He looked back as much as he looked forward. He knew where everybody was. He'd miss a scout, and you'd better know where he was. Course, we'd do all we could get by with. You always asked permission to use a scout when he was judging.

"Some dogs don't learn to handle and always needin' a scout because they never have to. Somebody's after 'em all the time.

"Mr. Proctor didn't associate with any dog trainer and he didn't smile about many things. Fact was, we used to call him Napoleon. He had his ways and if you wanted to win under him you'd better do it his way.

"Any time you're out there running a dog and want to win, you'd better be tryin' to please them two fellas settin' back there.

"It wasn't what I thought about it—but what he thought about it. When he told me to do somethin', whether I thought it was wrong or right, I done what he said. For I always wanted it to pay off in the end.

"We run in the Texas Championship one year. I had a little bitch. Called her Little June. Placed her 32 times. Had a find on a turn and flushed those birds. He told me to heel her up and bring her to the front. We started across a corn patch, and there was a fence row over there. I knew a covey of birds stayed in the woods. I turned my horse toward 'em and kinda whistled. She went over there.

"He was loping along there, and I was along behind him. I sent her around that away apurpose.

"I told him, 'Mr. Proctor, I got a point back here.'

"He pulled that horse up and turned. 'What'd you say?'

" 'Bitch standin over there pointin'.'

" 'I told you to heel that bitch up.'

" 'Yess'r, I know what you told me. But she got away from me.'

" 'No, she didn't get away from you. You sent her over there.'

"Well, anyway, she's standin' over there pointin'.'

"Dr. Killman was president of the trial and he was behind with us. I started to crawl through the fence, and Mr. Proctor said, 'Bring the bitch and come on.' He rode on off. I said to Dr. Killman, 'I can't even get him to look at my dog.'

"Dr. Killman got him to come back, and he said, 'Go ahead and see if you can flush 'em now.'

" 'I know I can. I can see 'em settin' right there in that briar patch.'

"One flew right over his head, and I just wheeled around like that and shot the bird, and I just missed his head that far. I didn't give a damn about missing a'tall.

" 'Quit shootin them birds.'

" 'Are they yours?'

" 'No, but that's the reason there aren't any. You dog trainers kill 'em all.'

"He threw me out of the stake.

"One thing about it, and I always sure appreciated it, next day I run another dog with Ches Harris, belonged to a lady in Oklahoma City named Miss Witt. I had one find with him and won the stake. But he threw the one out that I thought I won with."

— — —

"What's the difference in an all-age and shooting dog?

"An example was Mr. Oliver's dog. John run him; Mr. Oliver don't run his dogs on Sunday, you know. What was his name? Oh, yea, Oliver's Mr. Ranger. I helped judge the stake up there at Inola. We had your dog with five finds, maybe more, without a bobble and a couple of backs. The other dog had run an all-age race and had two finds. Another run a field trial race and had one find. I call 'em field trial dogs and shootin' dogs.

"There was three of us judgin', and they called me over there. I never run shooting dogs and didn't know these dogs names. They began to tell me which dog won, which placed. I knew what dog did what, but I didn't know their registered names.

"One judge wanted to place the dog that run the field trial race and had one find, and the other one second and you're (Mr. Oliver) dog third. I said to 'em, 'That's impossible. What about this dog here. He had five clean finds and a back. What are you going to do with him. He run a shooting dog race. He won it, or he ain't won nothin'. He hunted all the way. Handled. John didn't have any trouble at all with him. I can't do that. Ain't no way I'm going to do that. If we had any other dogs to place I'd throw them other two out. But there ain't no more that's pointed any birds.'

"I left it with them. Mr. Oliver come up after they announced the winners and said, 'I sure was scared because I knew you liked a running dog.'

" 'I do. And if it'd been an all-age stake it would have went against you. It ain't hard to tell the difference.' "

– – –

Andy recalled a story told on his brother, John, who was helping his dad with Ranger's Gallant Man at the Missouri Championship. Woodcocks were migrating through, and Man pointed one, Bud flushed it. Shot. Went on. It was raining, and when Bud next saw Buzzy, he had the dog on a rope, backed up in the shelter of an igloo.

"What the hell are you doin'," Bud inquired without much patience.

To which Buzzy replied, "I'm holding this dog. There ain't no use riding out there in this rain. Them judges don't even know what a quail is."

– – –

Cov remembered Maverick's Hedgerow Jack.

"I was running him down at Caddo in a trial we had, called it the Bryan County. Raymond Rucker was judging. Jack'd get a little close to his birds and lay down.

"I had a boy (Jody) workin' for me that didn't know much. I told him, 'If you find that dog laying down, he does that some times, just ease down off your horse, pick him up, straighten him up, and he'll stay up. Get back on your horse and back off and call point.'

"Well, I heard him calling point. When we got close I could see he was off on the ground. I seen him bending over. Got up where we could see him good and he was getting the dog all straightened up. There sat Raymond.

"'Boy, what the hell are you doin?'

"'You said stand him up.'

"Hell, I didn't tell you do to it in front of the judge.'

"In another stake down there I saw him layin down in a little draw. I just rode right on by him. I wanted to get Raymond out of the way, and then I'd pretend like I was lookin for him and ride back there and straighten him up.

"I was acting like I was looking for him, and damned if Raymond didn't look around and say, 'There's your dog, layin down right over there in the ditch.'

"That took care of that."

— — —

"Course a dog ought to be tight, 'till you flush the birds. He should be tight when the judge gets there, standin' there solid, and stay that way long as he's got birds in front of him. But after you've flushed the birds the deal's done and over. The birds are gone and the dog saw 'em go.

"It's over. If his tail moves or drops or he looks around, fine. I've heard guys say, 'He was all right 'til the birds left, then he dropped his tail.'

"Well, so what. Dog's job is done. What if he marked them. If he's not interested enough to see 'em fly off, maybe wheel just a little, then he ain't likely very interested in finding 'em either.

"I'm not talking about going with 'em. Just marking 'em. Kinda wheel. Showing interest. That's instinct in a dog. Shows he ain't a trick dog like some of them that just keep standin' when the birds fly off. If he's not interested enough in birds to watch 'em fly off, he likely ain't looking for 'em out there when he's by hisself."

— — —

"I got throwed out of the National Free-For-All one time because Walt Wimmer, and a lot of these judges, got to thinking all dog trainers are trying to put something over on 'em.

"Thought I had it won with Catalpa Ridge Peewee. Braced with Phil Brousseau. His dog had give out of gas and went

65

to following along with me. I lost my bitch with five minutes to go. She went up over a hill in high sage grass and lost her right there. I didn't ride fast, cause I was afraid I'd ride over her if she was pointing and ride the birds up. So I had to walk the horse. Phil's dog was there.

" 'Can you get your damn dog away from here. I think I've got this thing won.'

"He took his and went on in the woods. Roger found our dog pointing there in a thicket. I couldn't really see her, just her tail stickin' up. When I got down one single bird went up. Walt always thought somebody as tryin' to pull something over on him. I thought, 'Now, if I shoot, he'll think Roger put that bitch on that single.'

"So, I went over there and tried to flush, and then decided to take the bird that'd left. I shot, and a whole covey got up behind me. When I reached down to get the bitch, a single bird got up right under her nose. She ducked and kinda squatted, and he threw her out.

"I don't think it was that bitch's fault. Actually she was just duckin' the bird, not scared of nothin'.

"Phil went on to win that trial. He had a find when he went in the woods. Little later, somebody said, 'See you bought a new truck, Phil.' And he said, 'Yeah, Cov bought it for me.' "

— — —

"There's only one time a stop-to-flush can be any good. That's when a dog's runnin' down-wind and runs over a covey. If he's running down-wind, he ain't got no chance to point 'em. If he goes down-wind and goes over them and stops, everything's fine.

"There's another way. If you ride 'em up and they fly over his head. Now a dog going up-wind, there's no excuse for him to have a stop to flush. That's a knock to stop, and it don't win field trials — or hadn't ought to."

— — —

Mr. Oliver interrupted for a break in the program. Cov decided to start back to Booneville. He didn't want to be out after dark.

From Ardmore he went by Caddo to see the "boys at the filling station," and on to Hugo to see his friend, dog trainer retired to game chickens, Stub Poynor.

On Wednesday he and Perry Mikles were planning to have a field trial at Booneville again, and in the afternoon Cov drove out to look over the old grounds where he had lived and trained. Coming down Henscratch Mountain he died and his station wagon rolled into a shallow ditch.

Book II
An Album

Lone Survivor is posed after his win of the 1955 National Championship at the **Ames Plantation**, Grand Junction, Tennessee. Lois Covington holds a silver plate. Standing by her are Leon Covington, Spot Settle and to the right is Rube Scott, the plantation manager.

Cov and a helper lead their dogs down a sand road.
Photo by Evelyn M. Shafer

The dog wagon in Canada.

Photos by Evelyn M. Shafer

73

The dog wagon in Canada.

Photos by Evelyn M. Shafer

Henry Davis, Evelyn Shafer and Cov chat alongside the dog wagon.

Housing in Canada for people and for dogs.
Photos by Evelyn M. Shafer

Commercial feeds were virtually unknown, so, handlers cooked their own dog food in Canada.

Photos by Evelyn M. Shafer

Cov puts dogs in the harness attached to the roading bars on the back of the dog wagon.

A helper in Canada with a favorite setter.

Photos by Evelyn M. Shafer

With leathers over their horses noses to keep away the insects, one helper releases a pair of dogs and Cov blows the whistle for them to start.

With dogs on the the roading bar behind the wagon, a dog in the harness and helper, they're off across the prairie.

Photos by Evelyn M. Shafer

A little water is vital in the prairie heat.

Cov works with his dogs on the prairie, teaching them to walk at heel, remain still for flush of game, to back—the fine points of summer training.

Photos by Evelyn M. Shafer

79

Photos by Evelyn M. Shafer

Photos by Evelyn M. Shafer

Photo by Evelyn M. Shafer

Cov on the spotted stallion he bought for Lois to ride at field trials.

A couple who worked with Cov in Alabama.

Ch. Marvelous Jack, winner of the 1950 All-America Chicken Championship for Cov and owner C. L. Little.

Ladies of the field trial on the prairie, in the '60s, included Pearl Lee Epperson (left) and Lois Covington next.

Cecil Proctor, discussed at length by Cov and Marshall Loftin in their conversation in Chapter 2, is second from left. From left to right are Jack Downs, who reported for the FIELD, Proctor, Frank See, prominent judge of the day, Sid Mitchell and Herb Schroers.

The group posed for their photograph across from the club house at Booneville, Arkansas, in the late 1950s during the running of the Southwest Championship. Kneeling at front are Jack Harper of Benton, Mississippi, Bud Epperson of Stillwater, Oklahoma, Leon Covington, Leon Cantwell of Little Rock. Standing: Bob Lee of Norwood, Louisiana, Marshall Loftin of Laurel, Mississippi, Heck Lannon of Texas, John S. Gates of Leesburg, Georgia, Spot Settle of Amite, Louisiana, and Dr. P. T. Killman of Malakoff, Texas.

Leon Covington and William F. Allen, Cov and Bill, sit by the kitchen of the summer training house at Mortlach in 1975.

Vic Eastmond, born on the prairie, worked out his years on the farm and with his property in Moose Jaw. He looks at a watering trough he'll use during the trial of 1975.

Mrs. Eastmond prepared lunch in the house where Vic was born, and the trainers, owners of the era came there. Tommy Davis, Criswell and Randy Downs are served lunch in '75, and Fred Arant Jr., idles a little time away. In '82 Joe Davis of Alabama, and Don Ryan, the Minnesota attorney, who never missed the trial, have lunch with Marshall Loftin and Garland Priddy.

The barn which Vic Eastmond's dad built in 1915 was a landmark. The enormous frame structure housed the draft horses in the days when farming was done by teams, plus cattle, and tons and tons of hay. Saskatchewan weather gave it a list to the south, and Les Eastmond had it torn down shortly after his dad died in 1985.

The summer camp house north of Mortlach.

Tommy Long has the horses saddled and tied to the porch.

The house where Vic Eastmond was born in 1912, and where lunch was served during field trials.

The pump and dug well at Cov's camp.

Saddles hang in the old out building.

Marvin Reid judged the Saskatchewan in 1975, and he was around at dog feeding time. The shelter belt in the background is where Cov's dogs were staked. On the truck with a tub of feed, Criswell and Cov.

Bill Risinger (near, horseback) and Freddie Epp are ready to start their dogs in a Saskatchewan Derby, Criswell with Special Duty and Roy Epp with the other.

The truck **gallery** trails across the prairie during the Saskatchewan in **mid-'70s.**

Bill Allen was at Mortlach to report the championship, and Bill Risinger (right) had summered at Cov's.

Mrs. Denton Sharp watches in deep prairie grass as Alan Craig check cords Harvest Moon.

The prairie falls away to far bushes, the expanse dog trainers seek, and the cover that holds prairie chickens and Huns.

Gary Parker of Montana, takes a break. Cov's silver dog wagon in the background.

Leon Covington, 1975.

David Johnson and Robin Gates at Mortlach in 1973. It was the first trial for Johnson to scout for Robin's brother, John Rex.

The inimitable Ed Butler of Texas, Judge of the 1976 Saskatchewan Championship.

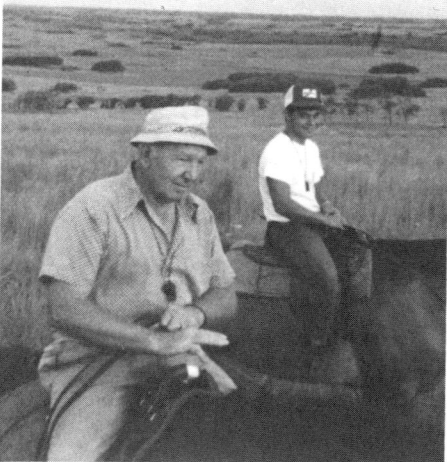

Raymond Rucker, judge of the Saskatchewan Championship in 1973 and '74.

Leon Covington rides with George Moreland of Leesburg, Georgia in 1971.

At Ardmore in 1972, Cov (seated) talked with Raymond Rucker, while behind them trainers Bud Daugherty and Bud Epperson visit.

G. W. (Stub) Poynor, handler of the 1970 Saskatchewan champion, Fugitive, talks with John Jackson.

Don Hickman and Arlin Nolen inspect the old dog wagon which once belonged to Jack Harper and was moved from Cov's camp to the starting place of the trials.

Years at Towner, North Dakota

Judges Rush Campbell of Washington, and John Ray Kimbrell in 1985. Kimbrell also judged the trial in 1983, '86 and '87.

In 1984, Bud Williamson (left) and Dan Clarke, Jr., of South Carolina judged Saskatchewan stakes.

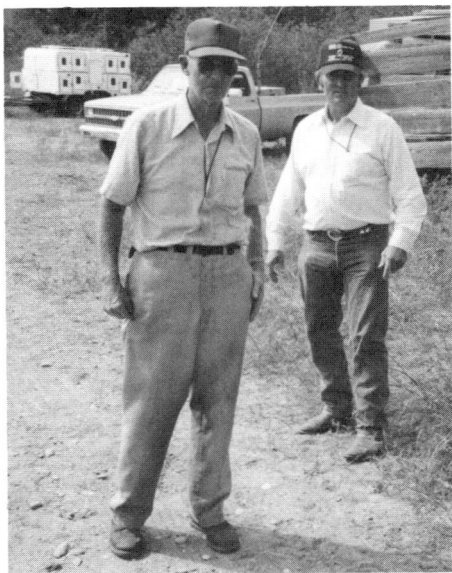

Left: Frank Thompson of Milledgeville, Georgia, judged the Saskatchewan of 1985 with Darrell Privett of Frog Jump, Tennessee. Right: Hall of Fame member Ed Mack Farrior attended the trial at Towner in 1983, staying at the camp of Kenny Robinson near Denbigh. Farrior first came to the area in 1921 with his trainer-father. Tony Terrell standing nearby.

Dr. Mike Furcolow, Boulder, Colorado, veterinarian and sportsman judged at the Towner trials, and Mr. and Mrs. Dave LaChance were regulars, handlers from California who established summer grounds nearby.

R. A. Weber, owner and club official from California, was at Towner, vising with Judge Rush Campbell.

O. G. Edwards of Oscaloosa, Iowa, was a director of the Saskatchewan, helped develop the grounds at Towner, and participated in every way making them work. The shade in front of the Little House was a spot he loved.

Don Hickman, Saskatchewan director, and handler Tony Terrell, during a Towner trial.

Dr. Alvin Nitchman, member of the Field Trial Hall of Fame, developer and trainer of champions, established a summer camp near Towner, and participated in the trials, where he place the superb Elhew Strike in the Saskatchewan shooting dog Derby of '85. He is here with Towner banker James Williams.

Doug Sellers prepares to start a dog for Marshall Loftin on the first course at Towner.

Joe Bush and Fred Rayl on the Towner prairie.

Wallace Sessions holds a Chinquapin Farm entry. Sessions manages the Florida preserve of the Baker family.

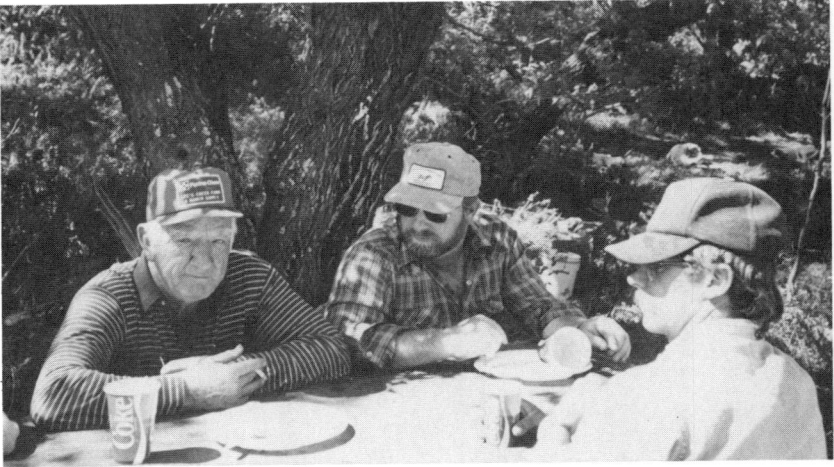

Senator (Sixty) Rayburn, senior member of the Louisiana legislature, has lunch with Dennis Jeffrey.

John Little and John Ray Kimbrell, both from South Carolina, were judges for the 1986.

T. Jack Robinson, Vernon Vance and Bob Napier in the Towner gallery.

Joe Hicks has champion-to-be Bisco Big Jack ready for the start of the Leon Covington All-Age stake. Handler Pete Hicks is mounted.

Lynn Bennett came north to help with the trail, including management of the rickety "dog wagon" on which he leans.

Trainer Kenny Robinson and son Greg. The Robinsons train on grounds near Denbigh.

Earl Connolly of Memphis, was at Towner to see his dog, Black Moon Rising, perform. With him is Dan Clarke.

Kevin Robinson scouted for his dad in the first championship at Towner.

Fred Rayl poses Ch. Fiddler's Pride after he had hunted impressively at Towner. Pride, owned by Dan Bonaguidi, was elected to the Field Trial Hall of Fame.

Winners of the 1986 Saskatchewan Championship, Ronco's Lucky Siete and Concerto Ace High are posed with a group that included Coda and Randy Downs, Mr. and Mrs. John Ray Kimbrell, Arlin Nolen, handler Robin Gates, Joe Hicks, Judge John Little, Tim Carpenter, handler Doug Sellers, Dan Clarke, Mr. and Mrs. Dennis Jeffrey, their son and John Criswell.

David Johnson, Robin Gates and Lynn Bennett pose K's High Rise and Thunderclap, champion and runner-up, following the 1985 Saskatchewan. Included in the group are O. G. Edwards, Doug Jess, Dennis Jeffrey, Judge Frank Thompson, handler Tony Terrell, Judge Darrell Privett, Arlin Nolen, Mazie and Colvin Davis and Rich Robertson, Jr.

Handler Tony Terrell has champion Double Rebel Jack, and Randy Downs poses Cumberland River Mark after a callback in 1987. Standing behind are Criswell, John Ray Kimbrell, Stanley Downs, Jackie Downs and Arlin Nolen.

Fred Arant Jr., holds Rambling Rebel Dan, 8 years old, after he was named champion in the 1964 Border International at Frobisher, Saskatchewan, Sept. 7. To his right is Leon Covington with Rampaging, the runner-up. The judges, Delmar Smith of Edmond, Oklahoma, and Maxon McGrady of Tallahassee, Florida, stand behind the handlers and their winners. It was the largest entry for a prairie championship—92. There were 110 in the all-age, and Dan won that, too. David Fletcher reported the long trial which also had 60 Derbies, Mingo the winner for Arant.

Lois and Leon Covington on the porch of the Mortlach camp house in the summer of 1966.   Photos by Dave Fletcher

110

Book III

Cov's Field Trials

Chapter 1

1934-41:
Those Early Years

ALBERT HOCHWALT and the field trial party stayed in a Moose Jaw, Saskatchewan, hotel and drove 25 miles north to the starting point on August 27, 1934, to begin the program which included the first Saskatchewan Championship.

Thus began a trial which would grow into the years of World War II, suffer abandonment until it was revived by Leon Covington in 1967.

The recounting of those first years is somewhat sketchy, but there are highlights and results.

Frank Walsh of Winnipeg, Manitoba, and Dr. W. A. Wilson of Edmonton, Alberta, were joined by C. T. Carney of Des Moines, as the first judges.

There were 16 pointers and 6 setters in the all age stake which started it all, Ed Farrior handling the winner, Evergreen Jersey Mack. Pete Pritchett was handler for Fort Dixie Proctor, second; Mack Pritchett with Spunky Creek Joann, third.

In the Derby, there were 8 starters, Ponciana, owned by Lebanon Kennel, the winner for Mack McGrady.

Eight pointers and 4 setters were in the championship. Kent Shartel of Oklahoma City, owned the winner, Fort's Dixie Proctor, and Pete Pritchett was the handler. There was no runner-up. The entry included Dr. Blue Willing and Spunky Creek Joan.

On August 28, 1935, Hochwalt was back to report, and there were three judges again, all from Canada: Walsh, Dr. Wilson, and J. M. Miller of Calgary.

The all age drew 27, and the previous year's champion, Fort's Dixie Proctor, won. Ed Mack Farrior handled Air Pilot's Sam to second, and third was divided between C. B. Black's Berry Hawk and O. S. Redman's King Genius. Clyde Anderson and John Parker had the first and second placed Derbies and, again, third was divided, this time between Anderson and Ed Farrior. Farrior's Dr. Blue Willing won the championship over 13 other entries.

The 1936 renewal started on August 30, and Hochwalt said of it:

"On the borders of picturesque Quapelle Valley, 30 miles west of Moose Jaw, it was an extraordinary large entry . . . marvelous region a half hour's run from town."

Dr. T. Benton King came from Tennessee to judge with J. M. Miller of Calgary. The winners:

1936
All Age: 14 setters, 41 pointers
1st – Highland Bimpkins, C. B. Black, handler.
2nd – Unca's Flying Devil, W. D. English, handler.
3rd – Sand Hill Dick, John Parker, handler. Spunky Creek Farmer, Mack Pritchett, handler.

Derby: 4 setters, 30 pointers
1st – Garwood, C. B. Black, handler.
2nd – Wayside Beck, B. F. Epperson, handler.
3rd – Sedgefields Topsy, Ed Mack Farrior, handler.

Championship: 4 setters, 23 pointers
Champion – Air Pilot's Sam, Ed Farrior, handler.
Runner-up – TenBroeck's Bonnet, Clyde Anderson, handler

Hochwalt wrote of the 1937 Saskatchewan:

"It was the fourth venture of the Saskatchewan Field Trial Club, and by far the most notable achievement that has yet been accomplished by this young and enterprising club. When in 1934 this new club was announced to run a trial near Moose Jaw, Sask., the world of bird dog people were not greatly startled. It was just another club to take its place among the many. But from the very beginning this new organization began to make itself felt. It was conducted just a bit different from the mine run kind; it proved to be a new note in the scheme of things. The astounding progress that was made in those few short years has been the talk of the country. The Saskatchewan club went from a small beginning to lead the clubs in the Canadian prairie country. This year the fourth trial of its career has broken records which may not again be equaled in Canada or elsewhere . . .

"Headquarters were made at Moose Jaw, but the trials took place some 30-odd miles north.

"Headquarters at noon were made at the John Moore farm . . . The grounds have frequently been described as gently rolling, with great open spaces where dogs may be shown to the best advantage."

It was a year of drouth, the trial beginning August 27, and there was an amateur championship on the program. For that stake, the judges were Henry P. Davis and J. M. Miller. They looked at 4 setters, 12 pointers and awarded the title to Spunky Creek Coin, owned and handled by E. J. Shaffer.

Hochwalt wrote:

"It will be recalled that Mr. Shaffer purchased the Spunky Creek dogs during the running of the Futurity at Mount Vernon, Ill., last November, and since then they have been handled very successfully by B. F. (Dutch) Epperson. A second series was run with Carl Duffield's Black Hawk Kid.

"At the end of the first series either might have been placed and no injustice would have been done to either. In the second series, Coin had a brilliant find, with birds beside a 'bonnie briar bush', but practically on bare ground, and they must have been visible to the dog. His manners were perfection. Kid backed and the question was solved."

1937
Open All Age: 68 starters

1st — Air Pilot's Sam; L. D. Johnson, owner; Ed Farrior, handler

2nd — Spunky Creek Coin; E. J. Shaffer, owner; B. F. Epperson, handler

3rd — Spunky Creek Boy; E. J. Shaffer, owner; B. F. Epperson, handler.

Open Derby: 48 starters
1st – Wayside Lulu; J. B. Daniel, owner; Howard Kirk, handler
2nd – Anthony's Betty Joyeuse; Charles Forrer, owner Earl Crangle, handler
3rd – Wayside Annie; J. B. Daniel, owner; Jett Crawford, handler.

Championship: 32 starters; 2nd series, 4
Champion – Highland Bipkins; Dr. L. O. Crumpler, owner; W. D. English, handler Runner-up – Bess Blue Willing; Park Farm Kennels, owner; V. E. Humphreys, handler.

The champion had four finds on chickens and huns in the first series, one in the second series.

It was Hochwalt's last year on the prairie, having died before the 1938 trial. George M. Rogers succeeded the revered FIELD reporter.

Rogers said the trial began Sept. 3, a Saturday, with Nash Buckingham of Tennessee, and W. T. Windsor of Akron, O., the judges. He wrote:

"Sloughs here and there were refilled. The old bloom appeared upon the cheeks of nature and green again became the predominant fashion note of spring. And yet, in the face of provincial economic disaster, the fine sportsmen and women of Saskatchewan fought for their wildlife resources. This season ye scribe wishes to report that nature returned to normal and joy has replaced gloom in the province."

Grant Hall Hotel in Moose Jaw was the headquarters, and the mayor addressed the opening night dinner. A. P. Mays of Corsicana, Texas, was at the dinner and said in his remarks that 17,586 dogs started in 1,236 stakes at 372 trials in 1937.

The grounds were still "30 miles north," but described as "better than they have been for the past two seasons. There are more birds on them and the foliage is much deeper due to the rainfalls this summer."

1938
Amateur Championship: 5 setters, 13 pointers
Champion – Norias Daisy; Carl Duffield, owner; Carl Duffield, Jr., handler

There was no count of finds, but Rogers wrote, "birds were plentiful, and on the course that Daisy drew, and while some were of the opinion too many birds were found, the judges did not concur."

Open All Age: 68 starters
1st – Ben Temple; C. A. Rugg, owner; Dewey English, handler
2nd – Mississippi Broomhill Jake; B. C. Goss, owner; George Payton, handler
3rd – Highland Bimpkins; Dr. L.O. Crumpler, owner; Dewey English, handler

Open Derby: 40 starters
1st – Island Park Boy; E. J. Shaffer, owner; B. F. Epperson, handler
2nd – Sedgefields Nigger; A.G.C. Sage, owner; Clyde Morton, handler
3rd – Olive Hill Topsy; E. S. Donovan, owner; George Crangle, handler, divided with Florita; Lebanon Kennels, owner; Jake Bishop, handler

Championship: 33 starters
Champion – Unca's Flying Devil; H. E. Eyster, owner; Dewey English, handler
Runner-up – Amazon's Village Girl; H. E. McGonigal, owner; Howard Kirk, handler

Jack Harper handled Gold Dot and Henry Gilchrist handled the dogs of G. M. Livingston.

Rogers was back in August, 1939:

"Emerging from a youthful organization that has served its apprenticeship for the past five years, the now mature club completed its sixth annual trials on Thursday, August. 31, after five days which featured some of the most exciting dog races ever romped over these Saskatchewan prairies."

Two trials were running at the same time that season, the Manitoba at Melita.

Rogers said:

"Never have the wheat fields of Saskatchewan appeared so golden. The stubble, and there were miles upon miles of it, has taken on a bright, dazzling brilliancy in the face of the

117

white sun. The rainfall has been more abundant this season, but it was early."

At the first-night dinner, Moose Jaw's mayor mentioned the good roads of the U.S., and called for such in Canada. But Dr. J. R. Hoag of Regina, president of the Saskatchewan Fish and Game League disagreed: "He felt that but for the fact that the roads were not too good, there would not be so many birds available for the field trials."

The judges were Harry Decker of Winamac, Indiana., and Paul G. Hatch of Moorestown, N. J. "Their decisions were generally accepted as correct, and while there were some far-off rumblings of dissatisfaction, this is to be expected in Canada," Rogers wrote.

Amateur Championship: 5 setters 7 pointers
Champion—Norias Daisy repeated a second year for the Duffields, having 6 finds and two stops-to-flush. Rogers thought a callback should have been held with Homerun Contact, owned by Miss Claudia Phelps of Aiken, South Carolina. There wasn't one.

Open All Age: 35 pointers 15 setters, 1 Irish setter
1st—Village Ben; Dr. H. E. Longsdorf, owner; Howard Kirk, handler
2nd—Florita; Lebanon Kennels, owner; Mack McGrady, handler
3rd—Amazon's Village Girl; H. E. McGonigal, owner; Howard Kirk, handler.

Open Derby: 20 pointers 6 setters
1st—Tennessee Daredevil; Albert Noe Jr., owner; W. D. English, handler
2nd—Tarheelia's Lucky Strike; Eugene F. Clark, owner; Earl Crangle, handler
3rd—Yankee's Village Lady; D. M. A. Blanchard, owner; Howard Kirk, handler

Championship: 20 pointers 4 setters
Champion—Spunky Creek Coin; E. J. Shaffer, owner V. E. Humphreys, handler Runner-up—Amazon's Village Girl; H. E. McGonigal, owner; Howard Kirk, handler.

An error in the drawing allowed Coin to run alone in the first brace of the stake, and he had four finds. Rogers reported: "Coin began to stretch out and his race to the finish was one of wonder. He was a picture of the skyline, always bending to the horses. Once he worked up a valley between two knobs or hills and could have very easily made the wrong turn, but he did not and swung out of there with everyone holding their breath, for at that distance he was just a dot. Working back, he circled a thrasher and jumped into the chaff that would be waist high on a man. For a moment there was a thought this would tire him. Humphreys rode to him and watered for the first time. Sent on, he finished his hour in a world of glory."

George Rogers was back in 1940, and with him were two judges from the U.S.: Dr. T. Benton King of Brownsville, Tennessee., and T. Dean Coridan of Fortville, Indiana.

The trial started August 25, and Rogers wrote:

"That their decisions were just and given full consideration is understood by the lengthy second series in both the all age and the championship, and these two men rode it out like majors, never once reverting to a wagon for rest."

Troops were in training at Moose Jaw, the Royal Air Force school nearby.

The AFTCA had assumed responsibility for authorizing championships, and the Saskatchewan amateur championship was reduced to an all age.

1940

Amateur All Age: 4 setters 2 pointers 1 Irish setter
Winner – Playgirl; C. E. Duffield and Earl Jackson, owners; Carl Duffield Jr., handler

Open All Age: 36 pointers 16 setters
1st – The Texas Ranger; D. B. McDaniel, owner; Jack Harper, handler
2nd – Lawless Boy; Dr. H. E. Longsdorf, owner; W. D. English, handler
3rd – Young's Billie; H. J. Yoakum, owner; V. E. Humphreys, handler

There was a 55-minute 2nd series between The Texas Ranger and Lawless Boy. Rogers liked Boy: "Boy was inclined to swing about the country, while Ranger selected the more straight line type of hunting. While it was not necessary to have a wider running dog than Ranger, we believe that Boy outfooted him considerably."

Open Derby: 31 pointers 8 setters
1st—Tarheel's Sassy Jane; Stanley Bayly, owner; Marvin Yount, handler
2nd—Mohawk Ginger Pal; W. F. Black, owner; R. D. Bevan, handler
3rd—Dean; Dr. Harry Ridley, owner; C. B. Black, handler

Championship: 13 pointers 2 setters
Champion—Young's Billie; H. J. Yoakum, owner; V. E. Humphreys, handler

A second series of four dogs was required to settle the matter.
For the 1941 renewal, Rogers and Coridan were back and James C. Griffin of Sedalia, Mo., joined as a judge. It started August. 30.

"These men held up over the miles of the prairie riding," Rogers wrote, "and never once did they take to the buggies. That their decisions did not meet with the whole-hearted approval of all is to be expected when the number of entries reach large figures. Their efforts were the results of their own opinions and their own eyes were justified. What more could they do?"

Rogers wrote this descriptive opening:
"The prairies. Impelling vastness seem to roll on and on. Wolfwillow, buck brush, bluffs, grasses and purple sage brave the glorious and burning sun. Acres of summer fallow, in preparation for next year's grain planting fade into slate-blue as they lift up the rolling hills to one side, or, far, far ahead. Skies are clear, but ominous gray-black clouds suddenly darken the day. Winds and rain follow, then the sun appears—and, lo, a rainbow magnificent, with both ends deep set in the horizon . . . the land of open spaces. The pinnacle of field trials is here."

1941
Amateur All Age: 9 pointers 2 setters
Winner—Jane Pepper; L. A. Henning, owner; E. J. Shaffer, handler

Open All Age: 42 pointers 18 setters

1st – Allegheny Sam; L. O. Crumpler, owner; Dewey English, handler

2nd – Spunky Creek Boy; E. J. Shaffer, owner; Dewey English, handler

3rd – Tarheelia's Lucky Strike; G. M. Livingston, owner; Earl Crangle, handler

Rogers wrote: "In our humble opinion, Tarheelia's Lucky Strike won this all age event and we are sincere in our efforts to make this opinion stick. Lucky Strike does not have the reputation of being a great running dog, but on this day he turned in a race that could be analyzed only one way, a superb prairie ground-working heat, punctuated with birds magnificently handled. He had two other opportunities in the championship to repeat this race, which he failed to do, but in spite of this, his performance in the all age was clearly before our eyes . . . it was clearly great and beautifully honest."

Open Derby: 30 pointers 4 setters

1st – Big Shot; A. G. C. Sage, owner; Clyde Morton, handler

2nd – Starry; A. G. C. Sage, owner; Clyde Morton, handler

3rd – Little Elva; Jacob Cooper, owner; George Crangle, handler.

Rogers called the Derby "disappointing. It would be jumping to conclusions to condemn these Derbies, after seeing them only once. We shall make excuse for them and blame it upon something not understandable, shall we say conditions?"

Of the championship: "Not since 1937 has the Saskatchewan Championship been run without any semblance of decisive work at the end of the first series. We have had a second series in this championship almost every year since that time, but the quality of the work in the first series was far below average, and the judges were justified, in spite of an almost 30-mile gale, to work this important event out to a logical conclusion in their own minds. Due to the elements and conditions which existed their task was a delicate one, for any dog which scored favorable marks in his first hour had the odds against him to improve that situation the second time he was put down.

"Young's Billie, the famous white and lemon pointer owned by H. J. Yoakum of Houston, Texas, and handled by the clever

V. E. Humphreys, defended his 1940 crown successfully late Friday afternoon. This feat of Billie's to return to Canada and stage a comeback, overcoming obstacles which were very difficult in the form of high winds and dry, mixed scenting conditions, is particularly significant in view of the dog's failure to show on the major circuit last winter.

"V. E. Humphreys was also handling the runner-up, Spunky Creek Coin, owned by E. J. Shaffer of Hutchinson, Kans. It will be remembered Coin won this event in 1939 and this pointer made a gallant bid for the title again. Few dogs running over the prairie in Saskatchewan have ever equaled the race which Coin turned in, not only in his first, but his second, as well."

The FIELD reported:

"Following a period of doubt and some uncertainty, the field trial curtain in Canada way rise again." It was at the Dominion, run at Pierson, Manitoba, starting Sept. 7.

Cecil Proctor judged with Frank Vestal. There were 51 in the all age, and Way Yonder won, Titan second, both handled by Dewey English. Texan Boy won the Derby, 33 entries, for Jack Harper. Tarheelia's Luck Strike was named Champion.

But it was to be more than 20 years before another Saskatchewan would be contested. There was a small ad in the FIELD:

"While the Saskatchewan Field Trial Assn. was not able to hold the program which had been scheduled to run at Melita, Manitoba, on August 30, the club sponsored a successful amateur meet at Buffalo Lake near Moose Jaw on Labor Day, Sept. 7. Conditions at Moose Jaw were conducive to successful trials and birds were on the courses in abundance. Jake Bishop and W. MacGuire were the judges of the 7 in the Derby and 9 in the amateur all age."

The Manitoba Championship did not run, though the All American did, V. E. Humphreys handling Titan for the title. Down in Wisconsin, John S. Gates handled Col. B. C. Goss' Mercer Mill Jake to the U.S. Open Chicken Championship. It was the middle of his three wins of the title.

The Dominion and All-America survived the war years. As trials bloomed in 1945, the Great Northern came into being. Cov handled Little June to runner-up, and Ches Harris had the champion, Ranger's Knolwood Dottie.

122

Chapter 2

1967:
The Renewal

THE SASKATCHEWAN OPEN Championship was revived in 1967. David Fletcher reported it in the September 30 edition of the FIELD.

As when run in the '30s, the trial started on the Monday before Labor Day, August 28, and was not completed until September 5.

Fletcher wrote:

"The reorganization of the Saskatchewan Club, or, Moose Jaw trials, colloquially, began with the foresight of Leon Covington and the eager enthusiasm and interest of local sportsmen. In 1967 the club was organized with Fred Freeman as secretary-treasurer; Harold A. Boyse, as president; and Sidney J. Glassford as vice-president. Perhaps the functional duties belonged to Leon and Lois Covington. They engineered the affair, and saw to such things as courses, judges, horses, dogwagon, noontime lunches, headquarters, drawing and accommodations."

He described Mortlach as "virtually a ghost town with almost all of the former places of business boarded up . . . The decline of the quaint little village came about when the Trans-Canada Highway was improved and paved about 1950." The new road by-passed town.

Victor Eastmond's place was headquarters and Mrs. Eastmond and Mrs. Ken Stephenson cooked lunch. The Midway Motel was operated by the Moens — Nelson and Eunice. Most of those attending stayed there, with some at the Park Lodge Motel on the edge of Moose Jaw.

Fletcher mentioned a few:

"On hand to witness the new trial were old favorites Ruthie and Jules Franks of Philadelphia, Pa., to watch their pointers, Davant Carbide Imp and Davant Chief's Beedy. They were keeping tabs on proceedings for the other half of the ownership of these fine dogs, Mrs. Myra Berol of the Davant Plantation at Ridgeland, S.C. Bob Dry was in attendance looking at David of Caddo and a newcomer, Huckleberry Dan."

The judges were Delmar Smith of Edmond, Okla., and J. Harold Criswell of Ada, Okla. The Open All Age stake was won by War Detector, owned by Keith K. Gardner of Jackson, Mich., handled by Cov. He was credited with "three good finds and displayed a hunting pattern of the all age variety." Second and third were both handled by Bill Rayl. High Storm, owned by Eugene Loftin of Jacksonville, Fla., was credited with a pair of finds "on which his style and manners were something to behold. He did not have the huge, going-away finish that is so highly regarded in these prairie events. Possessed, third, was owned by Dr. T. O. Kennard, also of Jacksonville. He "likewise had two finds. The first was not overly stylish, but the location, intensity and manners were beyond reproach. The second was completely crisp. Possessed had a great hunting race, perhaps the strongest of the stake. Many of the gallery thought Possessed might with fairness have topped the stake, not to question the decision of the judges, but merely to mention some of the conversation, for actually the reporter was indebted to the two able arbiters for notes and descriptions of the all-age and Derby stakes, which were run while the All-America trials were still in progress."

Fletcher wrote of the Derby and the unrecognized junior all-age:

"The open Derby was won by Nip's White Knight, white and orange pointer, belonging to Nip Howard of Dothan, Ala., piloted by Herman Smith. Nip was not the widest or boldest Derby, but he put a lot of enthusiasm in his searching, handled to the course and pointed chickens like a mature prairie campaigner—out from the cover, testing the wind.

"Second place went to Storm Glider's Jess, white and liver pointer, belonging to Bill Coates of Richmond, Ind., and handled by Fred Arant Jr. Jess had a strong and forward race, plus a great finish and he had a game contact, bird work of

124

a character to earn recognition. Third was Rainbo's Slammin Sam, white and orange pointer, owned by R. H. Pritchett Jr. of Fort Myers, Fla., also handled by Arant. Sam was in a similar category to Jess. Sam's forte was his range, which was extreme. He lacked somewhat in staying to the front. Sam had what amounted to a stop-to-flush on chickens with one remaining to be flushed for him."

The old custom of running a junior all age – for dogs entering their first all age year – was not yet dead, at least with Cov, though the results were not credited by the Field Dog Stud Book. It was judged by D. Hoyle Eaton and Bob Dry. They placed Bar Lane Rocket, first; Homerun Jim, second; Warhoop Dapper Jack, third. Herman Smith handled Rocket and Jack, and Fred Arant handled Jim.

Both Dapper Jack and Homerun Jim would be placed in the trial in years to come.

There were 69 in the Open All Age, 34 Derbies and 76 in the championship.

The roster of entries in the championship was a who's who: Mingo . . . A Rambling Rebel . . . Gunsmoke's Yon Way . . . Royal Heir . . . Safari . . . Tooth Acres Hawk . . . Gunsmoke's Admiration . . . Sugarshack . . . Toronado . . . Homerun Jim . . . Endurance . . . Riggins' White Knight . . . Red Water Rex . . . White Knight's Bullet . . . Possessed . . . David of Caddo . . . Volcanic Butch . . . Highway Man . . . Flush's Country Squire . . . Paladin's Royal Flush . . . Warhoop Judy's Suzette . . . Satilla Virginia Lady . . . It was a year that would be circled on Setter calendars, for the winner was the nearly all-white Flaming Star.

Fletcher wrote of the performances:

"The revival of the Saskatchewan Open Chicken Championship was a high note and despite almost record-breaking temperatures, well-conditioned contenders made stout bids for the prized crown. Flaming Star's triumph will be hailed by setter fans everywhere. Many have been awaiting such a victory by the stylish longhair and to have him achieve the distinction under weather that would seem to wilt even the stoutest of hearts brings an extra measure of gratification.

"As has been said, the thermometer showed 95 degrees and what little breeze there was only seemed to worsen matters. But the gritty setter paid no attention to the heat and ran without a let up for the full hour, just as hard driving at the finish as when he started. He negotiated his country well, his casts were huge and directed intelligently to promising cover. He used the wind advantageously when he neared objectives.

"Flaming Star's first find was outstanding. It came as the result of a swing from a barren rise where he had completed a huge, forward cast. Star slanted across the gallery well forward and headed for a pocket of bluffs; he did not show and a scout was dispatched to find the lofty setter on an inspirational point. The work was flawless. Sent on toward another series of bluffs perhaps an eighth of a mile ahead, he rounded the upwind edge and pointed again, handling more chickens perfectly. Star, for the remainder of the hour, ran to the limits of the course, finishing strongly over a far rise.

"Homerun Johnny, the runner-up, was whelped June 29, 1960, bred by his fond owner, Mrs. Phelps, and he has been in Arant's hands throughout his notable career. Johnny began winning as a Derby on the prairies in the fall of 1961, captured top honors in the American Field Pheasant Futurity that season and went on to several more significant Derby wins. In 1962 he won the International Pheasant Championship and last spring chalked up his 22nd placement with his first in the Indiantown Gap Special.

"It would be difficult to find a flaw in his performance. He had three great finds on a showy course where all his ability could be seen and evaluated. And there was much ability to see and record. He made his huge swings along areas of cover that spell chickens here on the prairie. His points were executed out from the cover, nose into the wind, as the great chicken dogs are wont to do. He has leaning style of the breath-taking variety. It would be difficult to run the open prairie country which John ran over any bigger than he did and yet be seen. Flaming Star's superlative first find provided the wee margin he needed to take the stake.

"In any stake of this size there are always a number of performances that thrill those who witness them. Really this is what one comes to the prairie for. These are the things that become etched on one's memory and help to ease the tired muscles, the long grinding hours in the saddle and the sun, wind and dust-battered hide. Safari and Riggins White Knight had efforts that were as pretty as one can witness on the prairie. Susie Miller was utterly fantastic in the way she covered her ground (she was a daughter of Mercer Miller owned by J. J. Stark and handled by G. W. Poynor). These were strong bids that made the hour seem like scant minutes. Safari had no game contact. White Knight had one contact that was not entirely perfect, and Susie Miller had two finds on which her intensity was not of the highest order. Huckleberry Dan had a creditable first half and a tremendous final half, logging three finds where style and manners were the criterion.

"The weather for the championship was a decided factor in the final outcome. Take nothing away from those that thwarted adverse conditions, but the heat sapped some contenders. The wind was the toughest obstacle. At one point it reached a velocity of some 50-miles-per-hour and it was simply impossible to control a dog on those occasions."

The renewal was a success by all standards. And it was in quite a prairie season. Safari won her 10th championship, the Dominion at Gainsborough, after a 10-minute second series called with The Hurricane by judges Joe Hurdle of Holly Springs, Miss., and Paul J. Treadway of Berkley, Mich. Perhaps more auspicious was the placement of third in the Derby at the Dominion—an orange marked pointer owned by Dr. I. J. Hammond of Moberly, Mo., handled by Colvin Davis. He was called Oklahoma Flush.

Mortlach, Sask., August 28, 1967
Judges: J. H. Criswell and Delmar Smith
Open All Age: 62 pointers 7 setters
1st—War Detector by War Storm - Sugarplum. K. L. Gardner owner; Leon Covington, handler.
2nd—High Storm by War Storm - Cleopatra. Eugene Loftin, owner; W. F. Rayl, handler.
3rd—Possessed, by Tradition - Jubilee. Dr. T. P. Kennard, owner; W. F. Rayl, handler.

Open Derby: 32 pointers 2 setters
1st—Nip's White Knight by White Knight's Bill - Brenda's Candy. Nip Howard, owner; Herman Smith, handler.
2nd—Storm Glider's Jess by Mr. Glider - Jennie Gal. Bill Coates, owner; Fred Arant Jr., handler.
3rd—Rainbo's Slammin Sam by Rough House - Heir's Sassy. R. H. Pritchett Jr., owner; Fred Arant Jr., handler.

Saskatchewan Championship: 72 pointers 4 setters

Winner – Flaming Star by Turnto's Hightone Pete - Miss Boo's Loch. Mr. and Mrs. G. G. Jordan, owners; Herman Smith, handler.

Runner-up – Homerun Johnny by Rambling Rebel Dan - Homerun Bet. Miss Claudia L. Phelps, owner; Fred Arant Jr, handler.

Chapter 3

1968:
Red Water Rex

THE PATTERN was set. The courses were established on the grounds owned by Vic Eastmond and those managed by the Land Utilization Board which took charge of the parched prairie in the '30s and tended it back to use. The '68 renewal brought a big entry, 82 in the all age, 41 Derbies, 82 in the Championship.

There was, in addition, the Saskatchewan Open Shooting Dog Stake, which drew 16.

David Fletcher reported it in two sections, first the all age action, and, the next week, the other three stakes. He commented on the turnout, the entries "from every professional camp on the prairie." It all started Aug. 26 after a near all-night drawing at the Mortlach City Building. The Saskatchewan drawings became legend. The city hall's main room, also used for indoor ball games and dinners, was full. Canadians from Moose Jaw were helping, and attempted to read the strange dog names.

Lois and Cov yelled at each other across the room. It was the first real meeting of those who had been a summer at training camps, and the beer and liquor flowed. The trial was the first of the season, and it was the portender of many things to come.

In this his first adult year, Oklahoma Flush won the all-age.

Red Water Rex was back on the circuit, and he won the championship, starting his successful campaign to be dog of the year.

Fletcher called the Derbies "the greatest crop of youngsters this reporter has ever seen emerge on the prairie." He said that Herman Smith rode every brace and called them "the finest group of young dogs I have seen in many years."

Two among them certainly were. The Kansas Wind was placed third. Emma Jane's Dot, later to become famous as Wrapup, went unplaced.

Judges were William H. Jarrett of Zionsville, Ind., and W. K. Young of Tulsa, Okla. They picked among the entries in the four all-age stakes, and Bill Rayl and Weldon S. Denton of Ft. Worth, Texas, watched the shooting dogs. Jarrett campaigned a string, which he bred, with Roy Jines, perhaps the most noted, Ch. Attache. Young was often a partner with J. Harold Criswell and Star Taylor in their dogs.

It was a year of blustery, windy weather. Fletcher called the open all age winning performances "ideal".

"Topping the huge list of starters was Oklahoma Flush, a brilliant first-year all-age in the string of John Rex Gates. The youngster, in his first year of senior competition, already has polish, with little immaturity showing through. The white and orange pointer dog, owned by Dr. I. J. Hammond of Moberly, Mo., notched a pair of perfect finds to carry off top honors . . . Flush's handling response even while running a distant prairie pattern, is uncanny, and he is obsessed with hunting desire. Sure and polished attitudes around game are another of Flush's attributes.

"Gunsmoke's Admiration, 5½-year-old white and liver pointer bitch, owned by H. N. Holmes and handled by Howard Kirk, was second . . . Addie had two ultra-clean finds.

"Third was captured by Davant Carbide Imp, 4½-year-old white and black pointer dog, owned jointly by Mr. and Mrs. Jules G. Franks and Mrs. E. Myra Berol. The dog had one exquisitely handled find, pegging birds in sparse cover, with a world of style on point."

The Kansas Wind . . . Emma Jane's Dot . . . Librarian . . . were the ultimate major-circuit winners from the group of Derbies which Fletcher and Smith lauded so, though only Wind was rewarded at Mortlach.

The Kansas Wind won championships everywhere. Dot, or, Wrapup, became a down-south champion with her remarkable record at Grand Junction, and on her home grounds at

130

Sedgefields. She failed on the prairie, trying only one other time, in the Saskatchewan Open All Age. Librarian was of prairie caliber, but also won the Pheasant Championship.

It was the Derby Paladin's Rebel Heir which won in '68. Bud Brown, handling out of Florida, had him for owner C. W. Bradford of Westerville, Ohio. He was said to have "hunted with zeal" and late in the heat scored "mannerly while scattered chickens left low alfalfa cover."

Beth's White Knight was second. Collier Smith was the handler, Lt. Col. Harvey T. Ingram of Redstone Arsenal, Ala., the owner. He was said to be "blessed with great speed and determination to travel distantly."

Third was The Kansas Wind, owned by L. A. Gay of Junction City, Kans., and handled by the man who developed him, Bud Daugherty. This was written of the first major-league placement of a true major-leaguer:

"Wind . . . is a sparkling dog in action and his course was a long downslope with great visibility. Wind hunted with jump and purpose at prairie-filling range, natural in his ability to swing and handle. Topping a rise late in the heat, Wind was seen standing as bracemate dashed chickens to wing. This restraint lasted a few fleeting seconds and Wind joined the fray, gleefully jumping two singles after having been ordered up . . . "

Fletcher called the championship a "splendid" stake, but went on to tell of the weather which was windy, dry and then cold and wet.

The champion, Red Water Rex, was near retirement before the trial. He had won the season before, but the summer training was to decide his future. He had suffered a back injury.

Back he was. Fletcher said "Rex was certainly one of the strongest prairie all-age contenders, and he topped this stake going away."

He had two finds "razor sharp in execution."

"A huge prairie-filling ground pattern and a single remarkable find placed Hangman in the runner-up position. His performance drew praise and was so outstanding as to cast aside a host of challengers for the award." Hangman was just 2 1/2 years old, handled by Bill Rayl.

Fletcher singled out others for praise, especially Fugitive, which was hurt by a chicken leaving as he relocated. There was Mr. Jack Delivery, Flaming Star – two finds and then relocating through birds on his third – Doctor's Stormy Mack, Homerun Johnny. Lisa of Arkansas had five finds. Gunsmoke's Admiration had two.

Mortlach, Sask., Aug. 26, 1968
Judges: William J. Jarrett and W. K. Young
Open All Age: 75 pointers 7 setters

1st – Oklahoma Flush by Paladin's Royal Flush - Baconrind's Sandy. Dr. I. J. Hammond, owner; John Red Gates, handler.

2nd – Gunsmoke's Admiration by Gunsmoke - Colonial Rose M. H. N. Holmes, owner; Howard Kirk, handler.

3rd – Davant Carbide Imp by Carbide Tipped - Tarengo Delivery Girl. Mrs. E. M. Berol and Mr. and Mrs. J. G. Franks, owners; Fred Bevan Jr., handler.

Open Derby: 35 pointers 6 setters

1st – Paladin's Rebel Heir by Rebel Jackson - Paladin's Paper Dolly. C. W. Bradford, owner; Bud Brown, handler.

2nd – Beth's White Knight by Riggins White Knight - Misty Morn. H. T. Ingram, owner; Collier Smith, handler.

3rd – The Kansas Wind by Tiny Warhoop Jake - Ninnescah Sierra June. L. A. Gay, owner; Bud Daugherty, handler.

Saskatchewan Championship: 77 pointers 5 setters

Winner – Red Water Rex by Tiny Wahoo - Sea Island Gale. E. B. Alexander Jr., and T. W. Pruitt, owners; D. Hoyle Eaton, handler.

Runner-up – Hangman by Wahoo's Arkansas Ranger - Sharp Steppin. Mrs. Virginia W. Silvers, owner; W. F. Rayl, handler.

Open Shooting Dog: 12 pointers 4 setters
Judges: W. F. Rayl and Weldon S. Denton

1st – Ray's Rocket John by Hillsite Toby Boy - Hillsite Dinah. T. D. Sanford III, owner; Herman Smith, handler.

2nd – Home Again Boy by Pyson - Home Again Lena. G. C. Barlow, owner; Harve Butler, handler.

3rd – Glamorous Judy by Morgan's Boy Jake - Paladin's Lady Freckles. G. C. Barlow, owner; Harve Butler, handler.

Chapter 4

1969:
Jack and Sport

THE 1969 PRAIRIE season certified two Pointers which were to become major influences in their breed.

A Rambling Rebel and Flush's Country Squire. If you had been at Mortlach during the first two weeks of September you could have seen Red Water Rex and A Rambling Rebel braced together . . . a future National and Continental champion place in the Derby . . . Homerun Jim place twice with performances not to be forgotton.

Bill Allen of Jekyll Island, Ga., was the reporter, and two of Cov's favorites, Marshal Loftin, the Norwood, Louisiana, professional, and Wayne Cornelius, Fort Worth rancher and car dealer, were the judges.

The Saskatchewan was never so popular. Large galleries rode. The entries mounted to records: 91 in the all age, 57 Derbies and 85 in the championship.

Mrs. Berol and Mr. and Mrs. Franks followed every brace in a Scout, and Mrs. Mary C. Oliver had a Volkswagen modified to go anywhere. Allen mentioned that John Francis Brown of Commander Kennel fame, and John McClure from near Fort Worth came with Judge Cornelius, and Wayne Tyson of Sarasota, Fla., was there to watch his setter, Mr. Thor.

Of the all age, Allen wrote:

"A Rambling Rebel was a consensus choice after a fine exhibition with several finds credited to him . . . including an impressive relocation. He is a full brother of Homerun Belle, from a later litter. Rebel, despite Arant's confidence in the dog's

133

abilities, did not win until he placed second in the Indiantown Gap Derby in the spring of '67. But it is well remembered that the Steve Richardson stylist captured primer honors in the United States Open All Age stake that fall. The dog's versitility has been demonstrated with wins in amateur competition and two of these were of real importance — first in the Virginia Amateur All Age in the fall of '68, and his victory in the National Amateur Quail Championship over the West Kentucky Game Management Area near Paducah last March, when Clift Scarborough handled."

Two field trial favorites owned Homerun Jim — Dr. P. T. Fagan of Chicago Heights, Ill,, and A. W. (Scotty) Burgess of Hammond, Indiana Dr. Fagan was on the prairie, but went home early with a broken leg. Burgess was in Scotland for the summer.

Allen called Jim's race "spectacular . . . found by handler far to right pointing in meadow cover at 12 minutes, birds perfectly located. He went on to run well and hunt far ahead, scoutless and bending out of sight, then at about 24 minutes one could almost see him make up his mind that he had to run into that east wind whether he wanted to or not, and he did, finishing over prairie ridge a quarter or more."

Bud Daugherty had placed The Kansas Wind in the Derby the year before, and he was to earn a piece of the all age with Ranger's Gallant Man, owned by Lee Shull, this year. He had three finds, braced with Paladin's Royal Flush, and once backed Buddy on sight.

The Derby entry was unprecedented. Miss Merryway was from the cross of Flush's Country Squire and Flush's Royal Sally, littermate to the extraordinary Oklahoma Flush. They were bred by K. L. Keesee of Holdenville, Okla., and Miss Merryway had been sold by Cap'n John Gates to W. D. Cox of Thomasville, Ga. She had two finds that "smacked of all age finish."

Rob of Caddo was second for owner J. R. Dry of Wichita and Stub Poynor. Rob, like his sire, David of Caddo, was a strong dog and ran to the limits. He had a find at pickup. Dry had turned a small western store called "Shepler's" into a major establishment, one that he was to expand into a chain. Later, after a turn at Thoroughbreds, he started "Drysdales" in Tulsa.

The third placed dog, just as The Kansas Wind a year before, was to make history. Crossmatch was in ever sense precocious. Dr. M. E. Gordon of Claremore, Okla., bred him from Stormaker, entered in the the stakes for older dogs, and Cat Creek Sally. He was in the charge of E. B. (Bud) Epperson. He had one find, and a big race, and it was a start in the majors which was to culminate with titles at Dixie and Ames Plantations in the same season.

Rob of Caddo and Crossmatch were braced together. Also in the Derby were Double Rebel Dan, Dr. I. J., The Company.

The championship — first of the season — drew the best in training: Sugarshack, Tooth Acres Hawk, Hill's Stylish Sam, Librarian, Saladin, Mr. Thor, Mingo, Mission, Paladin's Royal Flush, Endurance, Ormond Smart Alec, Oklahoma Flush, The Kansas Wind, A Rambling Rebel, Flush's Country Squire, Volcanic Butch, Habderdasher's Royal Ace, Tradition's Peggy, Red Water Rex, Possessed, Bill Possessed, Flaming Star.

Homerun Jim's win was clear. Through the years there has been no rumbling or dissent, just more vivid recollections of how beautiful he stood on his game. Bill Allen wrote:

"Jim had a dream prairie race, starting strongly and with game on his mind. On the end of the bend of his first cast, at five minutes, he was seen by handler pointing far, far ahead on bald prairie with four chickens perfectly located, and very high, taut style. He had an absence then, and finally appeared most a mile-and-a-half away at house and garden bluff, ahead of our direction but off the field trial courses. The road gallery called point and Joe Odom allowed him to relocate to house garden in back of popple enclosure. He froze loftily and Huns were flushed for him directly where he said they were, then chickens were flushed, too — both kinds. At 50 minutes, Jim was traveling with the south wind, just a few yards in front of judges and he stopped and froze as chicken flew out ahead of him, he being downwind and some distance away. At 58, two minutes before pickup, he had magnificent style and manners on chicken in bush far ahead, and still had time to show plenty of heels, which he had done all the way. Few handlers doubted at this juncture what they had to beat."

The performance came on Monday of the second week, the second brace, a south wind and temperatures in the 80s. In the first brace of the day, Flush's Country Squire had started, lost and "found two days later approximately 35 miles away."

Why was Homerun Jim not the Rebel breeding dog to write his name indelibly? He died early, and this was before Pointer breeders, tied up with their own programs, saw much merit in what Fred Arant was doing. It should have been obvious before, but the light began to dawn, and his bloodlines began to attract attention in other parts of the country. A Rambling Rebel was young and caught the imagination.

Flush's Country Squire, equally young, had Derbies winning on the prairie this season, one in the Saskatchewan, two in the All-America. It was also a big season for Squire, or, Sport. He was placed second in the Dominion Open all age and runner-up in the championship. He was champion at the All-America.

The Gates, with the Cap'n in charge, were the better pro-motors. And they also had a good product.

When Cornelius and Loftin settled on the champion, it was still not over. Loftin began training dogs early in life, working for Bill Cosner. He came up in an era when second series, or call-backs, were a regular way of life. Judges let leaders that were close separate themselves, braced together over the same ground. Loftin and Cornelius called the black-marked Texas Allegheny Pete back to run again with Gunsmoke's Admiration. Handlers: John Rex Gates and Howard Kirk, youth and experience.

Pete had two finds in the first hour, as did Addie.

As Bill Allen saw the second series:

"It was in the heat of the day, after 1 p.m., when they were released. As it turned out, we had never seen the chicken 'bluffed up' like this, and Leon Covington said they showed him chicken he 'didn't know were on the grounds.' The dogs wound out at about the same distance away, and after about 13 minutes, we crossed the road at ragged bluff and headed into big country, fenceless and with few bushes, spread apart. John Rex called point far ahead at 18 minutes over to left at bush and Pete was a statue as handler flushed five chickens from bush. Then, almost immediately, Kirk's bitch was pointing at a bush about 17 yards farther ahead, six chickens flushed from it. They went on and Kirk had another find with Addie on single chicken at 23. That was all of her bird work. Young Gates sent Pete on, and had covey finds on chickens at bushes at 27, 30 and

36 minutes, all out ahead of us and on casts following finds. Judges asked John Rex to send his dog across far meadow and bottom to left as Kirk had his bitch traversing country to right. After two minutes of comparison, judges ordered them up and named Texas Allegheny Pete runner-up."

Two stories which Cov loved came as a result of the second series.

At one point, Pete was going toward one of the few fences on the grounds, on ahead. Race was one of the sticking points. He asked Loftin if he could send a scout because "he's gonna get under that fence."

Came the reply: "You'd better hope he does."

After it was over, Kirk went to the judges and gentlemanly questioned the decision. He said he didn't understand "because that dog trailed my bitch."

It was Loftin, as might be expected, who replied:

"Now, Howard, I like your bitch. Always have. She's a great bird dog, good nose. And I don't think there's a dog alive that can trail her and point four coveys behind her."

Mortlach, Sask., Sept. 1, 1969
Judges: Wayne C. Cornelius, Marshal Loftin
Open All Age: 80 Pointers 11 setters
1st – A Rambling Rebel by Rambling Rebel Dan - Homerun Bess; W. S. Richardson, owner; Fred Arant Jr., handler.

2nd – Homerun Jim by Homerun Johnny-Homerun Sis. A. W. Burgess and Dr. P. T. Fagan, owners; Fred Arant Jr., handler.

3rd – Ranger's Gallant Man by The Arkansas Ranger - Satillac. Lee Shull, owner; Bud Daugherty, handler.

Open Derby: 54 Pointers 3 setters
1st – Miss Merryway by Flush's Country Squire - Flush's Royal Sally. W. D. Cox, owner; John Rex Gates, handler
2nd – Rob of Caddo by David of Caddo - Tradition's Peggy. J. R. Dry, owner; G. W. Poynor, handler.
3rd – Crossmatch by Stormaker - Cat Creek Sally. Dr. M. E. Gordon, owner; E. B. Epperson, handler.

Saskatchewan Championship: 77 Pointers 8 setters

Winner – Homerun Jim by Homerun Johnny - Homerun Sis. A.W. Burgess and Dr. P. T. Fagan, owners; Fred Arant, Jr., handler.

Runner-up – Texas Allegheny Pete by Texas Allegheny Sport - Home Again Lou. Dr. Don Morrow, owner; John Rex Gates, handler.

Chapter 5

1970:
Backing, on the Prairie?

THERE HAD BEEN no more acrimonious trial at Mortlach than the 1970 renewal.

The stage was set early. Cov had invited two men who were well respected in their areas as amateur handlers. Neither was wise about the prairies.

Lee R. West and Dempsey Williams.

West was early to bed, early to rise. That caused the first disturbance.

Bright and early on August 31, the starting day, West was up before daylight, and in a booming voice hollered to others in the parking lot of the church motel at Caren, just east of Mortlach.

being awakened at what she considered too early an hour. U. L. took up the cause. The first person he saw was not the culprit, but Harve Butler, the Oklahoma professional who later died on the prairie flushing game for Saladin. He was an innocent bystander who had come out on the porch of his room to meet the morning. He caught the brunt of the tongue-lashing.

It was, by and large, downhill from there. The entry was 71 in the all age, 35 Derbies and 67 in the championship.

Anyone who has ever attended a prairie trial understands that late nights and good times don't mix with a week's riding, eight hours a day in the sun and wind and occasional rain. Williams liked to go to Regina at night, and, on some of the mornings, was barely on time for the start. In the afternoons he squirmed in the saddle.

But we can start this story even earlier. West and I drove north together, in tandem with separate rigs, each pulling two horses. My father was to join us. We visited the Gates camp near Melita, where I had broken a leg the year before on the third day out. We went to Eaton's.

Riggins White Knight was loose in the yard and heisted his leg while West was talking, Eaton laughing that he could always spot a judge.

Next day, Eaton worked Red Water Rex. It was short, for the dog pointed a covey of chickens in minutes. It was bird work that I will never forget, for he was so intent, so impelled into the scent that it looked as if he might explode from the excitement. As Eaton went in front of him, nothing flushed, and the dog stood taller and reached for more scent. Hoyle crossed a wire fence and a covey lifted beyond. He walked back to Rex, brushed him, picked him up and carried him to the horse.

He had a Derby which Williams owned, he told us, a good one. He ran him for a time and he was impressive. West told him that I had a Derby which John Rex was working and we were going to run her. He had never had any ownership in the bitch, Whileaway Royal Ann, a litter-sister to his Barshoe Cuz.

Little was said about it, though West wondered just how one went about judging his own dog, and speculated that it might work so only he would watch him.

On to Mortlach. One of our four horses was injured in the pasture at Cov's house, and that didn't help.

Bill Allen was the reporter.

The all age went along without great event, only wearing on the judges, who were the only two men — as usual — who rode it all. At Mortlach road galleries are large. It is easy to haul horses and be in view, behind the dog wagon ready to start.

It was my first time to meet John O'Neall Jr. I had sensed from reports that Sentry wasn't much of a running dog, and expressed that thought to West some time earlier, to which he admonished me that I shouldn't make judgments about things I hadn't seen. O'Neall was roading the white pointer in the gallery and talking all the time about his strength and other prowess, "the most dog we've ever had."

140

Perhaps he shouldn't have roaded him, for he was very short. West motioned me to come to the front, where, uncharacteristically, he said, "You sure were right."

Bud Daugherty won the all age with Kansas City Jake, owned by Joe Heindrikson and Bill Coddington of Paola, Kansas. Second and third were the Gates' champions, The Texas Squire, owned by Edwin Brown of Troup, Texas, and Oklahoma Flush, then owned by Roger Kyes of Bloomfield Hills, Michigan. All were credited with prairie races and good finds.

In the Derby, Admiral Knight, the dog which Eaton had told us Williams owned and bred, was braced with Ursus, Dr. Jim Nickles' son of Sandstorm Jake and Ripley Creek Renee, handled by Gates.

Allen wrote:

"Knight had a strong race, stopped to flush ahead on chickens at 21 in light cover and then pointed covey of Huns across big gravel road, the Huns leaving as dog was cautioned by Eaton, moving; he was mighty attractive. Ursus, with a huge race, was a strong contender with a far-out, wide-swinging race in a two-bend half hour and one chicken contact, birds leaving before formal flush. He had a stronger finish."

Mr. Revelation and Whileaway Royal Ann were braced together later in the afternoon. Said Allen:

"Revelation was gone, out of judgment after his first huge cast. Ann had a perfect all age find, according to the judge and road gallery, and even though the judge (Williams) rode and looked at her, she was declared out of judgment because she was gone too long, handler informed after time was up."

The information actually came that night in the motel as Gates and Scotty Burgess, Dr. Fagan and I were enjoying what we took to be a win of the Derby. Lois Covington and Mrs. J. Harold Criswell had found Ann pointing near the main road and called the scout.

Rex's Trouble ran the next morning. Allen said of him:

"Trouble had a brilliant early race and an acceptable stop-to-flush on chicken, moving some but heeding command at about eight. Trouble did not point from outside the bush, but got in, birds leaving; he still looked all right."

Admiral Knight was first; Rex's Trouble, second; Ursus, third.

That night, Allen was told that General McIllhenny of Avery Island, Louisiana, had bought Admiral Rex and he had been so transferred. 141

It was during the running of the championship that the real uproar started. Judge Williams announced a dog watering policy. Herman Smith went to town threatening to leave. There were huddles and conversations. All angry.

As Allen wrote it:

"There was a great deal of complaining at this field trial because during the championship handlers were told the scouts could only water the dogs ahead of the gallery when aiding the handlers. Judge Dempsey Williams was very explicit that he did not approve of scouts watering dogs, because he suspected them of training while the trial was going on, using choke collars while ostensibly watering the dogs.

"Having been on the prairies for about 20 years, and this being the first year either of these men have judged up here, I feel that I must say that any time anyone wants to water a dog on the prairie under any circumstances, it should have no bearing on the judge's decision for or against the dog. Many a great dog has been burned up on the Canadian prairie and has never been able to run 15 minutes again. Many a dog has been ruined by 'pumping him out' in bringing him to the gallery—especially young dogs, and it was during the Derby when Judge Williams decided to impose this rule against scouts watering the dogs away from the gallery.

"Truly, to limit or prohibit watering mitigates against getting a good performance by the dogs—especially on a place like Cov's grounds, where there is no water, ever, in any year, anywhere except for about 20 minutes along the edge of Pelican Lake. In other words, on only 4% of the course is water available naturally. This is usually true in any field trial or workout on the prairie. So, handlers and scouts should be allowed to water any time and any where they want to without impunity.

"On the other hand, if a scout is caught chastising a dog while he pretends to be watering the dog, or if a handler is apprehended correcting a dog with any instrument, the dog should be immediately disqualified and the handler notified . . .

"Unnecessary suspicion can get a judge in a great deal of trouble. He must judge what he sees and knows he saw—not what he suspects . . ."

All was far from happy. Especially me. Fred Bevan Jr. was equally angry after this incident with Davant Carbide Imp:

"Imp stayed out on well-directed sweep down right, bending as we did and crossing after first cast to rise on our left, heading toward fence corner on rise near bushes. Judge Williams rode up rise, and this reporter (Allen) did not follow when larks were sighted, however, Williams reported Imp was moving and Hungarian partridge flew, and he reported Imp was still moving. Frederick Bevan Jr. complained – for the first time this reporter has ever heard him complain during a field trial – claiming no game birds flew. Still Williams advised him that Imp was out of consideration and Bevan picked him up."

I was standing across the rutted prairie road where the second half hour usually ended, when Bevan came to the trucks, furious. He let out a string of expletives about the judges, looked my way and added, "That goes for you, too." Little did he realize I was on his side.

It was quite a stake. Hours with Homerun Jim and Red Water Rex, The Kansas Wind and Texas Allegheny Pete, Ormond Smart Alec braced with Haberdasher's Royal Ace, A Rambling Rebel and Oklahoma Flush.

Three were singled out. Allen wrote of Flush's Country Squire:

"For the first time in this reporter's memory, Flush's Country Squire ran for an hour without being scouted or handled by his scout. He had two finds, the first one far ahead on course, a hard ride away, maintaining lofty style, taut throughout ride to him and flush. He bored on out, swinging back and forth, just a speck out in front. He was never away from a cone of less than 40 degrees ahead of his handler, and his second find was an outstanding prairie find, farther away than Sweet Bippie's, which I still had in mind as definitive or comparative, as a forward, individually handled find, with no help from scout or handler. Squire had the same kind of finish as Tradition's Peggy and Fugitive, handler letting him ramble on, gambling somewhat dangerously."

Of Red Water Rex:

"Rex ran a perfect chicken race, though his finish in the heat was less than desirable in a prairie performer. Still, if there was anyone there who did not know how chicken should be handled – especially on an 85-90 degree afternoon – Rex showed them."

He had three perfect finds, at 40, 44 and 48, game flushed for him, precisely located. Allen said of his first, "He was found dead ahead of us more than a quarter of a mile away, outside bushy bluff, standing motionless, tail and chin erect, and obviously self assured.

" . . . With 12 minutes left, we could not help but note that Rex slowed, and as he was sent through grain field at end, he was pressing ahead, but was a very hot dog. Still, he pulled away and over the hill out of sight ahead."

Allen wrote of Fugitive:

"Fugitive ran a strong race, charging and busting ahead with individuality and bird hunting desire bristling from him on every cast. His first find came at 22, with perfect location and lofty style throughout flush and flight. Poynor sent him ahead and at 40, on far cast to left, out of sight over rim, Poynor came back for judge and they rode 7 minutes to the dog—probably the farthest find of the trial so far, and Fugitive still had the chickens in front of his unmoving, erect-tailed stance. Scout joined them and Poynor flushed. This dog had an extremely strong finish, reaching out of sight across low land at pickup time, still with speed."

There was a single brace left in the stake, late afternoon. Gates had fed his dogs. He, Arant and I were in a pickup waiting for the party to cross the road. A young Mortlach man was helping marshal, and was sent with a message. He pecked on the window and asked if "Mr. Gates is in there." He said he was told to tell him the judges wanted him to get Flush's Country Squire ready to run in a callback after the last brace.

John Rex thought the trial was already Sport's. The news was met with fury, but it didn't take long for Gates to ask Arant to help, and "we'll just win it again."

The judges were divided. West had Country Squire champion, and Fugitive runner-up. Williams had Red Water Rex champion, and Fugitive runner-up. After conversations, they reached a compromise devoid of logic. Fugitive would be champion. Rex and Sport would run again, with no agreement as to time or what was sought, on a course near Pelican Lake where birds always stayed. Both had showed they could find and handle game. The only issue could have been the stamina to complete the time. That was the logical issue. Not so in the callback.

Allen wrote:

"Judge Williams announced the two were running for 'second, no matter what happened,' and he said 'only one scout

144

will be allowed,' although neither of the dogs was scouted in their first appearance. The dogs sped away to objective bushes to right, Squire the farther in turn to left and away down center of course. Rex turned more sharply across at right angle and pointed at nine. As we rode, Judge Williams ordered Gates to bring Squire in to back Rex. Gates had to go around Rex and beyond him to left, and as he spoke to his dog, Squire pulled up into point toward thin grass. They told Eaton to flush and he did flush chicken for Rex. Now, West asked Eaton to have Rex back Gates' dog, which Rex did after some firm cautioning. Eaton dismounted and Judge Williams ordered the dogs up while Gates went to flush. Leon Covington warned that it might not be considered fair if Gates and Squire were not allowed to relocate—the relocation being as important as the original find in handling chickens and Huns on the prairie to most experienced trainers. Although somewhat startled that they had overlooked this point, the judges allowed Gates to send Squire on to relocate and after he tried for two minutes, they ordered him up and the decision was announced."

In conclusion, Allen wrote:

"The running speaks for itself . . . The championship dogs, though, should have special mention. It should be emphasized that Flush's Country Squire had the very best hour on the prairie of his career, and the only unscouted hour that I can remember, clean and powerful with a massive finish. This reporter . . . would place the champion, Fugitive, and this dog in one compartment, and Red Water Rex in another.

"If Red Water Rex was the champion, then, certainly, neither of these two dogs were close enough to him and his kind of performance to be named runner-up . . . If either Fugitive or Squire was champion, then the other one was close enough to be a really close runner-up, and that takes nothing from either."

In his report, Allen had a line that Raymond Rucker often chuckled about: "West will make a good judge."

Disgruntled, the handlers went on down the road to Stoughton and the Border International, where: "Flush's Country Squire, 5½-year-old white and orange pointer male, was powerful, wide-ranging and tireless in his hour, with three finds on prairie chickens and a magnificent unscouted race, always to the front, to top a field of 59 in the 1970 renewal . . ." Oklahoma Flush was runner-up.

Mortlach, Sask., August 31, 1970
Judges: Lee R. West, Dempsey Williams
Open All Age: 66 pointers, 5 setters
1st – Kansas City Jake 682504, pm by Hytail Hypo - Paladin Warhoop Daisy. W. D. Coddington and J. J. Heinerikson, owners; Bud Daugherty, handler.
2nd – The Texas Squire 815520, pm by Flush's Country Squire - Flush's Royal Sally. Edwin Brown, owner; John Rex Gates, handler.
3rd – Oklahoma Flush 782916, pm by Paladin's Royal Flush - Baconrind's Sally. R. M. Kyes, owner; John Rex Gates, handler.

Open Derby: 35 starters
1st – Admiral Knight 863806 pm by Riggins White Knight - Anastasia Lynn. W. S. McIlhenney, owner; D. Hoyle Eaton, handler.
2nd – Rex's Trouble 868675 pm by Red Water Rex - Rogers Rangerette. L. P. Marshall, owner; D. Hoyle Eaton, handler.
3rd – Ursus 843110 pm by Sandstorm Jake - Ripley Creek Ranee. J. F. Nickell, owner; John Rex Gates, handler.

Saskatchewan Championship: 61 pointers, 6 setters
Winner - Fugitive 714797 pm by Wayriel Allegheny Sport - The Druggist's Pat. W. S. Denton, owner; G. W. Poynor, handler.
Runner-up - Red Water Rex 690437 pm by Tiny Wahoo - Sea Island Gale. E. B. Alexander Jr., and W. T. Pruitt, owners; D. Hoyle Eaton, handler.

Open Shooting Dog: 33 starters
1st – Ridgeland 809215 pf by Texas Allegheny Sport - Home Again Lou. Quail Capital Kennels, owner; Bill J. Martin, handler.
2nd – Easy Mark 734806 pm by Prairie Smoke - Royal Line Sue. M. C. Casado, owner; Dean Lord, handler.

Chapter 6

1971:
Derbies to Remember

IT WAS TO BE a season of the young dogs. Cap'n John Gates had engineered the gathering and early work on the last group of Derbies he would send to the prairies. They were formidable. And they would endure for many another season.

It was a Saskatchewan when two Texans with good reason to believe in the future of their dogs came to the first trial and watched. Joe Harrington of Plano. was there to see a liver-marked dog he had bred and raised, Palariel Stormy Clown. Clown moved with the reaching, smooth stride of a Thoroughbred and he could crack his tail high in cadence. He had already earned fans among those who had stopped at Broomhill and watched him in workouts.

Edwin and Evelyn Brown were there to see The Texas Squire, already a champion, and a Derby. K. L. Keesee of Holdenville, Okla., bred The Texas Squire, and J. C. Meek, also of Holdenville, raised the Derby, Texas Fight.

The Gates Derbies also included The Sultan and Haberdasher's Millionaire, owned by Dr. McCall.

Collier Smith brought a setter, Wiregrass Thor, and a pointer called Torquay. James Norris had the Derby Breakthru and Bud Daugherty entered Warhoop Express Doc.

When the Derby at Mortlach was over, the judges picked The Sultan, Bliss' Plantation Beau and Breakthru for Gates, Fred Bevan, Sr., and Norris.

In his critique, Allen wrote:

"The main reason for someone to come to the prairie is to see the Derbies – some of which are sure to be tomorrow's stars and the day after tomorrow's producers. The only way this reporter can improve on his average in picking some good ones each year is to be noncommittal and let the dogs speak for themselves in the running. Of course, bird work separates the Derbies for judging purposes, so it will be permitted, will it not, for a few of the birdless Derbies to be recognized here? First of all, though, let the writer disabuse himself of a thought.

"Whatever influence is bringing it about, the requirements of August up here on the prairie, before a dog has had any appreciable quail killed for it, certainly should not be so stringent as those of November when, among other things, a young dog must be able to ignore geese and deer as well as hunt birds. Anyone who has ever worked a Derby they really like or live in Canada, will be perfectly satisfied if the Derby occasionally chases game, or at least runs in generally the same direction, rather than in the opposite direction, or into a hole or flat on the ground with tail curled under.

"We had better watch ourselves if this is a breeding thing, or we will force competitors to flagrantly disregard the whelping age of pups in order to have a 'more mature' vessel for cramming bird sense into, or we will be breeding mediocrity to mediocrity, under which practice the chances are astronomical that the get will be any better than either individual, or, for that matter, both together.

"Certainly, thousands will say, 'he's living in the past,' when this writer says that the first dog in the Derby set the criteria by which Derby stakes on the prairie should be judged. And, these two judges, whether they knew it or not, were coerced by circumstances (and their sum total experience) into using Palariel Stormy Clown as a measuring stick. Then, when other dogs came along they had clean bird work, and were strong and reaching and eager, they still had Clown to look back on, and divine with. May we preserve and not downgrade the Clowns of August. For, Casey Black had Titan as a puppy, and fondled Tyson's ears. Clifton Scarborough followed Rambling Nellie thousands of miles on horseback."

Of others that became prominent:

Texas Fight – "was shorter than in his previous show in the all age, and found no game."

Haberdasher's Millionaire—"could not get to the front, came through the gallery twice and, unheeding of Gates, jumped into the lake and chased ducks."

Palariel Stormy Clown—"split the wind and soared away, coming back across on his own, wheeling to look for his handler, then speeding away, tail cracking high. He found birds, almost out of sight at about six minutes, far over, and handler rode to rise and pointed him out ahead, crossing. Clown pointed more than a quarter mile ahead at about 13. He stood, tail almost curled over his back, until Gates got almost there, then jumped at the nearest chicken and chased them off, barking at them. He then found where one had lit and took it out after flash-pointing. He ran on, popping up in front and just before pick-up time we could barely see him, but the dog turned right at time."

Breakthru—"handles well and reaches out to far bushes, hunting all the way. He got just an edge when he made the bottom turn and threw his head to point . . . tail straight up, head outstretched . . . Breakthru finished on a far cast."

The Sultan—"performed nobly with a driving race out of sight straight away twice, scouted back, and crossing in front by himself, then searing the hay fields toward buckbrush cover at lake rim. He went away after crossing and pointed, on his own, in sight. It took two minutes to ride to him, standing with upright tail, trembling like an overtight spring, only marking flight of birds with his head as they flew—one still there for Gates to flush. This was a half minute before pickup time."

Warhoop Express Doc—"The wind was really tough on us now. These two were lost, although Doc was returned—too late."

The next week, at the Border International, The Sultan won again, Texas Fight was second and Front Runner, owned by G. G. Jordan and handled by Collier Smith, was third. Clown was again Allen's brag dog, "a real star, behaving like a Derby, with fire in his eyes and supershine in his gait . . . "

At the Dominion, Floyd Hankins and Carl Lippard placed Clown, first; Texas Fight, second, and Johnny Crockett's Boy third for W. C. Kirk and owner H. P. Sheely.

In addition to Texans Harrington and Brown, it was quite a gathering at Mortlach. Allen listed Louis Tippet, Dr. W. H. McCall, Lee Cruse, Jim White, Mr. and Mrs. Allan Jacobs, Don Ryan, Tate Cline, Dr. H. T. Fisher, Mr. and Mrs. Blue Morrow,

149

Mr. and Mrs. Weldon Denton, Rich Fowler, Mr. and Mrs. John O'Neall, Jr., Mrs. Collier Smith. Rod Cowan was spending the summer at Cov's.

It had been a hot summer, with only Bud Daugherty and Bill Conlin having the least wet weather trouble on their grounds some 100 miles north of Regina.

There were 80 entries in the open all age. Lee Shull of Cameron, Mo., was present to see Bud Daugherty win with Ranger's Gallant Man — a beautifully bred dog with great desire. He never had a just opportunity to produce his like. He had three finds and a "good handling race." Second was Warhoop Dapper Jack, owned by Pete Mixon of Cottonwood, Ala., and handled by Smith. Third was Broken Arrow, handled by Gates for Tommy Walden of Albany, Ga.

Allen singled out two others:

"Flush's Country Squire, with two finds, and Ormond Smart Alec had the most magnificent Canadian prairie hunting half hours in the stake, in this writer's opinion, and their finds were far off, difficult to handle, and the bracemate put up Alec's game before his unblinking visage. Squire was just getting warmed up to sail at the end of the half hour."

He liked some others: Handicap Mike and Fairview Boy for Conlon, Doctor I J, Super Star, and he called a find of The Texas Squire's the "outstanding one of the stake."

Of one Country Squire find, he wrote: "After being watered and sent on, he wheeled in midair and pointed again mid-course in four minutes, and never relaxed as chickens flew around him."

As if a rule, the best met at Cov's. The championship had 76 starters. Among them: The Company, Sentry, Haberdasher's Royal Ace, Rob of Caddo, Orion Flush, Ormond Smart Alec, A Rambling Rebel, Mission, Homerun Jim, Doctor I J, Paladin's Royal Gold, The Kansas Wind, Tradition's Peggy, Double Rebel, Crossmatch, Double Rebel Dan, Fugitive, Librarian, Oklahoma Paladin Pache, Oklahoma Flush, Mr. Thor, Saladin, Flush's Country Squire, Texas Fight, Endurance, Bill Possessed.

It was Stub Poynor who was most opposed to the order of the finish. The judges placed The Texas Squire champion and his Sweet Bippie runner-up. She was owned by Dr. Jack Huffman of Memphis.

Of the winners, Allen wrote:

"Squire, flying through the long bottom country, pointed down-wind of willows and covey was flushed for unblinking eyes. He was sent on to bend beautifully around the hook behind Cov's house – then he used up the course toward Mortlach and was found far ahead with a covey of Huns nailed under his nose, and he had been there some time. He finished strong and hunting out . . .

"Monday's wind (eighth day of running) was very strong, and it was uncomfortable even at 55 degrees. Bippie came from left sidewind at five minutes to low place ahead, throwing up head as Lisa Again roaded directly into wind. Bippie pointed, and Lisa scooped one out, then followed the rest while Bippie stood. Sent on, Bippie went left, crossed high to right and disappeared ahead. Approximately eight minutes later, Poynor, with Marion Gordon lost behind, called point at 37 and Bippie was a picture, tight and getting more intense, until he returned and flushed five chickens in her face, and she did not twitch. Sent on she drove over hill top and Poynor found her about five minutes later, down under pothole ledge, pointing with high chin that got higher at attempted flush. Six Huns were above and directly upwind of her on the rim of the ledge above. She went on to hunt every bush carefully, then finished into the meadow far to right."

Poynor's strong feelings brought something of a lecture from Allen in his article about handlers not riding to see the competition. Then he assessed the leaders, as he saw them, in order of appearance:

"First, Haberdasher's Royal Ace had a fine race, three finds in about 24 minutes on two coveys and a single, style elevated, and he was gone from two minutes before pickup time to about 19 minutes after time was called.

"A Rambling Rebel had a wide, thrusting, vigorous race with two well spaced finds, the last of which the bracemate was in the vicinity of the bush and a single remaining bird flushed far at other end of bush; he finished strong.

"Double Rebel had a nice race, very snappy and classy with magnificent style on three chicken finds. Toronado's Peregrine had three finds and a very strong half hour, plus a finish of some consequence . . . his range was showing some wear, he was gone quite awhile toward the end . . .

"Sweet Bippie had three finds, every one of them with the smile of the gods upon her ... Double Rebel Dan had a monstrous race and three finds which lacked some fire ... Rebel Knight had two finds and a remarkable finish in 97-degree heat, a blast furnace wind blowing 25-plus ... Repetitious had two finds and a magnificent finish. Then, just two braces from the end, The Texas Squire uncorked the two-find performance those people had been talking about ... "

Fred Arant said he thought he'd been overlooked, and through the years, as he told the story, said he believed the judges just forgot a day's running.

Mission won the Border; The Kansas Wind, runner-up. Saladin won the Dominion; The Texas Squire, runner-up. Allen chastised the judges for placing Saladin, and said he was "given" the title. Allen said Saladin "ran over a chicken, then ran the opposite direction then returned to just in front of this reporter in a buffalo wallow slough and put up another in the same area after milling around. Then he pointed ... " He liked Oklahoma Paladin Pache and Sentry, and said Flush's Country Squire "had three perfect finds and the most mammoth untiring race of all with certainly the farthest cast of all ... "

All of this resulted in an altercation at the Dreamland Motel in Melita between reporter Allen and judge Hankins.

Oklahoma Flush won the All America and Susan Crockett was runner-up.

The Saskatchewan shooting dog stake was scantily reported, all three places going to dogs handled by Dean Lord.

Mortlach, Sask., August 30, 1971
Judges: Casey Black and Clifton R. Scarborough
Open All Age: 80 starters

1st — Ranger's Gallant Man 775450, pm, by The Arkansas Ranger - Satillac. Lee Shull, owner; Bud Daugherty, handler.

2nd — Warhoop Dapper Jack 772981, pm by Warhoop's Dapper Dick - Jacqueline. Pete Mixon, owner; Collie Smith, handler.

3rd — Broken Arrow 869329, pm by Oklahoma Flush - Mike's Madonna. Tommy Walden, owner; John Rex Gates, handler.

Open Derby: 52 starters

1st — The Sultan 895786, pm by Oklahoma Flush - Madonna's Kate. Dr. D. E. Hawthorne, owner; John Rex Gates, handler.

2nd — Bliss Plantation Beau, pm by Cobb's Red Rex - La Belieza. F. M. Flanders, owner; Fred Bevan, Sr., handler.
3rd — Breakthru 905316, pm by Peter Rinsky - Fanta. J. T. Payne, owner; James A. Norris, handler.

Saskatchewan Championship: 71 pointers 5 setters
Winner — The Texas Squire 815520, pm by Flush's Country Squire - Flush's Royal Sally. Edwin Brown, owner; John Rex Gates, handler.
Runner-up — Sweet Bippie 839599 pf by The Hipster — Paladin's Royal Missie. Dr. Jack Huffman, owner; G. W. Poynor.

Chapter 7

1972:
Year of the Scouts

ENTRIES WERE SOLID, both of number and quality, and the results little in dispute for the '72 renewal.

Cov took Rod Cowan north with him, slight and a Tennesseean who had his best days on the West Coast in the '50s and '60s, where he won 11 championships. And he invited Henry Havens, the Ardmore, Okla., postman, and Wayne Cornelius, a Fort Worth car dealer and rancher, to judge.

Bill Allen was the reporter, and it was another successful event for the Gates organization. John Rex handled winners of both the all age and championship.

Oklahoma Flush was six years old, and the title was the eighth for him. He was then the property of a premier owner, Sellers H. Vredenburgh of Montgomery, Alabama. Runner-up of the 61 entered was Tradition II, also six, owned by Thomas M. Woodside, Sr., of Jackson, Louisiana., and handled by Marshall Loftin. He was also second in the all-age, behind Texas Fight, handled by Gates for Edwin Brown of Troup, Texas.

It was an exceptional year for game.

Oklahoma Flush had six finds in the championship, Tradition II, four. Tradition II handled three coveys in the last five minutes of the half-hour all age.

I had stopped at Melita before going to Mortlach, and one afternoon helped with the roading chores. I got the Cap'n's old horse, and Oklahoma Flush. The route was around a Canadian section, and both horse and dog knew exactly where they were going, where the water was, and when to turn to get to it. I was just a passenger, something of a tourist. I was sure they could have done it on their own.

Marshall Loftin once pointed out that it took a better dog trainer to keep winning with an old dog, than to train a young one. At Broomhill, the older dogs in Oklahoma Flush's category were roaded daily, but not off the rope until the last week before the trial, and then only once or twice. Roading keeps the muscles toned, and those brief works help the lungs.

In the all age at Mortlach, Oklahoma Flush was getting loose only the second time that summer. It was hot, and at about 15 minutes he stopped in a small shade and rested. I wondered why John Rex didn't pick him up. He knew why. Shortly, the dog went on and finished the half hour. It was all he needed. A few days later he cut the hour and won the championship.

The roading process was not just to avoid speargrass, but to keep from hassling a broke dog on game that isn't their favorite anyhow.

There was some door-slamming over the Derby, but the fun of the Saskatchewan was the group of scouts. Gates had Tommy Long. Joe Odom was with Fred Arant; Joe Nahr with James Norris; Tobe Bailey with Bill Conlon; Joe Bush with the Rayls. Robert Burris was not there, but he belonged to their company. They knew their dogs, for they helped train them; they knew their handlers, where they would be, what they expected — a team of three.

They were full of themselves, aggressive, riding hard, happy to be there. Underpaid for the hours and hardships of the job. To a man they loved it. They loved the dogs, and the prairie. They were sportsmen, competing with each other, and doing it with such good will, with respect for the other guy's good dog, his good job. They'd shake a lead rope at the other scout and laugh when both knew they weren't getting the job done. They'd tell the other he did well — when he did. With their laughter, their spirit — infectious — they put fire in the sport. They were daring on a horse, anxious to ride where more timid souls would go reluctantly. They would call point for any man's dog, and bring him back if they found him. Theirs was a code to admire; theirs were talents to respect, enjoy and be heartened by.

They were not just black helpers or scouts who helped make success, place Andy Daugherty in those ranks, turning his Dad's fortunes. Also the team of Epp and Epp, Roy and Freddie, and Rod Smith.

The era of the scout has passed, and field trials are lesser for it. Here and there are the remnants. David Johnson, handlers helping their handler friends, and wives.

Overall the performances are less. The change has come from the lack of new men trained for the job. Handlers plead economics. A hollow plea. Able scouts made money, attracting owners and their dogs, and providing the margin in winning trials. Almost anyone will call point when he finds the dog of a competitor he's helping. But the edge is the scout helping the dog find game. Some judges contributed, too, those timid men who never understood the role of the scout, how to marvel at them rather than cringe and fear them. They are the men who worry about coming back next year, who worry that someone's trying to put something over on them. They are the insecure which so many handlers seek.

Of the all-age, Allen wrote:

"Most everyone thought the open all-age judged itself, but Tradition II could have beaten Texas Fight with an early find. He was gathering up a lot of country in objectiveless land, looking for a bush.

"A Rambling Rebel ran strongly, as did Warhoop's Last Stand, Handicap Mike with two finds, Torquay with one find, and Palariel Stormy Clown without bird work. High Heels showed she was at home. Birdie Belle reached far and wide and was impressive. Also impressive were Paladela's Delivery, Ranger's Gallant Rex, Double Rebel Dan and Tombigbee . . . "

The Derby:

"Granted, Joe Odom and Mighty Sentry got chicken located twice, and handled them cooly and smartly like an all-age dog. But it was behind and the dog was not in front ten of the thirty minutes. Certainly he was the best 'broke' Derby back there and back here in August. But in August on the prairie, I'll take Accutron, with five contacts, including three all-age pieces of work and two chases, all out in front and streaming away to find some more excitement.

"Peaches Sweet Sam also was this kind of dog. He wanted to go with his birds, and Collier Smith should have let him go with them. When Collier hollered at him, he sat back – not laid down, but sat back . . .

"But eagerness and love of game and knowledge of the fore – of the front of the gallery of the front of a horse, is the reason a Derby goes to Canada – to see whether he has the absolutely necessary eyesight and brains to know that you want him always in front when he is not on birds."

Lee West and I had Call N' Raise with Daugherty, and he was something of a talk dog. He was to run just after lunch. As John Rex and I rode back to the grounds together, the gale-force wind was the subject, and he assured me "the only dog that would run into that was Susan Peters, and she's dead."

But he saddled his horse, as did the other trainers, and roaded dogs. He had wanted the dog, a son of Flush's Country Squire, but West was anti-Gates and insisted on Daugherty, who did well with him early, but whose training resulted in the dog's acquired habit of getting away. The dog was a natural front-handling individual.

It was a big gallery, Allen wrote:

" . . . We started into a 20-25 mph wind that must have burned the nostrils. The nostrils of Call 'N Raise did not burn, however, but the prairie around him might have due to his speed . . . he ran out of sight into the teeth of the wind and ran as big as or bigger than any dog we had seen in either stake. He was never behind. He could not hear his handler, and had to be handling from sight all the while . . . Finally, he split, ran through, knocked and chased seven or eight coveys of chickens in the half hour, and we could not see how many singles out of sight. He stopped to flush one time (Daugherty aiding him with a whoa) as one covey flew away, and he finished past the windmill where Sweet Bippie had her find a year ago, and that was more than a half-mile straight into the wind."

West, with little to do but watch, helped George Clark with several dogs in the all-age, and the more lithe scouts had enjoyed their competition. As Call 'N Raise ran, the co-owner who had handled him to many amateur placements got more and more excited and rode further out front. Tommy Long called to him, "Say, Judge West, I didn't know you rode in front of the judges except when you scouted."

During his "helping" period, he volunteered to scout Paladela's Delivery, who was being handled in the all-age by his owner,

157

Clyde Queen arriving later on. Delivery and bracemate were strong, and West and Long rode atop a rise. West pointed the dog out to all who were interested. And after about the third "there he goes," Tommy said, "That's not your dog. That's mine. Yours is back there and pointed straight to the rear, the dog just a dot."

"How do you know?"

"I've been watching. Besides ours is orange and yours is liver. The liver one's way back there."

Of the championship:

"There were a great many fine performances in the championship, and little argument about the champion, with six finds and the kind of race Oklahoma Flush had—hunting.

"After Tradition II, there was certainly Right Royal, with a very lengthy relocation that could have generously been termed a reconsideration of foot scent direction, and had a good race with some weakening at the end. There was Scatman with a strong finish, and he, like Oklahoma Flush, got stronger as he ran, with his last five minutes better than his first.

"Still, Tradition II's coolness around game, his immense range and his hunting direction to every likely spot and handling forwardly were in the pattern of the champion.

"Double Rebel and his kinfolk, the great sire and champion, A Rambling Rebel, did outstanding jobs of handling the country, and Double Rebel had two finds. But the breaks did not come."

Like most years at Mortlach, the entry included the best in training: Homerun Jim, Davant Carbide Imp, Palariel Stormy Clown, Breakthru, Warhoop Express Doc, Orion Flush, Pat's Monster Mike, Macon, Torquay, Texas Fight, Mission, Tradition's Peggy, Monte Bello Peggy, Librarian,, Rebel Hawk, Mr. Thor, The Sultan, Saladin, Double Rebel Dan, Crossmatch.

Allen's report of the brace of Rudy's Wonboy and Oklahoma Flush:

"They sped away independently and each was shown on lengthy forward casts through bluffy, rolling hayland. Flush was seen to point first at twenty, downwind, outside the fourth really large popple bluff he had visited on the south prairie. It was at the end of a mammoth cast, mid course, The bluff was large and he used the wind carefully to hunt to the end of it, never entering it, finally nailing chicken at far end in willow clump as others were ridden up by gallery following him from downwind of his search. It was good relocation, no fault, more really laudable than critical. The setter was very forward and very strong, the durability and forwardness being a mark of George Clark's setters. Wonboy had a wonderful find with high deep flag tail and good location. John Rex rode up on Oklahoma Flush through fence gap and a bit to left on rise, the dog standing high and with perfect location, where he had been seen running to hunt three minutes before. He had perfect location here. The setter added a good find to the right as we turned north, and Flush charged away to disappear over far rise at bank of narrow ditch. Gates called point and a chicken rose from in front of the dog as we rode to him, and he was tight and high, turning his head slowly a bit to the right, and five more chickens flushed from right and behind him. He was sent ahead and he disappeared far to right, made a swing just in sight and rose and fell over far dunes crowning haymeadow. There we rode up on him pointing, with lofty style much in the manner of a sight-point. He had seven or eight chickens perfectly located, and now he was playing a hot hand, finding a covey on each cast. He added another similarly to the right again, and then one dead ahead, just barely visible, at pickup, both crisp and clean with four and three chickens."

Mortlach, Sask., Aug. 28, 1972
Judges: Wayne C. Cornelius, Henry Havens
Open All Age: 55 pointers, 12 setters
1st – Texas Fight 903387, pm by The Texas Squire – Bar Lane Dot. Edwin Brown, owner; John Rex Gates, handler.

2nd – Tradition II 786990, pm by Tradition – Lemon Drop Survivor. T. M. Woodside Sr., owner; Marshall Loftin, handler.

3rd – Pat's Monster Mike, 887645, pm by Frederick The Great – Dixie Dell's Darling. John Patterson, owner; Collier Smith, handler.

Open Derby: 22 pointers, 1 setter
1st – Mighty Sentry 912419, pm by Sentry - White Knight's Belle. LeRoy Franks, owner; Fred Arant Jr., handler.

2nd – Accutron 917410, pm by Texas Allegheny Mike – Titan Candy. F. G. Wardlaw, owner; Marshall Loftin, Handler.

3rd — Peaches Sweet Sam 938066, pm by Dividend — Eufaula's Keepsake. Ernest Allen & Jay Clark, owners; Collier Smith, handler.

Saskatchewan Open Championship: 53 pointers, 8 setters
    Winner — Oklahoma Flush 782916, pm by Paladin's Royal Flush — Baconrind's Sandy. S. H. Vredenburgh, owner; John Rex Gates, handler.
    Runner-up — Tradition II 786990, pm by Tradition - Lemon Drop Survivor. T. M. Woodside, Sr., owner; Marshall Loftin, handler.

Open Shooting Dog: 19 pointers, 2 setters
    1st — Shore's Sir Richard 792841, pm by Hound's Cry - Miss Doone. Stephen Harwood, owner; Dean Lord, handler.
    2nd — Harwood's Killer 917974, pm by Harwood's Red Knight - Elhew Gin Again. Stephen Harwood, owner; Dean Lord, handler.
    3rd — My Big Gun 837801, pm by Pow Wow - Doc's Dedee. A. J. Johnson, owner; Dean Lord, handler.

Chapter 8

1973:
George Clark Hill

COV BELIEVED IN saving money, wherever. Judges are considered an expensive part of a field trial – especially in Canada. So, Cov solved that problem by inviting friends, and limiting the expenses to $300.

In 1973, Tommy Long and I spent the summer at Mortlach, arriving at the bird dog paradise several weeks before the trial. I had a group of young dogs staked under the south and west line of shelter belt trees that edged the yard of Vic's old house where Cov and Lois stayed. Tommy worked three coming Derbies in particular, My Main Man, Smooth Sailin and Greener Pastures. By the end of the season he had Greener Pastures, a daughter of Riggins White Knight, trained, polished – as compared to broke.

It had been the plan for me to judge the championship and the all-age stake with our friend, Raymond Rucker of Yukon, Oklahoma, and someone else would judge the Derbies. That plan went awry, as did many other things during the trial.

Tommy was the first point of contention. He had come to work for me from John Rex Gates in April, and David Johnson was pressed into his first trial scouting job. He wanted to do everything right, and after I had asked some members of the gallery to get back with the group, he thought I was speaking to him. Later in the day John Rex came over and said, "Will you please tell David you didn't mean him. I can't get him out of the gallery." In the all-age stake Oklahoma Flush had two finds, as good as one could ask, and the dog was running with the power of a diesel engine. Sent from his second, he flew toward Pelican Lake. David didn't understand the route to intercept him, and, as we watched, it was John Rex who faded out of sight, Tommy, who broke the dog and could predict his every move, was riding in the gallery. Someone opined, "I wouldn't be surprised if he killed you."

There were 63 dogs in the all-age, including Wrapup in the first brace, her singular adult prairie appearance. It started as a happy event. Everyone there. The best in training competing. But by the second night, after the first group of winners were announced, it went sour.

The Kansas Wind, owned then by Pete Frierson and handled by Garland Priddy, had been bitten on the tail while roading with another male, and could not point with his high style. Bill Allen said of him:

"Wind had the first really powerful on-his-own field trial find of the stake, when he was found more than a half-mile from breakaway, standing ears thrown over head, chin up into wind, and seven chickens lined up in front of him. His style was not 90 degrees, but better than level . . . Priddy rode on out and called point at bush at 21, better than a quarter dead ahead . . . Collier Smith rode up over rise while Priddy was calling point, and he, too, called point. When we arrived, Sue stood in front, flagging as some chickens flew and some remained, but Kansas Wind was still tight until the last chicken flew . . . "

We placed him first.

Warhoop Dapper Jack was black-marked, and ran a huge race. He had his second game near the dump ground that is actually off Cov's grounds, seen standing to the far right. He, too, had style problems. Allen said of him:

"Jack had a whale of a ground heat, fiery and wide-ranging, hanging out and returning on the right side twice, then whirling to point outside bush ahead at about 20 with birds directly in front of him, two remaining of six, some relaxation of level style, but taut indication in the foreparts. Jack ate up a huge chunk of country and had very good style and again perfect location on chicken during his swing of the ending buttonhook."

Joe Harrington was in the road gallery, and laughed with Collier years later that he watched the second find through field glasses as Smith tried, before I got there, to get Jack's tail to stay up. 162

The third place dog, Cheeno's Red Rock, was certainly not one of the many household names in the stake, and he ran just before lunch. Thus, most of the party, and all the handlers, went to Vic's for lunch. Rock, handled by George Clark, had two finds, a forward race.

The stake was scheduled to end that day with a bye, Knight's Homerun, which Robert Burris thought had a good chance at winning. But, as Hoyle and I went behind a truck to use the prairie facilities, I said that I hoped he could get something done with this one.

He bristled, and asked, "You mean I'm not in it?" I said, "No." He was furious, went around the truck and told Robert to put the dog up, that he was going to scratch his dogs.

That ended the running, and, very near, the field trial. Hoyle and I had been friends. I had bought dogs from him and bred to his dogs. He was a totally dependable man to do business with, fair and honest in everything he said. I thought he would appreciate knowing where he stood. Not so. He had run a dog over the first course, Arkansas Spicy, as I recall. She pointed game twice, and was gone some eight minutes, according to Bill's report. No one could but admire her style on the game. But at the end of the half hour, Hoyle took her beyond the open prairie, across the choke cherry bush trail, and stood on a rise pointing her out as if a great distance at pick-up time. I was not in a position to see her, and Hoyle knew it. But Rucker was riding across the prairie and had a different angle. As we came together shortly, he said, "You can forget that last dog. When Hoyle was holding his hand up so high, you couldn't see, but she was just a little way in front of him."

That night at the Midland Motel there was a good bit of drinking after the announcement. The Kansas Wind was the only name dog selected. And he had only shortly before been in the Daugherty string, leaving under less than happy circumstances. The focus went to Tommy. He had ridden the stake, and was accused of judging it.

It got so loud around the motel that later in the evening I took Tommy and went to a motel in the edge of Moose Jaw. Next morning we were back early. It was customary that handlers say they're scratching their dogs to signal the judges and club officials to beg them to stay. I was both judge and president of the club—if president in name only.

During the long evening John Rex also announced that he was scratching. Bill Allen relayed this message next morning, and I told Bill that was fine with me. If they wanted to stay, they could apologize and we'd continue. Otherwise, they could go back to camp. John Rex had a Derby for me, one with which he won the Georgia Derby Championship that winter. Shortly he came to the room and after a short visit he sent David back to the grounds with the dogs.

According to Robert, Hoyle had left Mortlach during the night, and Robert went back to camp with the dogs, At the Futurity that Fall, Robert said he thought his boss had been wrong, that he thought their best shot was left, and he hated to miss running him. Things were better in the Derby stake. The winner was clear as could be, a superb performance. Montana Rod had two excellent finds. He was the equal of his breeding, by Paladin's Royal Flush out of the daughter of A Rambling Rebel, Montana Cross Over. Fred Arant, Jr., bred and developed him. He later came back to Mortlach under the whistle of Marshall Loftin, who won the Texas Championship with him before his sale to James Ray and his eventual tragic loss a few years later.

Astounding had what Bill Allen called "the find of the stake." I have since had doubts. Joe Nahr was with the young dog, not far from Vic's house, across the road. One bird was there. Joe Odom had Flush's Rebel Dan and had been in the same area. We met him coming to us as we rode to his bracemate, which had one chicken. Joe Nahr, I later found out, could sound precisely like chicken flying. He could do it on the other side of a bush, or he could do it in the motel room kitchen. And Joe Odom said he could "keep a bird sittin', I don't know how."

Santa Rosa Star ran on a hot afternoon and the half hour was far and forward. Garland Priddy had a Derby in the cooler part of the day, and about the same sort of race, perhaps a tad more. And we gave a little to the weather, some say incorrectly, some say otherwise. Allen said Star "rambled through the big country, reached to the very limit under control, going to the bushes and doing a workmanlike job, and finishing very smartly . . . "

There was an entry, then called Barshoe Rebel, which became the successful Buckboard. Allen said, "Rebel had classy gait to uphold his breeding, but he was coming in some, breaking up casts that should have been exhaustive and more fulfilling. Both, however, had plenty of range and showed hunting ability above the average."

The trial had settled back to prairie normal for the championship, which drew 54. I had owned the eventual winner, Call 'N Raise, in partnership with West, having bought him from T. R. Miller as a puppy. We ran him his first season and sold him to Brad Calkins of Denver, as Allen put it:

"The white and orange first-year all-age had one of the most consistently far-reaching, sustained efforts seen in many a year on the Canadian prairies, certainly the best in a championship by such a youngster in a decade and a half . . .

"It is strange and somewhat ironic how things come back to someone. John Criswell and Raymond Rucker could have gone no further to find a better champion than Call N' Raise. But John Criswell, who bought him from T. R. Miller less than three years ago, rejected him from his breeding plans and asked Bud Daugherty to sell him because he had been beaten three times in open Derby competition by the same dog and because Call N' Raise was not developing on schedule. So Brad Calkins of Denver bought the pup.

"If, indeed, John made an error in judgment then, Patrick forged a reshuffling of assessments at this trial for he got the highest formal accolade a young dog could have before he left Mortlach: every other professional trainer – even those in the majority who were in warm trucks or bedrooms when he ran – had some flaw to pick in him. That is the mark of a dangerous champion."

I wanted Pat to go to Leesburg and John Rex, where his sire stood, and where his brothers had done well. West, who wasn't a Gates person, insisted that he go to Daugherty, who wasn't a fan of the Gates dogs. Though it worked out at Mortlach in '73, it never worked out for the dog in the future. He was exceptionally smart. Bud could yell once, as the dog got older, and Pat went to other country. Bob Duncan came so close with him at Inola in the Region 8 all-age Championship, a perfect race. Frank Mudd ran him in the same stake a year or so later in Kansas, and the front-handling performance was spectacular. He would do it for Andy. But not Bud. It was a classic example of dog and handler, both good, simply not getting along, though he was Daugherty's first prairie champion.

The running said of Pat:

"Raise outdistanced his more experienced bracemate (White Knight's Button) on the first cast, and came back looking for the gallery. At 15, he was hammering away with flashing tail at the course middle, when he climbed a hill ahead and whirled into point, taut and immobile until we got within 100 yards when he raised his tail and locked-stepped twice more to stop. We had to ride past Button to get to him, and he had the quarry nailed dead under his chin, with growing stature and interest at flush. Button pointed and corrected at hayfield and then we found him pointing in willow bushes on west side and he was inside, but nevertheless had birds flushed for him by Smith. This was at about 34, and Raise was just a dot crossing in front. Bud Daugherty sent Andy to find Raise down under the crest of a half-teacup sand cliff, surrounded by wolfwillow and buckbrush. A bird flew as we arrived, and then four more. Still, Raise was chin high, and tail up, better than 60 degrees, and alert at flush. This was even farther than his first find and just a few degrees off course. He proceeded to outdistance Button and all of us, sweeping and pausing once on lark scent in large pasture, then finishing with a three-minute final cast dead ahead. Button finished well to the front, but the distances were much different."

Oklahoma Flush was at the peak of his remarkable career. I was watching The Texas Heir, Rucker with Flush at the start. When I caught up with some 20 minutes remaining, Rucker said, "This dog has run the finest all-age race I've ever watched, and had one find." We crossed the main road through the gate and he was swinging toward a pond to the far left before we went out of the pasture on the east and into rough country. The dog missed no bluff. John Rex pulled his horse to a walk and pointed him out. It was thrilling. The dog was, indeed, running the perfect all-age race.

In the rough area he pointed, high, intent. Nothing was flushed. He relocated fast ahead. Still nothing. He moved up again, fast and seemingly certain. This happened either three or four times, and at the edge where the rough cover met the mowed prairie, a hen duck fluttered out, dragging one wing. Allen wrote of his performance:

"Flush was found at the end of his first cast far ahead, past where The Kansas Wind had his find in the all-age, and

166

he had high chin, tail lofty and curled, and eight chickens in front of him. Sent on, he mastered every corner of the course, as far ahead and as far to the side as one could see, hunting bushes and hollows . . . Flush went on to finish his hour fading away out of sight. Gates' novice scout almost ruined the picture, but Flush was unheeding and finished his last cast away and correctly."

James Norris ran two dogs of exceptional ability, and it is altogether possible that others might have placed one or both. We obviously didn't. We thought Breakthru failed in the wind test, as the course turned into it a couple of times. Allen said:

"Breakthru, and especially Macon, should have stood James Norris proud. They both handed in stellar performances worthy of accolades any year. The Kansas Wind, with a long absence at the end, a tactical error probably, also was great and worthy of comment. The last half of Mr. Thor's hour was tremendous and as good as last year's runner-up effort by the pretty setter. But the races and stature of the finds of the first two dogs were a bit more than the others had to offer in the opinion of the judges."

At lunch time, Cov's helper, Jody, arrived at Vic's headquarters with a Canadian horse which had been kept around a season or so, not ridden, and with a crippled shoulder that gave him a decided limp.

I asked Cov what he was going to do with him.

"I've rented him to this falla." He pointed to John McClure, a Texas rancher in his late 60s and owner of a dog Cov had brought north. I could hardly believe it.

Mr. McClure got on the big-footed horse in the gravel road, and, as could have been predicted, he met the rider in the air and bucked on toward the starting point. Mr. McClure rode him until he stopped, turned and brought him back to where we were standing. "I didn't know I could still do that." After an hour or so, he forfeited the remainder of his $20 rental fee and gave the old horse back to Cov.

George Clark was feeling good. He had placed Rock in the all-age, and in the championship he had been "doing a good job of running and hunting," as Allen reported it. Then Rock went to the top of a knoll that rises out of the flat prairie near the trail the road gallery uses. A small bush stands alone near the crest, and Rock pointed there. On stage. With spotlight.

His bracemate, Warhoop's Last Stand, had two finds, and was coming across from the far left. Clark was riding slowly toward his dog, his back to Stand, enjoying the view and allowing everyone horseback and in the car gallery that gathered closer an opportunity to enjoy it, too. But Stand saw Rock, and at the instant he recognized what was happening on the knoll, picked up speed.

Collier was too far behind the dog to turn him. George dismounted, took his time, oblivious to what was about to happen. Just as he started in front of Rock, Stand flew past him, ran up the chickens and both dogs chased them. Thus, there is a George Clark Hill at Mortlach.

A few days after I got home, the mail had a manila envelope from Alabama. Inside was a full color photo of Mr. Thor, a brochure or two and a two-page letter. Insulting was the kindest description I could find for it. Mr. John O'Neall Sr., who had not been at the trial, was outraged that his dog didn't win. Likely he hadn't been told about the unproductive where the hawk flew by, and the chipmunk ran out, or where he established point along an old fenceline, left and came back to point the birds as we approached. His last paragraph said he wanted to hear from me, and he didn't want to hear that his dog was third. I picked up the phone, and he answered. After the acknowledgments of who was calling:

"Mr. O'Neall, I wanted you to know that your dog wasn't third. When Mr. Rucker and I sat on the bale of hay to finally talk about the dogs we were carrying, yours wasn't mentioned. He certainly wasn't third."

Mortlach, Sask., August 27, 1973
Judges: Raymond Rucker, John Criswell
Open All-age: 57 pointers, 6 setters
1st – The Kansas Wind 810781, pm by Tiny Warhoop Jake - Ninnescah Sierra June. Mr. and Mrs. Pete Frierson, owners; Garland Priddy, handler.

2nd – Warhoop Dapper Jack 762981, pm by Warhoop's Dapper Dick - Jacqueline. Pete Mixon, owner; Collier Smith, handler.

3rd – Cheeno's Red Rock 908204, pm by Night Train Cheeno - Long Shot Bess. G. G. Jordan, owner; George Clark, handler.

Open Derby: 34 starters

1st – Montana Rod 960731, pm by Paladin's Royal Flush - Montana Cross Over. Mr. and Mrs. Gary Dowdy, owners; Fred Arant Jr., handler.

2nd – Astounding, unreg, pm, breeding not given. James Norris, agent and owner.

3rd – Santa Rosa Star 932323, pointer male by Riggins White Knight - Satilla Peggy. Jack Fiveash, owner; Collier Smith, handler.

Saskatchewan Championship: 47 pointers, 7 setters

Winner – Call N' Raise 898053, pm by Flush's Country Squire - Red Water Sugar. B. H. Calkins, owner; Bud Daugherty, handler.

Runner-up – Oklahoma Flush 782916, pm by Paladin's Royal Flush - Baconrind's Sandy. S. H. Vredenburgh, owner; John Rex Gates, handler.

Open Shooting Dog: 41 pointers, 5 setters, 1 German Shorthair.

1st – Bill's Discard 876364, pm by Red Water Rex - Wayriel Paloma Phoebe. Stephen Harwood, owner; Dean Lord, handler.

2nd – Oklahoma's Red Water 871886, pm by Red Water Rex - Wayriel Paloma Phoebe. Mike Weaver, owner; Dean Lord, handler.

3rd – Little Shiver 888905, pf by Peacepipe, Smokepole's Fran. Thomas Ennenga, owner; Dick Williams, handler.

Chapter 9

1974:
After the Coldest Winter

V IC EASTMOND was not a man to indulge himself. It would
take a record winter to cause him to buy a snow mobile to
drive from Mortlach to his ranch a few miles north. The winter
of '73-74 was that sort.

The road from Moose Jaw, Canada's Highway 1, was kept
open, but the gravel road that leads to the place where he
was born and raised during the years of drouth, was snowed
in enough days to cause him to take this drastic action. As
he rode to the farm, only tree tops were above the snow, and
he would see sharptails on the limbs.

It was called the worst winter of the century, and Cov
thought the summer was the "coldest and wettest" he could
remember. The result was a short crop of game. "If this isn't
the bottom of the cycle, I don't want to see it."

Bad as it was, the bad was relative; relative to the prairie
in years of plenty. On these superb grounds such a summer
as '74 is better than most places when they're considered
"good."

There was enough game for an eight-and-a-half-year-old
Pointer, handled by an 18-year-old boy, to have four finds and
win the Saskatchewan Championship. Fifty-seven of the big
names of the sport were there.

Mission, with liver spots and many ticks, found the game,
and Fred (Buddy) Arant flushed them, the last a covey of Huns
so small he almost stepped on them. He was easily the youngest
man to win such a title on the prairie.

He and Mission had the help of Joe Odom, the 25-year veteran of the northern summers who helped Buddy's dad win the championship with its greatest entry. A few years later, Joe would help another young man, Scoot Terrell, win both the championship and runner-up of the Texas Open.

The runner-up was The Texas Heir, with a hunting hour that took him to faraway places, and twice he pointed coveys of chickens, his last one bringing down the controversy that seemed inevitable at the first trial of the prairie season.

The judges were both from Oklahoma, Raymond Rucker, who had judged the year before, and Bud Epperson, the trainer from Stillwater.

The Derby stake had done nothing to help matters, at least not for me. I had thought Paramount Squire won something. But it didn't come his way, and over the years I've concluded they were probably right. There was a general feeling that Epperson had his prejudices among the handlers, and the feelings mounted as the long days wore on. The long days and long rides take a toll on a young man in shape for the ordeal, and that toll is more obvious on an older man, like Epperson, not conditioned.

As Bill Allen saw that part of the trial: " . . . Rucker did his level best, with his own good horseflesh, to see and adjudicate what was going on. But Judge Epperson, perhaps lacking a good horse, was either unwell or unwilling, repeatedly did not see birds visible to the gallery, and would not allow certain trainers to show him singles that had left their dogs, allowed other trainers to do so, and took eighteen minutes, by stopwatch, to go to the runner-up's last find.

"It is an axiom of prairie field trials that, in the words of that philosopher of the prairie, John Gardner, 'When you are going to a find on the prairie, give your heart to God, your behind to the horse — and come on!'

"If a man's fairness, or enthusiasm, or ability to fulfill the awesome responsibility of judging these most important of stakes is impaired in any way, by prejudice, ill health, age or any other inability, he should not accept an invitation to judge on the prairie.

"This is not necessarily 'young men's country.' But it is for the free spirit who is prepared to pay the price, as Coach Frank Leahy said. It is a fact that the judge at a field trial is not paid, but pays in strenuous effort that can never be recompensed. Thus, the great judges are the richest among us."

As it turned out, there was some confusion between the two judges when point was relayed on Heir, the judges having been separated, and it was technically "Rucker's dog."

Allen wrote of the Derby:

"There were, besides the outstanding first-place winner with two finds, only four other Derbies with the class races in the same category of extreme excellence.

"Colfax had a powerful forward effort, very classy in gait, high-tailed and vigorously enthusiastic. He also loved his game, knocking his Hungarian partridges and then pointing and holding one of them at good distance, individually without handler or scout help.

"Barshoe Ingenue and Hobo's Last Chance, braced together, put on a beautiful duel, separated from one another all the way, but did not finish so very far away from their hard-riding handlers.

"Paramount Squire was off on a cast, then hunted through birdy country by handler and then had the stake's outstanding finish directly into a 30-mph wind, fading out of sight ahead for his last 14 minutes, still biddable."

Of the all age, which drew 61, Allen wrote:

"Scat Man had a beautiful piece of bird work, but for the first seven or eight minutes he was unnaturally spooked and did not want to come to his handler at all. When he got his head together, he was a very creditable performer, but his handler had another dog that did a much finer and happier job of wide-reaching hunting, Oklahoma Paladin Pache, with a very good find, and an unproductive.

"Mighty Thor was the class of the stake with find, race, pattern, hunting application and endurance far and away outclassing the other entries. This is as powerful a setter and as thorough a searcher of country as you will see, anywhere under any conditions.

"Royal Squire had a very good piece of bird work, but a rather elastic race, with more constrictions than stretches. He looked very good on his game, but there were better races with prettier bird work — by Berol's Danbury Wahoo, for instance, or Texas Fight (where the judge did not see birds but everyone else did) or First Class Delivery, or Wonsover Slicker."

There was no real question about Mission's championship. He found more game, handled them correctly, and ran aplenty. Allen enthused some about Heir: "Heir's finds were on large coveys of chickens, his style truly inspiring, and his aloof unconcern for chickens leaving him and certainty of his achievement shone through every long-strided thrust he made through the densest cover – for he is a bird hunting dog par excellence."

Heir's last find which is so often recalled, was not on the course, but a very great distance. Some of his fans thought he should have been the winner, but that was a minority, and during discussions on the question, Cov asked, "What was he doing over there anyhow, we were going the other direction?"

Allen wrote about the championship:

"The winners pretty well isolated themselves . . . Texas Silver Spur and Torquay had a brilliant brace effort, striking fire and dueling one another independently, with Spur having two finds, and Torquay one, all three finds immaculate. Had The Texas Heir not come along, these two might have been considered.

"On bird work alone, Scat Man would have been of considerable importance, but Andy Daugherty hid him in a bush his last five minutes though he nor his father could get their hands on him and he was spooked and went to the kennels unroped.

"Miss Cindy C proved for Bobby Vaughn and everyone that she is not a shooting dog on this prairie, handling well at far, far distances. Knight Templar had two stylish finds and a very strong race, and was in the running until Mission and Heir came along."

A couple of weeks later, at the All America, the full impact of Flush's Country Squire was felt on the lists of winners. In the all age, Royal Squire, a son, won; Texas Silver Spur, a grand-son, was third. In the Derby, Poseidon Sam, by his grandson, Texas Fight, won. In the championship, Texas Fight won and Royal Squire was runner-up.

Mortlach, Sask., August 26, 1974
Judges: E. B. Epperson, Raymond R. Rucker
Open All Age: 55 pointers, 6 setters
1st – Scat Man 893390, pm by Kansas City Sammy - Jake's Prissy Susie. J. D. Spears, owner; Bud Daugherty, handler.

2nd – Mighty Thor 920118, pm by Mr. Thor - Commander's Skypoise. J. S. O'Neall Sr. & Jr., owners; Bill Conlin, handler.

3rd – Royal Squire 855649, pm by Flush's Country Squire - Stormy Becky. K. L. Gardner, owner; John Rex Gates, handler.

Open Derby: 43 pointers, 6 setters

1st – Colfax 1735, pm by Texas Fight - Tradition's Rx. Pete Mixon, owner; John Rex Gates, handler.

2nd – Barshoe Ingenue 980062, pf by Mr. Perfection - Gunsmoke's Elhew Dancer. R. L. Duncan & L. R. West, owners; Bud Daugherty, handler.

3rd – Hobo's Last Chance 968239, pm by A Rambling Rebel - Barshoe Barfly. R. E. Bellows, owner; Roy Jines, handler.

Saskatchewan Championship: 54 pointers, 3 setters

Winner – Mission 808657, pm by Vendetta's Jake - Jeannie Mae Go. Dr. M. J. Bennett, owner; Buddy Arant, handler.

Runner-up – The Texas Heir 921604, pm by Royal Heir's John - Palariel Wahoo Kate. Pete Frierson, owner; Garland Priddy, handler

In the open shooting dog stake, which Rucker judged with David Suitts of Boulder, Colorado, two young Oklahoma-based handlers, each making their first field trial appearance on the prairie, won first and second – John (Buzzy) Daugherty and Steve Downs.

Open Shooting Dog: 37 pointers, 3 setters

1st – Sammy's Ace 883277, pm by Kansas City Sammy - Jake's Prissy Susie. J. D. Spears, owner; John Daugherty, handler.

2nd – Wynoka 915276, pm by White Knight's Bud - Rambling Rebel Patty. B. H. Calkins, owner; Steve Downs, handler.

3rd – Paladin's Indiana Duke 871527, pm by Amos Duke - Running Tina. C. W. Word, owner; Dick Williams, handler.

Chapter 10

1975:
Amateurs At Mortlach

NO AMATEUR STAKE had been contested on the ideal field trial grounds at Mortlach. It seemed a shame. The grounds were at the height of their popularity. But, at best, only one day could be afforded.

I convinced Cov that a one-day stake, an "Invitational" would be fun. So, sixteen of the best all-age dogs occasionally run by amateur owners or handlers accepted. As it wound up, only 12 competed on a very cold, drizzly August 24.

Bill Risinger and I had been on the grounds most of the summer with Cov, and with us were Alan Craig, Jr., Raymond Rucker and Thom Brower came north shortly before the trial and they judged the amateur stake. U. L. Hudson of Georgia, and Marvin Reid of South Carolina, had been invited to judge the open stakes.

Mr. and Mrs. Denton Sharp of Duncan, Oklahoma, made their first trip north. He was to judge the Border stakes, and they brought Hiway, their black-marked American Field Quail Futurity winner which had won all-age stakes for Denton and Ernest Allen. It had been tentatively agreed that during the next season I would handle him and Denton would be the scout.

The afternoon they got to Mortlach, it was a must to see Hiway on chickens. He had a reputation for getting away, sadly it's a reputation many dogs have got wrongly. They were simply being run in wooded country and weren't found in time. Bill Allen, Risinger, Sharp, and Craig were riding. I sent the dog away from the corner by Cov's old camp, somewhat backward of the regular course. He crossed the prairie to the choke cherry lane, and we could see him at the big second half-hour bush. He turned and came with us north, handling far, but beautifully. He went to the first half-hour corner where square hay bales were stacked until they looked like three-story buildings making up a small town. I turned him beyond them and immediately found him pointing, high, intent and the chickens right in the bush ahead.

My theory that he shouldn't be worked again, just roaded, until the trial three or four days hence, didn't last. He had done so well they couldn't resist running him. In the amateur stake, as Bill wrote it:

"It was a premiere performance for Hiway, which had never been run in competition on the prairie before, and he showed a great deal of aplomb and appeal to everyone. Handler Criswell was particularly astute at three points, erasing an unproductive stain with an immediate find, and handling a stop to flush with ancien regime to suit the most demanding, pressing for a very good finish."

He was second to Blackbelt which "just hung out ahead, had a perfectly handled find on which we rode up on him standing haughtily, and a very strong finish."

Billy Lang handled Blackbelt. And Gary Pinalto handled his Paladin's Spunky Knight to be third.

I didn't get to run Hiway the next season. Risinger got him for the championship, and John Rex Gates got him to go on down the road, eventually to win the Georgia and Oklahoma Championships. Truly a bird-finding all-age dog.

It was a season that brought many to the prairie, among them: Don Ryan, on his 34th trip; Dr. Nicholas Palumbo, owner of Riggins White Knight, from Hawaii; Dr. James Nickell, John S. Moore, Mr. and Mrs. Arthur Curtis, Joe Harrington, Rockybull Robin Fowler, Mrs. Marion Gordon, Jack Fiveash and Jack, Jr., Harold Dean Arant, Ken Forster, Mrs. Joyce Burdeshaw and family, Bill Doherty, Bob Duncan, Lee R. West, Dr. Jack Huffman, Dr. Minor E. Gordon and Al Kern, Mrs. Bud Daugherty and Pat, Mrs. Sharlene Daugherty, Pete Reiman, Dr. and Mrs. W. L. Humphries, Nathan Sholar, Ray Fields, Mr. and Mrs. Bob Stark, Mel Babcock and daughters, Dave Myers, Paul Stuckey, Ruth Ann, Roy and Ed Epp.

The open all-age went smoothly, Texas Silver Spur, first, Palariel Stormy Clown, second, and Doherty's Crackerjack, third. As Allen saw it:

"The best of the 76 contestants in the open all-age was Texas Silver Spur, with one find called for him far ahead by bracemate's gentlemanly handler, Bud Daugherty, and a wide searching race, very courageous in view of Spur's torn footpads, under John Rex Gates' direction and the property of Serafin Suarez of Mexico City. Palariel Stormy Clown, owned by Joe H. Harrington of Plano, Texas, and handled by Gates, was second with a brilliantly stylish find as he almost fell off a road bank and hollow; third was Doherty's Crackerjack, owned by William P. Doberty, Lake Charles, La., and handled on a great find on sharptail by George Clark . . .

"The dogs seemed to pretty well place themselves in this stake, with only two other dogs of the entire field of 76 in contention with the top three.

"Many could have rewarded Monte Bello Peggy for her beautifully handled Hungarian partridge find, for she did well on this difficult chance. But she had a simple course to run and her application was rather unfortunate for both her and her handler.

"Rebel Hawk had two contacts and a strong race, true, but handler was off his horse on Hawk's first find just before calling point; and Hawk walked as birds flew, while handler showed the judges a sharptail wallow on the second find. The judges preferred to place clear-cut bird work . . . Barshoe Ingenue had a brilliantly handled independent find on chicken with a great deal of maturity . . . "

When the first stake was over, as was the pattern, the judges were the target of scrutiny. Lofton thought Peggy should have been on the list. Arant was upset with Allen on his assertion that Rebel Hawk walked on the game. But there were no affronts, yet.

In the Derby, Button's Bracemate had a huge race, forward and was found pointing by Rod Smith, high style, intent and the game precisely located. He was a popular winner. The second-placed The Southern Planter also had a strong race, and pointed chickens "far ahead in hay meadow, tail straight up, chin high and proud." He moved up, pointed anew, and as Arant stepped down and spoke to him, he took them out. Third was Gail

Possessed, which "flash pointed" and had a forward race, not as strong as the judges thought, and the bird work hardly that, in my opinion and Loftin's.

We both had dogs with strong races, no game. As the results were announced, the fire flew from Marshall over Prairie Breeze, and Risinger because of Specialty. Lofton accosted Hudson near the water trough, and Risinger spoke to Reid at the motel. Both were loud. And both handlers gave Allen credit for influencing Gail's inclusion.

Of it, he wrote:

"The winners were placed on their class of gait and hunting and producing ability, as well as range and nascent all-age potential. To do a creditable job of judging a prairie Derby, one cannot get so preoccupied with bird work that one brings back 75% of the entry to get 'definitive' bird work, as one pair of judges did up here nearly twenty years ago. Neither should bird work, or the flashing, cracking, sparkling gait be forgotten in a Derby. It is rare for judges to take it all into consideration and come out with a semblance of order.

"At Mortlach, good Derbies were rewarded by hard riding, hard looking judges.

"Specialty, handled by Bill Risinger, had a grand, far- ranging race to the limits, and Prairie Breeze, handled by Marshall Lofton on the same course, did a very creditable job of running, and running great distances. Specialty, in most opinions, far outclassed Loftin's entry. Neither contacted game . . . These two were not, as someone suggested, penalized for not finding game. The three Derbies placed were chosen not just because they found game or contacted it – but for the way they did it, the way they looked doing it and what they transmitted to the spectators when doing it."

If the handlers were firm with the judges, so Cov was with me. Furious more like it. During the Derby we stopped after being unable to see because of fog, and lost a half day. He could see the dollars going in costs for housing and feeding judges, and an extra day was a serious matter to him, even though the Midland's rates were low.

Allen said, "When we arose and walked out, low clouds scudded from the southeast and during the first half hour this turned into fog. We had to hold up and lost half a day running the Derbies and completing them Thursday afternoon."

The Nimrod became the champion with "three faraway finds and a thrilling and indefatigable hour of hunting" for G. W. (Stub) Poynor, The Texas Heir again runner-up with "three finds and another contact." There were 71 entered.

When point was called at 14 for The Nimrod, owner Pinalto, who was also scouting, started to the dog. His horse rolled over a square bale and rider, breaking ribs and leaving Pinalto on the ground with suspected more serious injuries. Poynor went on with the dog, which Joe Odom had found. He stayed with the eventual winner to the detriment of his own charge, Rebel Hawk, which, as a result, was gone too long. As Bill Allen wrote:

"When judge arrived, Rod was swiftly correcting to get wind from covert. The dog stopped as chicken flew and some remained, the dog with good style, location of remaining birds exact. Help (Risinger) was dispatched for Gary and Marion Gordon filled in as scout, finding Rod far, nearly to house, across summer fallow lumps near prairie trail. Rod had a covey of Huns pinned without correcting, just nailed with high style and trembling intensity. This was at 32. Thirteen minutes later, coming back from promontory into Pelican Lake, Rod again was found pointing and had his chickens initially located with good style and tight attitude throughout flush. He was running with the wind, but checked at bush momentarily, then checked in field, corrected on and sped over hill to next bush where was picked up. Handler said he was pointing, although judge saw him at pickup time, and it was a strong finish, faster and with more verve than any with exciting bird work yet seen."

Of the runner-up:

"Gusts were nearing 25 mph this hour. Knight did an excellent job of hunting, but he seemed to be on the inside of Heir's range. At sixteen, far out ahead, point was called for Heir, and after a serious flush attempt, Priddy asked for relocation. Heir went to his right on his side of the tree row, sifting wind from his left cheek, coming back on our side of the bushes moving into the field, back toward trees and establishing a solid, quick point several rods downwind from his original stand, a great location of game. Sent on, he sped across fence corner and was inside badger pasture when he was mauled by a young bull which had him down. He was checked and watered by Priddy and sent on. At 42 both dogs were far ahead through gap and in bottom, hunting. We saw birds in the air and Heir made a seeming correction forward at sound of Priddy's voice, halting to point stylishly. Tennessee Knight went on, and birds were flying in the same direction. We could not see what occurred, but Heir had pointed and had a chicken perfectly located when it left him. Judge advised Priddy to run the dog on, indicating his knowledge of the occurrence. Knight was picked up. Heir had a find at bush on hill at 50 with high style and closed-mouth intensity. He added another at 54 at the next bush on course, and finished bearing sidewind out of sight. He had run all except the last ten minutes directly into the wind."

In his evaluation of the stake, Allen wrote:

"It became evident as we went along for the nearly 10 days of this trial that the chicken population on Cov's grounds had more than doubled — probably tripled since last summer. The sharptail did not get more scarce as we ran, but seemed to become more available. The more that was at stake, the more cooperative in separating the dogs the game birds became. Almost too cooperative.

"For both the champion and the runner-up had flaws in their performances, due to birds we had not seen in the particular place before and the general emergence of game.

"Similarly, a close competitor to the winners, Buckboard, was undone by a huge covey that we knew lived near where he pointed and that we had ridden up, that his handler was fully conversant with, but which Buckboard could not relocate on his second find.

"As can be seen from the running, the deserving champion, The Nimrod, wanted to pin his running birds and moved as the judge and gallery rode to him, stopping and pointing just before or just as the first of several birds flew. He had been there quite a while, his handler was on the ground and his scout-owner was badly injured, which had held up the whole operation of attending to the find for awhile. Rod's second (Hun) find and third find were excellent, and he was stronger than Texas Heir at the end of his last cast.

"The Texas Heir's bobble came when chickens left him, and he and bracemate were both moving as chickens flew, but Heir moved only in a brief circle and pointed one remaining one as bracemate went on. Then he stood as we rode and the bird left. His first find and relocation was a masterpiece and his third and fourth were clean and stalwart – all of them stylish, intense and lofty.

"Buckboard's first find was a great one. The Texas Squire's patterning of the country without game for the hour was masterful.

"There were others, some lost and some that erred. Cementer had an initial find, even better than Buckboard's; farther on a cast on the same course.

"But the dog probably closest to the two winners was Hiway, the prodigious white and black pointer having his Canadian debut. Ernest Allen can take pride in whatever work he's done with 'Ole Bill' on those panhandle 'yaller leg' chickens, for the Denton Sharp family pride did well on two chances in this event and had a great finish. He was prodigious, if you wonder why that word crept in, because he had never been to Canada before. I have been coming many years, and I saw Bill handle not only the first of five chances he ever had in a Canadian field trial with distinction, but I can tell you he is the only dog I ever saw handle the first sharptail he ever smelled in Canada exactly right."

I wrote of the shooting dog stake:

"Texan Bob Langford's valiant campaigner, so genuinely misnamed, Bill's Discard, fairly wrote the chapter on how it should be done on the prairie. Three times he was found ahead statuesquely pointing. He patterned that ground heat which is neither too far nor too near, ahead without help, save the song of his handler, Dean Lord."

Second placed Volcanic Trail Boss, brother of Ch. Volcanic Express, found game three times, and Barshoe Bartender was third, handling chicken twice in the hayfield alfalfa.

Mortlach, Sask., Aug. 24, 1975
Amateur Invitational Classic
Judges: Raymond R. Rucker, Thom Brower
1st – Blackbelt 967632, pm by Flush's Country Squire - Quailwood's Sally. Dr. W. O. Pardue, owner; Billy Lang, handler.

2nd – Hiway 853672, pm by Gunset-Silencer. Mr. and Mrs. D. C. Sharp, owners; John Criswell, handler.

3rd – Paladin's Spunky Knight 902678, pm by Fisher's White Knight - Heir's Royal Kate. Gary Pinalto, owner- handler.

Open All-Age: 70 pointers, 6 setters
Judges: U. L. Hudson, Marvin A. Reid
1st – Texas Silver Spur 942127, pm by The Texas Squire - Pinewood Gussie. Serafin Suarez, owner; John Rex Gates, handler.
2nd – Palariel Stormy Clown 898139, pm by Palariel Stormy Pat - Missie from Plano. Joe H. Harrington, owner; John Rex Gates, handler.
3rd – Doherty's Crackerjack 821146, pm by Four Aces Frank - Storer's Allegheny Lady. W. P. Doherty, owner; George Clark, handler.

Open Derby: 39 starters
1st – Button's Bracemate 25490, pm by White Knight's Button - Dundee Patty. G. R. Quigley, owner, Collier Smith, handler.
2nd – The Southern Planter 26729, pm by Double Rebel Dan - Hawk's Dot. Dr. P. T. Fagan and W. S. Richardson, owners; Fred Arant Jr., handler.
3rd – Gail Possessed 6414, pf by Bill Possessed - Blythe Ferry Flack. Al Blanton, owner; Freddie Epp, handler.

Saskatchewan Open Championship: 66 pointers, 5 setters
Winner - The Nimrod 932791, pm by Volcanic's Nimrod – Oklahoma Nimrod. Gary Pinalto, owner; G. W. Poynor, handler.
Runner-up – The Texas Heir 921604, pm by Royal Heir's John - Palariel Wahoo Kate. Pete Frierson, owner; Garland Priddy, handler.

Open Shooting Dog Classic: 38 pointers, 3 setters
Judges: Bill Risinger and John Criswell
1st – Bill's Discard 876364, pm by Red Water Rex - Wayriel Palomo Phoebe. Bob Langford, owner; Dean Lord, handler.
2nd – Volcanic Trail Boss 952270, pm by Volcanic Butch - Enloe State Belle. Dr. W. L. Humphries Jr., owner; Marion Gordon, handler.
3rd – Barshoe Bartender 909553, pm by Texas Allegheny Pete - Barshoe Cuz. F. H. French, owner; Dean Lord, handler.

Chapter 11

1976:
Year of Realignment

THE WINTER HAD not been a good one for Cov. When he moved back to Oklahoma from the south he located on the Stuart Ranch near Caddo, not far from Denton and where he was born. It was a grand place to train bird dogs. Ideal for field trials. Some thought the best in the state.

Ronnie Smith trained there before Cov. The owner, Bobby Stuart, a polo player who ran a family-owned, old-line insurance company based in Oklahoma City, was not at all a demanding person. He provided a frame house in good repair and the kennels had been built for Smith only a year or so before Cov arrived. Stuart wanted to bring friends to the ranch to hunt three, maybe four times a season, and he wanted the trainer to have dogs to hunt behind. He also wanted a couple of dogs of his own kept year-round.

Cov found even these meager requirements hard to meet. He didn't like to hunt, and had little use for meat dogs. He and Lois were the least tidy about where their bottles went in the yard. The kennels were in disrepair. There were no dogs to hunt over. And Cov called Stuart instead of the ranch foreman when his water heater went out. It added up and during the winter Cov had to leave Caddo.

Stuart had given permission for field trials, and Cov and I had organized the Bryan County club, which ran twice a season, and each was a free-wheeling fun event. The AFTCA Region ran amateur championships there. The grounds were typical of Cov's choices – ideal for his purposes.

There was a more profound change in the 1976 Saskatchewan. Bill Allen would not report the trial. For the first time Linda Hunt would perform those duties.

Allen was the veteran, having spent his early bird dog years with John S. Gates. He had a strong background in reporting. His incisive mind had been educated with care before he started his days as reporter and outdoor writer for the Atlanta Constitution.

He had not the slightest reluctance to report controversy, or, on occasion, to be a part of it. Readers of the FIELD could hardly wait until the report appeared to see what Bill Allen wrote about the prairie trials. He made heroes of dog and man. Dogs didn't perform all the same to him. There were villains, and there were super-stars. As a consequence there were dogs that came off the prairie with their own galleries — and that translated into stud business for their owners. It would also mean that some were watched more closely, and, thus, won more for their handlers. Allen didn't say something was "thrilling," he made you feel it was so. He was accomplished at his craft.

The wife of an active dog trainer becoming a reporter of field trials launched something very new, and it would set a trend. When Hochwalt reported for the FIELD he was required not to have dogs or to have them in competition. That customary journalistic rule of impartiality had been bent, if not broken.

It should be noted that during the war years and for a very short time, Pearl Lee Epperson reported a few trials. She filled in an emergency.

Hochwalt was an employee of the FIELD, commissioned to cover the major stakes. As time moved along and the major circuit expanded not only into more and more all-age championships, but unto a circuit for shooting dogs, it was impossible for the magazine to afford full-time reporter-employees. Canada had been something of an exception, in that reporters like Allen kept their expenses other than motel and they were divided between the trials they reported by the FIELD. Every trial became responsible for selection of a reporter, and must shoulder the expenses for same. It simply boiled down to economics.

Few were those with the ability to write and ride willing to give the time, and, like the judges, hear the complaining.

Linda Hunt was blessed with intestinal fortitude, an acknowledged ability with young dogs and a willingness, even desire, to work. Her devotion to the sport was true. Albeit she had no formal training or background for writing or reporting she was anxious to try her hand. She rode every brace of the trials she reported. She rode close by the judges, and was always an aggressive part of the official team. She was proud of her position, and its importance.

Unfortunately, because of the lack of writing and reporting experience and an ambition to please clubs and some fellow handlers, there was a sameness. At times it was difficult to discover why all the dogs entered didn't win.

The one certainty was that her riding and reporting changed their family fortunes. She and her husband, Bill, trained out of Missouri. Luck had not often come their way. They regularly went to Canada, to grounds in Alberta, Bill with a string of older dogs, Linda with a string of young ones. They made the circuit, with dogs that were occasionally placed. But it was not until '76 that he won a championship, coincidental with Linda's discovery of reporting.

They lived in horse country, and Bill's horse-trading ability was relied on, though they were not always the fattest around.

In '76 he handled Miss Warsmoke to the All-America Quail title.

Linda was available. She brought another handler with additional dogs to the trial, and the list of trials they attended grew. Over the next 10 years they won 10 championships and 12 runners-up.

Whether true or not, the perception was that judges often were made aware of her views, even likely what she would write. The charge of influencing the outcome grew to the point that Andy Daugherty spearheaded an effort to have her banned from reporting major trials. Nothing much came of it, and Marshall Loftin was her strongest defender:

"It would knock another handler off the circuit, because Bill couldn't make it if she wasn't getting their expenses paid. Besides who'd be riding all these miles if she doesn't?"

The Daugherty and Hunt camps buried their differences. Hunt kept on reporting major stakes until she became secretary of the AFTCA. And her husband kept winning, the ball had gathered momentum with her invaluable help. It was she who, when Bill wanted to take a state job managing a field trial area, said no. Her life was with field trials.

The pattern was set, and trials, in need of someone to write something about them, abandoned the old precepts. The Hunt success, where reporting was the reason or not, encouraged other wives and girl friends to write about the home team. It proved to be the turning point of other careers. Impartiality fell to economics.

U. L. Hudson of Demorest, Ga., he of the handlebar moustache, and the truck decorated with antlers, was back to judge at Mortlach. His partner was Ed Butler of Sunset, Texas, his considerable bulk trussed in overalls, and laced with a sense of humor of rare quality. If they had any problems it was not reported.

Strongman was the winner, described as being "at the tender age of four has captured his third all-age championship in less than a year. He put down a thrilling hour here to walk away with the title uncontested over a field of 71 for owner D. C. Moses of Arthur, Ill., and handler, young Freddie Rayl. He had two sterling pieces of bird work and a blistering race from start to finish."

The runner-up was Forty Grand, handled for Arthur Curtis of West Paducah, Ky., by John Rex Gates. "He ran in scorching heat which did seem to subside toward the end of the hour; had three finds, two real limbers, and an unproductive."

In the Open All Age, Hiway had two finds and a back, as owners Jo and Denton Sharp watched him perform for Gates. He was first. Second was The Texas Heir, also with two finds, for Garland Priddy and owner Pete Frierson. Texas Silver Spur, which won the stake the year before, was third with one find for Gates and owner Serafin Suarez, the Mexico City field trialer who bought him from Edwin Brown during the winter. Brown's Texas Fight drew praise for his ground effort. But he only had an unproductive. Brown sold Spur before he won two prairie titles in one year, and establish himself as one of the superior prairie bird dogs.

In the Derby, two of the winners were littermates – Warhoop Express Boy and Country Express Doc – which would eventually win prairie championships. Boy, owned by R. L. Duncan, was first; Doc, owned by Don Faller, was third. Bud Daugherty handled both. They were sired by Warhoop Express Doc, owned by Duncan and Springfield sportsman Lee Cruse. Their dam, Gwinn's Little Jan, was bred and owned all her life by Gwinn Williams of Sulphur, Okla. She was placed in one trial, and subsequently bred with great success. She became the only female to have produced three prairie champions when her daughter, Michael's Express Babe, won the Saskatchewan in '82.

Daugherty also handled the second placed winner, Agenda, a daughter of Dr. M. E. Gordon's Continental and National Champion Crossmatch. She was owned by the Claremore doctor and subsequently produced his winning male, Headstone.

Mortlach, Sask., August 30, 1976
Judges: U. L. Hudson and Ed Butler
Open All Age – 63 pointers, 4 setters
1st – Hiway 853672, pointer male, by Gunset – Silencer. D. C. Sharp, owner; John Rex Gates, handler.
2nd – The Texas Heir 921604, pointer male by Royal Heir's John – Palariel Wahoo Kate. Pete Frierson, owner; Garland Priddy, handler.
3rd – Texas Silver Spur 942127, pointer male, by The Texas Squire – Pinewood Gussie. Serafin Suarez, owner; John Rex Gates, handler.

Open Derby – 42 starters
1st – Warhoop Express Boy 31777, pointer male, by Warhoop Express Doc – Gwinn's Little Jan. R. L. Duncan, owner; Bud Daugherty, handler.
2nd – Agenda, 44632, pointer female, by Crossmatch – White Knight Trudy. Dr. M. E. Gordon, owner; Bud Daugherty, handler.
3rd – Country Express Doc 33353, pointer male, by Warhoop Express Doc – Gwinn's Little Jan. Don Faller, owner; Bud Daugherty, owner.

The Saskatchewan Open Championship
66 pointers and 5 setters
Winner – Strongman 981135, pointer male, by Lem Ripcord – Stylish Sam's Ginger. D. C. Moses, owner; Freddie Rayl, owner.
Runner-up – Forty Grand 952242, pointer male, by Paladin Heir – Rex's Tiny Red. A. S. Curtis, owner; John Rex Gates, handler.

Open Shooting Dog

1st — Bill's Discard 876364, pointer male, by Red Water Rex — Wayriel Palamo Phoebe. Bobby Langford, owner; Dean Lord, handler.

2nd — Oklahoma Pache Sue 920871, pointer female, by Oklahoma Paladin Pache — Sherwood's White Lady. Dr. F. F. Simmons, owner; Dean Lord, handler.

3rd — Everton's Moby 974559, pointer male, by Beeline Trooper — Stone Hill Rudy. Gordon Schroeder, owner; Gary Parker, handler.

Chapter 12

1977:
Like Father,
Like Wrangler

LINDA HUNT WAS back to Mortlach for the second year, and Cov invited L. D. Hayes of Bartlesville, Okla., and W. C. Kirk of Bowie, Texas, to judge. The field was again representative of the best in training.

Oklahoma Flush won the Saskatchewan in 1972, and this renewal was to go to his son, Flush's Wrangler, owned by Dr. Ron Deal of Macon, Georgia. He was with John Rex Gates, who had him since he was placed in the American Field Quail Futurity at Inola. The same male line was represented in the runner-up, County Seat, a son of Texas Fight, owned by Frank Sallee of Missouri, and handled by Bill Hunt.

The report said:

"Wrangler had one find to compliment a splendid ground effort. Seat had three pieces of work and a true prairie-filling race. The championship drew 59 contenders.

"The open all-age stake saw 47 toe the mark and a standout winner emerged in Texas Fight. He scored twice and put down a far-flung race. He is owned by Edwin Brown of Troup, Texas, and was handled by John Rex Gates. Man's Knighted Squire, white and orange pointer male from the string of Bud Daugherty, was second for owner Tom M. Schooley of Tulsa. He had one contact on game. Third was Texas Silver Spur, likewise a white and orange pointer male, having one contact. He is owned by Nishimura of Tokyo, and handled by Gates.

"The open Derby attracted 42 promising youngsters and was dominated by a white and orange pointer female, Michael's Express Babe, piloted by Andy Daugherty for Michael Faller of Springfield, Ill. She had two finds and showed a desire to range and handle. Quailcrest Rambler was second for Hoyle Eaton and owner Richard Hall, Jr., of Memphis. Rambler had one well-done piece of work. Third was Snow Cloud, a female Pointer, also in Eaton's string, and owned by Lester C. Shepard of Conroe, Texas.

"A shooting dog classic ran prior to the all-age events this year and 49 competitors made it a quantity as well as quality stake. The winner was a white and liver pointer female, Miss Warhoop Express, owned by L. D. Hayes, and handled by John Daugherty. Second was Pete of Caddo, from the Marion Gordon camp for owner Dale Perryman of Springfield, Mo. Amos Mosley, owned by Woody Thompson of Batesville, Ark., and handled by Dean Lord, was third. Lord said that Hank P. Sheely of Denton, Texas, had purchased Amos."

Of the open all-age, Mrs. Hunt wrote:

"Texas Fight, prairie dog supreme, ran in the fifth brace and set a standard that was not equalled in the stake. He scored two finds, the first being a most outstanding one that will remain in mind for a long time. It was far on a limb directly in front and Gates called point on the crest and Fight stood in the bottom land along an unmowed strip looking twice his size. Chickens began leaving at intervals and it seemed that minutes passed as we rode and still more remained as Gates dismounted to reach the motionless Fight. His second find also was pretty and well done. Needless to say, the first find would have quit sufficiently assured him the top spot in the stake. His race, in short, was forward and far flung. What more can you ask?

"Man's Knighted Squire wasted no time in his heat as he scored on a very praiseworthy piece early. He was standing tall and proud as handler went in to flush and retained the same tall and proud stance as he watched the birds leaving. His race had been sufficient the first part, but the last 10 minutes he really established himself as a prairie contender to be reckoned with.

"Texas Silver Spur, for the second year in a row, captured third in this stake and, if memory serves, it was on the same course. It was one find that was pretty and sharply done along with a good ground effort that brought him reward. He did not have his usual speed and drive, but gallant performer that he is, he went the route without wavering."

The three placed were all grandsons of Ch. Flush's Country Squire – Fight and Spur by Ch. The Texas Squire and Man's Knighted Squire by My Main Man. Mentioned as "contenders" were Knight's Triple Play, Rex's Cherokee Jake, Buckboard and Doc's Paladin Babe.

The Derby winner would return in '82 to win the Saskatchewan Championship, and would go to Grand Junction to win the National. Mrs. Hunt wrote of her:

"A standout winner for young Andy Daugherty was Michael's Express Babe. She made some beautiful swings, displaying a desire to stretch while never once losing contact as she seemed on the end of that string. She tallied two praiseworthy pieces of bird work, remaining motionless as she watched the birds leave, and once this occurred before handler was with her. After a short time on both finds, she took a few short steps, indicating only that she still had the desire one likes to see in broke Derbies. The last find was on a covey of Huns, an accomplishment for a dog of any age, and it was as if she had it planned waiting for all the road gallery to be on hand to see her perform.

"Quailcrest Rambler had a find that showed a very well mannered youngster quite capable of handling his game. His ground work was admirable and he did not cause a lot of riding to keep him directed after the first cast. Snow Cloud had gained favor with her light speedy way of getting over the ground, and her casts had carried her to great distances."

High Fidelity, who would win the championship in 1981, was singled out for mention, as were Constant Comment, a Derby which Brown bought during the summer, and Chief Moon Mountain. Also in the group were Bar C Rebelette, Arcanum's Aspasia, Fiddler, Blackbelt's Fargo, Stampin Kate, The Cajun Rebel and Heritage Premonition.

Of the championship:

"Wrangler performed in the 19th brace, which drew the third course along the big hay fields and around Pelican Lake. He had been running the country in good form in the early going, but after his find that was far across the big unmowed prairie, it would have seemed that you could have drawn a map and not have planned it any better. His last cast carried him far across the ridge and at 58 he was seen just hitting the bluff at the northern most part of the course. He was picked up just on out after time had expired. True, he only had one contact, but combined with the splendid ground work, it was all that was necessary for the judiciary to award him the title.

"County Seat, first-year all-age, again showed himself to be a prairie threat. Seat does not have a long list of placements, but among them was third in the Border International all-age during his Derby year . . . After a fast and furious hour it was generally felt that serious consideration would be given him. There were those that questioned an incident that took place on the breakaway where both dogs went competitively straightaway for the top of the hill. Both were out of sight and birds were seen to lift and fly to the south. At breakneck speed the judges were the first to arrive at a vantage point and Seat remained in high gear never having veered from his course. Hunt, arriving in the area, went on in search and called point some distance. Seat's second point proved unproductive from one point of view, but the judiciary related that they had seen birds lift just seconds before but could not be certain of their exact lift off. His third was in a hay field as he was regaining the front where several birds were seen in the are, and when seen he was rigid in a spun position with a bird directly in front as Hunt walked in. His race was fast, forward and distant for the first half. After crossing the road he made a sweep far past the sand dune ridge and quite a bit of time elapsed before he was gathered up and brought on to finish with plenty left, going straight away to the sand dunes on the next edge.

"Evolution had put down a performance that received much consideration as he ran in the first afternoon brace on the final day. He had two finds and a good race . . . Knight's Triple Play had to sterling finds but his ground effort was not quite on the level with that of the winners. Miller's Happy Choice had three well done pieces of bird work with average style. The Texas Heir and Over There had been early performers that remained in the limelight for some time."

Mortlach, Sask., August 17, 1977
Judges: L. D. Hayes, W. C. Kirk
Open All-Age — 45 pointers, 2 setters
1st — Texas Fight 903387, pointer male by The Texas Squire — Bar Lane Babe. Edwin Brown, owner; John Rex Gates, handler.
2nd — Man's Knighted Squire 12696, pointer male, by My Main Man — Sunday Clothes. T. M. Schooley, owner; Bud Daugherty, handler.
3rd — Texas Silver Spur 942127, pointer male, by The Texas Squire — Pinewood Gussie. Haruo Nishimura, owner; John Rex Gates, handler.

Open Derby — 38 pointers, 3 setters
1st — Michael's Express Babe 59153, pointer female, by Warhoop Express Pete — Gwinn's Little Jan. Michael Faller, owner; Bud Daugherty, handler.
2nd — Quailcrest Rambler 75495, pointer male, by Montana Smoke — Montana Cross Over. G. V. Hall, owner; D. Hoyle Eaton, handler.
3rd — Snow Cloud 75195, pointer female, by Miller's White Cloud — Lester's Sugar Bee. L. C. Shepard, owner; D. Hoyle Eaton, handler.

Saskatchewan Open Championship — 53 pointers, 6 setters
Winner — Flush's Wrangler 978947, pointer male, by Oklahoma Flush — Susan of Arkansas. Dr. D. R. Deal, owner; John Rex Gates, handler.
Runner-up — County Seat 46262, pointer male, by Texas Fight — The Matador's Patador. Frank Sallee, owner; Bill Hunt, handler.

Open Shooting Dog Classic — 43 pointers, 6 setters
Judges: W. C. Kirk, Frank Mudd
1st — Miss Warhoop Express 974054, pointefemale, by Warhoop Express Doc — Sherwood's White Lady. L. D. Hayes, owner; John Dauerty, handler.
2nd — Pete of Caddo 1279, pointer male, by Caddo's Man — Warhoop's Gleaming Girl. Dale Perryman, owner; Marion Gordon, handler.

193

3rd — Amos Mosley 20192, setter male, by Thor's Pacesetter — Fancher's Flame Brigte. Woody Thompson, owner; Dean Lord, handler.

Open Derby — 18 pointers, 1 setter

1st — Ann, unreg pointer female, by Blackbelt — Salome. Ronald Thompson & Mark Coward, owners; Marion Gordon, handler.

2nd — Greenbriar John, unreg pointer male, by Greenbriar Blaze. Bud Walters, owner; Dean Lord, handler.

3rd — Micro Wave Express, unreg pointer male, by Warhoop Express Boy — Miss Warhoop Express. Robert Hensky, owner; Marvin McDowell, handler.

Chapter 13

1978:
A Daugherty Sweep

BUD EPPERSON judged the Saskatchewan in '74 with Raymond Rucker as his partner. Cov invited him back for 1978 with Don Powell.

There was a perception that Cov was listening to counsel from the Daugherty camp, a thought not too far off the mark. The year before the entry was down some, to 59 in the title stake, but the '78 entry of 41 was to be a blip on the graph, coming back the next season to the normal 60s.

It was to be Linda Hunt's third trip to Mortlach, and her last for Cov's trial. As her report reflected, it was not a bumper year any way it was figured:

"Cover was shorter here on the Mortlach grounds than has been the case for the past few years, and with it came fewer chickens. The heavy alfalfa growback areas offered a good retreat for some but the barren areas were not so laden."

Dr. D. E. Hawthorne had organized a caravan to go north that summer, and one that generated a good deal of speculation about the trial. But the doctor's presence or enthusiasm for a project often raised questions about motives.

As Mrs. Hunt reported it:

"Barshoe Ingenue, 5½-year-old white and orange pointer female, owned by Brad H. Calkins of Denver, Colo., and handled by Bud Daugherty, captured both ends of a twin bill as she was named the 1978 Saskatchewan Chicken Champion and first in the companion open all age. She had three finds and a stop-to-flush during her championship hour.

"Runner-up honors went to her kennelmate, Man's Knighted Squire, four-year-old white and orange pointer male, owned by Tom M. Schooley of Tulsa, and also handled by Daugherty. He had three finds to his credit and an unproductive point coupled with a good ground effort.

"Barshoe Ingenue topped the open all-age field of 33 with a find on Huns. Second was Anonymous Belle, white and liver pointer female, owned by Robert E. Wallace of Memphis, and handled by Tommy Davis. She had one find on chickens. Third was Charismette, white and liver pointer female owned by R. L. Feaman of Lebanon, Mo., and handled by Pete Hicks, which scored near the end with a dandy find and had a good ground effort to her credit. She had a sterile stand on her tally card that marred."

Of the Derby:

"My Man Izzy sewed up the top spot with a find that complemented his big forward race. Although he was not class personified, he pointed chickens on his own in alfalfa, no easy task for a young dog, and as the first one flushed of its own volition he stayed, then went a distance with the others, but such is considered by most within proper conduct for Fall Derbies. Probably of all the qualities to look for in a good prairie dog, toughness is most sought. The prairie is no place for pantywaists, and it was great to see the heart and stamina displayed by the winners as well as several others that did not make the cut.

"Monty ran with the winner and put down a ground effort from start to finish that left no doubt where he stood. His carriage was eye-catching and he ran and handled like he was on a string throughout with a sterling finish in the midday heat.

"Warhoop Boy Express drew the first morning brace and displayed some outstanding qualities; however, his race was not a consistently showy effort. His running could have equaled the others, but not until the final cast did he put his performance in the showcase."

More detail of the champion and runner-up:

"Barshoe Ingenue, appearing in the third brace, lost her bracemate early and had the advantage of setting the pace for her running. She ran a consistent effort, not far-flung, but business-like and of little trouble to handler and scout. Her four contacts were fairly evenly spaced with the final contact coming just as the clock was about to run out. The judiciary had stated that they wanted a dog that you could send from one objective to the other rather than the rangier type that made the bigger swings and chose its own destination, and Ingenue filled the bill. She runs with class and pointed likewise, and such was the case on this occasion. Ingenue entered the record books for the prairie competition a year ago when she placed in the All America all age stake.

"Man's Knighted Squire, in the fourth brace, encountered a temperature that had climbed to a blistering level as midday approached. His first find came early in his hour and in the shelter strips along the lake that had served us well with bird work. It was not until 44 that he had his second, and it was the best of the lot, Man having made a huge swing and gaining much favor on the ground. Andy Daugherty had been sent to the top of the hill to check, but as the dog had begun to swing merely watched and raised his hat as he established point. His unproductive point at the far north end of the course could have been costly in the eyes of the judiciary. His third contact was a highly controversial one, but nonetheless creditable, and had to be looked at from that point. His ground effort had been acceptable for the first half where the going had been none too conducive; after the half it was all-age in caliber and his finish denoted the heart that it takes for a great prairie dog. Like the champion, Squire made his presence felt among prairie contenders in 1977 when he placed second on these grounds in the all-age stake.

"Blackbelt had been very impressive and had he been able to be located on his second find on the first tour through the area, it could well have been a different story. Builder's Free Boy and Heritage's Premonition both had good ground efforts and bird work."

Ingenue started her prairie days with a placement in the Saskatchewan Derby. In addition to his all age placement the year before, Man's Knighted Squire won the Dominion Chicken Championship.

The shooting dog stake at Mortlach often came as an afterthought, but not this season. The judges were enthusiastic about their chores and their choice for first, Bisco Landau Tat, was to have her named shortened to Bisco Tat and, in 1990, be elected to the Field Trial Hall of Fame for owner Barry Carpenter and Hicks – whose dog she really always was.

Mortlach, Sask., August 25, 1978
Judges: E. B. Epperson, Don Powell
Open All Age – 30 pointers, 3 setters

1st – Barshoe Ingenue 980062, pointer female by Mr. Perfection – Gunsmoke's Elhew Dancer. B. H. Calkins, owner; Bud Daugherty, handler.

2nd – Anonymous Belle 74396, pointer female, by Anonymous – White Knight's Prissy. R. E. Wallace, owner; Tommy Davis, Handler.

3rd – Charismette 944236, pointer female, by Out Going Up – Knight's Lil Lee. R. L. Feaman, owner; Pete Hicks, owner. Daugherty, handler.

Open Derby – 31 pointers
1st – My Man Izzy 94369, pointer male, by My Main Man – True Value's Gold. Gary W. Reid, owner; K. L. Keesee Jr., handler.

2nd – Monty 87028, pointer male, by Blackbelt – Kansas City Streaker. E. E. Jones, owner; Freddie Epp, handler.

3rd – Warhoop Boy Express 94387, pointer male, by Warhoop Express Bud – Paladin's Lady Fancy. R. L. Duncan, owner; Bud Daugherty.

Saskatchewan Open Championship – 36 pointers, 3 setters
Winner – Barshoe Ingenue 980062, pointer female, by Mr. Perfection – Gunsmoke's Elhew Dancer. B. H. Calkins, owner; Bud Daugherty, handler.

Runner-up – Man's Knighted Squire 12696, pointer male, by My Main Man – Sunday Clothes. T. M. Schooley, owner; Bud Daugherty, handler.

Open Shooting Dog Classic – 40 starters
Judges: Dr. M. E. Gordon, Albert Kern
1st – Bisco Landau Tat 101446, pointer female, by Fast Gun Pete – Bisco Candy. R. L. Feaman, owner; Pete Hicks, handler.

2nd – Huckleberry Foots 4571, pointer male, by Huckleberry's Butch – White Cricket Rexann. L. L. Davis, owner; Dean Lord, handler.

3rd—Kainai Warlord 29326, pointer male, by Elhew Copper Strike—Carter's Dixie Babe. J. C. Hoyt and E. S. Hopper, owners; Gary E. Parker, handler.

Open Derby—17 starters
1st—Sue, unreg pointer female, breeding not given. L. D. Hayes, owner; Dean Lord, handler.

2nd—Matt, unreg pointer male, breeding not given. L. Garner, owner; John Daugherty, owner.

3rd—Driftwood Squire 100545, pointer male, by Flush's Wahoo Dan—John's Rosy Lee. Joe Colley, owner; Dean Lord, handler.

Chapter 14

1979:
Country Squire's Season

IT WAS A GOOD YEAR for the dogs, but the owners scarcely got to read about it. Cov didn't have a reporter, and finally the FIELD got the raw information from the judges and a short report was prepared in Chicago.

Cov was living on the farm of Bill Burris in Arkansas, and Bill was asked to judge. With the decline in entries for the two years before, it was thought Jim Cohen's presence could cause a return of some handlers. The entry was up.

Sixty-four started in the championship, which went to Texas Silver Spur, the first of two titles he would win on the prairie that summer. He had been sold by Serafin Suarez to another international sportsman, Haruo Nishimura of Japan. He was still under the whistle of John Rex Gates, whose season was one of his very best. In addition to Spur's two titles, Texas Fight won the All-America for him, the dog's ninth championship.

It was a season of Flush's Country Squire, for he was the male ancestor common to Spur and Fight and the runner-up of the Saskatchewan, Blackbelt, and to the first and third placed Derbies at Mortlach.

Blackbelt, a son of Country Squire, was owned by Dr. W. O. Pardue and handled by Freddie Epp, who developed him. Details of what they did were not included in the report.

In the Derby, Tommy Davis handled Man's Sailin Ann to win for Robert and Sarina Craig. It was a prediction of things to come, though Davis sent her home during the winter. She was placed with Marshall Loftin and won the Southern Championship, at an hour and a half, twice, the All America Quail

Championship, at the same endurance time, and the Southwestern Open Championship. And Blackbelt, of course, was elected to the Field Trial Hall of Fame.

Second was Bluff City Mike, owned by R. E. Wallace of Memphis, and also handled by Davis. Mike also won in older competition. He would win the National Championship. Third was Campbell's Fabulous, like Ann, sired by My Main Man who was by Flush's Country Squire. His Florida owner had him in the string of Bud Keesee.

The sketchy report included this paragraph:

"It is regretted that a complete report of the Saskatchewan events is not available. In years past the Mortlach trials have always been hotly contested and have enjoyed extreme popularity, both because of the quality of competition and because it is the 'lead-off' event of the major circuit all-age trials for the new field trial season. This abbreviated account appears so that those winning prairie contenders might receive a measure of recognition for their performances as well as credit for their placements in the permanent records of the Field Dog Stud Book."

Mortlach, Sask., August 24
Judges: Dr. M. E. Gordon, Albert Kern
Open Shooting Dog Classic – 49 starters

1st – Silver Strike 42968, pointer male, by Elhew Copper Strike – Red Water Topaz. Rush. M. Campbell, owner; Gary Parker, handler.

2nd – Oklahoma Pache Sue 920871, pointer female, by Oklahoma Paladin Pache – Sherwood's White Lady. M. J. Long, owner; Dean Lord, handler.

3rd – Snow Cloud 75195, pointer female by Miller's White Cloud - Lester's Sugar Bee. Lester Shephard, owner; Dean Lord, handler.

Open All Age – 44 starters
Judges: Bill Burris, James E. Cohen.

1st – Jaws 6271, pointer male by White Knight's Possum – Sandstorm's Candy. Pete Frierson, owner; Garland Priddy, handler.

2nd – Snake Creek Warrior 998004, pointer male, by Red Warrior – Second Creek Lou. Pete Frierson, owner; Garland Priddy, handler.

3rd – Country Express Doc 33353, pointer male, by Warhoop Express Doc – Gwinn's Little Jan. Faller Kennels, owner; Bud Daugherty, handler.

Open Derby – 38 starters
1st – Man's Sailin Anne 112686, pointer female by My Main Man – Set Sail. R. E. & Sarina Craig, owners; Tommy Davis, handler.
2nd – Bluff City Mike 121890, pointer male, by Admiral Rex – Paladin's Royal Cheryl. R. E. Wallace, owner; Tommy Davis, handler.
3rd – Campbell's Fabulous 116412, pointer male, by My Main Man – Thou Swell. Tommy Campbell, owner; Bud Keesee, handler.

Saskatchewan Open Championship – 64 starters
Winner – Texas Silver Spur 942127, pointer male, by The Texas Squire – Pinewood Gussie. Haruo Nishimura, owner; John Rex Gates, handler.
Runner-up – Blackbelt 967632, pointer male, by Flush's Country Squire - Quailwood's Sally. Dr. W. O. Pardue, owner; Freddie Epp, handler.

Chapter 15

1980:
Buckboard's Championship

Buckboard HAD WON the Purina Dog of the Year award for 1976-77, with six championships to his credit, but none since the National Chukar Championship in the spring of '77. He had not won since the fall of '78, but the Saskatchewan was his after the 65 had run in the opener of the '80 season at Mortlach. He was eight years old, the property of Dr. D. E. Hawthorne of Tulsa, handled by Bud Daugherty of Inola.

The runner-up was Mardi Gras, a four-year-old pointer owned by Dr. and Mrs. D. C. Diefendorf of Baton Rouge, La., and handled by Marshall Loftin.

After no real report in '79, Marc Appleton undertook the job, as well as that of judge with Bill Burris, of Arkansas.

It was one of the big-entry trials, but it was the one which signaled the sharpest decline. Only 34 entered the grand old title stake the next fall.

Appleton wrote:

"His (Buckboard's) was a performance that kept all who were riding in stone silence as his effort unfolded ... he put down a superb race, reaching to the horizon. He was lost at six, then point was called at 15. Judge Burris exclaimed that it was one of the most breathtaking finds he had ever witnessed. Rebel was high and lofty at the edge of several bushes and Bud Daugherty produced three chickens from directly in front of the dog. Buckboard continued to carry the mail hard, fast and forward for the next 40 minutes. He was lost again at 50, and point was called at 58. A 4½-minute ride elapsed before the dog was sighted standing at bush edge. Fifteen to 18 chickens were put to flight and the dog was ordered up.

"Mardi Gras, the runner-up, used the treacherous prairie winds as though they were his friend. He ran into the wind, across it, and it seemed the wind did not exist for the white and liver pointer. He exhibited great ground speed and one had to watch him all the time just to know where he was. His range was as far as the eye could see, yet he never seemed out of touch with Loftin. Scout L. P. (Buzz) Marshall was kept busy the hour, but the dog really did not need his services. At 45 after long absence, Loftin called point directly in front, on course, when he happened to espy Mardi Gras standing 100 yards off grid road at edge of buckbrush. Loftin and the judge were the only ones there because of the cropland. A covey of young Huns was put to flight and then Mardi Gras went to work like a master to complete one of the strongest hours of the stake. Interestingly, this is the dog's first all-age placement of record; he had three Derby wins during the 1977-78 season.

"The championship was not a two-dog trial. There were others that had performances of note and that could have won other trials. Among those dogs with superlative efforts were Snake Creek Warrior, Bisco Tat, Michael's Express Babe, Nimbus, Flush's Wrangler, Heritage's Premonition and Big Sky's Rebel. All had impressive races and good clean finds."

Nothing was written of the performances in other stakes, but the usually conservative connections of Big Sky's Rebel were vocal through the years. They thought the title should have been theirs, but that they "came from the wrong part of the country"—Montana.

Buckboard was whelped at my kennel, as was Big Sky's Rebel. Buckboard was first named Barshoe Rebel, that after he had been offered at the going $200 puppy price and there were no takers. He was a bright, quick, happy pup, whelped late in the year and not big enough to compete in puppy stakes against the bigger ones. But he was so much fun, I took him to Caddo and ran him in the Oklahoma Puppy Classic despite the age handicap. Lee West, had him at Ada running loose on his Barshoe Ranch.

Tommy Long worked dogs for me the spring Buckboard was a coming Derby, and he was to start a group of young dogs, and break them while we were at Mortlach. West was scheduled to move to Washington, D. C., that spring, but there was a delay.

Tommy had the young Rebel going well, yard worked so he would stand, stop at "whoa", and watch a pigeon fly off. West came to Stigler to see him and some others we had. A few days later he decided to make a trip to Nebraska and wanted to take Rebel with him. I harbored the theory that if a man was to work a Derby, expected to break him, that he should be something of the sole trainer, and objected to Rebel going for a few days on the jaunt to Nebraska.

The result was a division of our dogs. Buckboard was sold by West to Hawthorne after Bud Daugherty saw the young dog handle the prairie country at Inola. It was a complicated transaction, with the sale of The Nimrod to Gary Pinalto involved, both eventual Saskatchewan winners. From that time on, Buckboard was truly Bud's dog. He was the only one who roaded him, and the dog's consummate fan and promoter. If Rebel had flaws in the eyes of others, they went unseen by Bud. They were a formidable team, especially when linked with his owner.

Mortlach, Sask., August 21, 1980
Judges: Marc Appleton, Bill Burris
Open All Age – 44 pointers

1st – Blackbelt 967632, pointer male, by Flush's Country Squire – Quailwood's Sally. Dr. W. O. Pardue, owner; Freddie Epp, handler.

2nd – Country Express Doc 33353, pointer male, by Warhoop Express Doc, Gwinn's Little Jan. Faller Kennel, owner; Bud Daugherty, handler.

3rd – Pine Briar Rex, unreg pointer male, breeding not given. Garland Priddy, agent and handler.

Open Derby – 21 pointers

1st – Warhoop Express Penny 139574, pointer female, by Warhoop Boy Express – Gwinn's Little Gal. J. K. Baker, owner; John Daugherty, handler.

2nd – Hard Time 140134, pointer male, by Rex's Cherokee Jake – Spaceglider's Miss Dot. Mack Largen, owner; D. Hoyle Eaton, handler.

3rd—Mac's Gunnery Sergeant 141821, pointer male, by Mississippi Rifle—Snow Cloud. W. S. McIlhenny, owner; D. Hoyle Eaton, handler.

Saskatchewan Open Championship—65 starters
Winner—Buckboard, 970478, pointer male, by A Rambling Rebel - Barshoe Cuz. Dr. D. E. Hawthorne, owner; Bud Daugherty, handler.
Runner-up—Mardi Gras 85521, pointer male, by Montana Rod—Rebel Fantastic. Dr. and Mrs. D. C. Diefendorf, owners; Marshall Loftin, handler.

Open Shooting Dog Classic—27 pointers, 3 setters, 5 Brittanies
1st—Bar C Rebelette 64221, pointer male, by Buckboard—Bar C Knightette. Larry Garner, owner; John Daugherty, handler.
2nd—Elhew Tex 83234, pointer male, by Elhew Knickerbocker—Elhew Ball's Nell. Stephen Harwood, owner; Dean Lord, handler.
3rd—Blackbelt's Sensation 75933, pointer male, by Blackbelt—Salome. Meredith Long, owner; Dean Lord, handler.

Open Derby—3 pointers, 3 Brittanies
1st—Knight Line 140785, pointer male, by Miller's White Cloud—Dillon's Lady Knight. C. G. Greenhorn, owner; Marvin McDowell, handler.
2nd—Ken's Wahoo Joe 115959, pointer male, by Ken's Joe Wahoo—Riggins White Gypsy. K. L. Brown, owner; John Daugherty, handler.
3rd—Texas Express Betty 141796, pointer female, by Warhoop Boy Express—Gwinn's Little Gal. DeVoe Treadwell, owner; Dean Lord, handler.

Chapter 16

1981:
Second Hand Notes

Cov INVITED TEXANS Ed Butler and his neighbor, professional trainer W. C. Kirk, to judge the 1981 renewal of the all-age stakes. But he didn't bother about a reporter. After it was over, I wrote what appeared in the FIELD based on notes from the shooting dog judges' and Butler's notes and memory.

It was a low point for entry, only 34 in the championship, 30 in the all age and 19 in the Derby.

The trial had fallen on bad times, and that primarily because Cov had tried to cut corners, save on judging expenses, reporting and the like. Plus the perception was that he was setting it up for certain trainers. Cov never intentionally set anything up for anyone. In later years he may have been misled. He drew only the faithful. The Gates dogs, which had won so regularly in years before, stayed in Manitoba.

The report said:

"There have been times — this year in the wind — when the weather is such that running should be stopped in order to give all of the dogs an equal opportunity. A storm can blow in as a brace goes on in September, and there are days when strong winds make it impossible for a dog to be tested fairly. The rush to finish forfeits the owner's dollars.

"For the shortcomings, the grounds and the game are more than equal . . . the magnet, the special something that has made Mortlach ring magic to the handler who has worked to get ready, the owner who wants to win something genuine, and the judge who gives his time and tired muscles to witness what should be the best.

"Those who are unkind about Canada are those who have never been to Mortlach – more often than not. They usually handle or own dogs they like to call 'all-age,' but in a second-class use of the term; dogs that 'can't cut it at Cov's.'

"... Mortlach is an historic centerpiece of major competition that neither owner nor handler nor fan can afford to lose. It is raw, and limits itself to those who raise their sights to true worth."

Of the all age stake:

"The half-hour all-age stake has always opened the program on Monday morning. Blackbelt was braced early in the day with Man's Knighted Squire. Each had a find of chicken in the first 10 minutes, both stylish and mannerly. Shortly, Blackbelt pointed again and Squire voluntarily backed him. Epp's dog hunted forward, going bluff-to-bluff and twice more he found and pointed game with his customary style and behavior. Squire continued a searching race, but had no further game contact.

"Second-placed Snake Creek Warrior appeared in the 11th brace, on the same course as the winner, starting at the end of the second hour and coming to the corner at Cov's camp, finishing in the pasture in front. He ran extremely strong and took in the rough pasture country that is to the north and west, Terry Walker riding for him. Twice during the time he pointed game and was correct in every respect. His handler thought his race was sufficient to elevate him to first, but the judges reasoned that Blackbelt's race was enough to establish him as an all-age dog, and his four correct finds established him the winner."

Of the Derby:

"The 19 Derby entries had the worst of it. The winds came out of the west like a gale and none of the placed dogs, Judge Butler emphasized, was required to go into it. 'None of the winners had to run into the strong headwind. They either were going with it, or were fortunate to run at a time when the gusts were not so strong. Perhaps there were those who drew courses into the wind that are as good or better, but simply couldn't show it,' he said.

"None of the three placed was shown on game. They patterned forward and reached to bluffs reasonably. It was on their seeming interest in finding game and attractiveness of carriage that determined the winners.

"Canaberry Cap is owned by John Sayre of Richmond, Ind. It is the third consecutive year that a dog owned by a member of the Indiana group has won this Open Derby. Detailed information on the other two placed Derbies was not made available.

"It is a pity. For the Canadian Derbies have long been thought a preview of things to come. In the halcyon days of Bill Allen the Derby competition was fierce. It goes in part to his ability to create a mood of interest, and his reliance on the effective ways of the late Capt. John S. Gates, who considered the Derby stakes in the North to have impact throughout the life of the all-age championship contender.

"When a dog had a registered name and was talked about in Canada and won there he was establishing himself as one to watch. The best example was that exceptional season when Sultan, Texas Fight, Palariel Stormy Clown Haberdasher's Heir (Millionaire) and Rebel Hawk were attracting so much attention in the North — a pattern that continued to set the crop apart.

"But, then, Capt. John understood those things."

The championship:

"Dr. Jack Huffman bred and raised Paladin's Royal Cheryl on his Whippoorwill Farm near Grand Junction, Tenn. He eventually bred her to Dempsey Williams' Admiral Rex. Tommy Davis started working the resultant litter early, and he singled out a lightly marked male and prepared him for the puppy classic at Union Springs. He won it.

"The next year he was back on the same grounds and won the Dixie Derby for Tommy Davis. Then the dog was runner-up in the All-America Derby Championship. The next season he was runner-up for Huffman at the National Amateur Chicken Championship in Alberta. He came back the next season to win that amateur title. Three times he has won titles for Davis — the Missouri and the Southern, each at an hour and a half, and now the Saskatchewan . . .

"His placements have been north-south, on various game and certainly in differing terrain. He has established himself as an important all-age champion. In doing so, he has enhanced the solid base of respect that young Davis has earned for himself. He started in the north Mississippi school, shepherded first by his uncle, Martin Davis, and then Hoyle Eaton.

"In a few years he has carved for himself a certain and impressive niche. He has clearly shown the past two seasons that he comes out of Canada with young dogs ready to win. He has now had time for his first young dogs to become older dogs, and they are solid, also ready to win. His attitude and his sincerity have always been impressive. It is not too early to understand that he had the capacity to learn what his teachers knew, and the tenacity to apply it as well—or better.

"This report is written from the notes of Judge Butler and he explained that he may not have recorded every game contact for all the entries, but the running is the way the judges saw it.

"They were in agreement that High Fidelity won the championship to himself. Judge Butler thought that his second and fourth finds were among the very best that could be seen on the prairie—which translates to 'anywhere.'

"They also thought the runner-up was clearly above the others, though they gave consideration as the running progressed to Little Maverick, and to Merryway Blackbelt. Judge Butler singled out Little Maverick, another Davis entry, as the 'one dog that ran into the teeth of the wind and did it right.' "

Comments on the short entry:

"The entry has fluctuated from the high of 85 through such big entries as 71 in 1975 to this year's low of 34. It is not that there aren't a great number of all age dogs in training. There were 82 drawn for the Border International. A number of major trainers decided not to go to Mortlach, regulars Gates, Rayl, Collier Smith among them, and Eaton, who attends occasionally.

"Reasons for going or not going change from year to year. The most common is that the judges aren't to the liking. Sometimes increase in entry fees is given as the reason, or excuse. The cut of the purse is used, all the time knowing that the percentage paid in Canada trials is consistently higher than those of major trials in the U.S.

"Often the unspoken factor is that the dogs 'won't look good at Cov's.' Some 'name' dogs that won well in the woods of the south dodged the prairie altogether; others tried just once.

"It has been the rule the last decade and a half that owners knowledgeable in the all-age circle—in that list of trials known as the major circuit—have harbored hope of winning at Mortlach. Why? Because the keen competition is there; because of the grounds; because of the high game population. An hour in this open, beautiful demanding terrain can be equal to three down-south hours where there are places to hid and rest and the fields require less. Scouts in Canada are for a different purpose. This year the game population was the equal of the wonder years at Quitman, considerably greater than is ever expected at Grand Junction. Severe high winds on the days of running made handling them tough."

Cov varied his program, running the shooting dog and the companion Derby first. Judges Butler and Kirk were traveling together and because of truck trouble took six rather than two days to get there. Jon Anderson and John McKinley were recruited to take care of the shooting dog part of the program.

Mortlach, Sask., Aug. 31, 1981
Judges: Ed Butler, W. C. Kirk
Open All Age – 28 pointers, 2 setters

1st – Blackbelt 967632, pointer male by Flush's Country Squire - Quailwood's Sally. Dr. W. O. Pardue, owner; Freddie Epp, handler.

2nd – Snake Creek Warrior 998004, pointer male, by Red Warrior – Second Creek Lou. Pete Frierson, owner; Garland Priddy, handler.

3rd – Man's Knighted Squire 12696, pointer male, by My Main Man – Sunday Clothes. Don Fox, owner; Bud Daugherty, handler.

Open Derby – 19 entries

1st – Canaberry Cap 160775, pointer male, by Canaberry Butch Boy – Snicker Doodle Dew. J. M. Sayre, owner; Marshall Loftin, handler.

2nd – Fred, unreg, pointer male, breeding not given. Dr. T. O. Kennard, owner; Freddie Epp, handler.

3rd – Beaux Rip, unreg, pointer male, breeding not given. Marshall Loftin, owner and handler.

Saskatchewan Open Championship – 34 Pointers

Winner – High Fidelity 72738, pointer male, by Admiral Rex – Paladin's Royal Cheryl. Dr. J. D. Huffman, owner; Tommy Davis, handler.

Runner-up – Snake Creek Warrior 998004, pointer male, by Red Warrior – Second Creek Lou. Pete Frierson, owner; Garland Priddy, handler.

Open Shooting Dog
Judges: Jon Anderson, John McKinley
26 pointers 6 Brittanies 1 setters 1 Irish setter
1st — Blackbelt's Sensation 79533, pointer female by Blackbelt — Salome. Meredith Long, owner; Dean Lord, handler.
2nd — El Sauz Ginger 61722, pointer female by Atascosa Pete — Perseids Babe. F. C. Thielepape, owner; Dean Lord, handler.
3rd — Bar C Rebelette 64211, pointer female, by Buckboard — Bar C Knighette. Meredith Long, owner; Dean Lord, handler.

Open Derby — 9 pointers 1 Brittany
1st — Knickerbocker's Rip, unreg, pointer male, breeding not given. Fagan Mullins, owner; Marc Appleton, handler.
2nd — Bill's Hustlin Buck, unreg pointer male, breeding not given. C. F. Thielepape, owner; Dean Lord, handler.
3rd — J. R. Kojak, unreg, pointer male, breeding not given. F. C. Thielepape, owner; Dean Lord, handler.

Chapter 17

1982:
Sundown at Mortlach

NO ONE COULD KNOW that 1982 would be the last year
for many things. For it was a good summer. A renewal of sorts.
At least for me. I was back at Mortlach after an absence of
several summers, invited to judge with Bill Burris, and to report.

Some change had come. Cov and Lois, the year before, moved
to a house in town from the frame two-story camp house at
Vic's, the place of history and stories and summer fun. Vic's
son, Les, had joined him on the farm and he had tidied up
the place which had known little tending.

Les moved into a new home, his wife planted flowers around
the front yard. There was an electric pump on the new well.
A neat, small barn stood where the other out buildings had
fallen from disrepair. A board fence marked the lot for her
saddle horse, and, to the dismay of the senior Eastmond, the
boards were painted white. One wouldn't know the place except
that it was at the same spot where the shelter belt had been
haven for so many dogs so many summers.

Cov's dogs were down the road, scattered among the shade
of a large bluff. He didn't bring a horse. He hadn't had a drink
in a year, and seemed quite at peace with his Canadian neighbors.

Marc Appleton had engineered the move to town, not endearing himself to Vic, who had collected the $300 summer rent
for quite a number of years. Arlin Nolen and I had a small
house in Mortlach, a pleasant change from the Midland Motel
which had also gone down hill since the days of the Moens.

I asked Vic about the pump from the old dug well. He priced
it and said he'd get it for me when I left. A bucket had been

hung nearby to have prime water. It had a distinctive long wooden handle, to bolt here, wire there.

I flew to Alberta for the first shooting dog championship there, and Nolen paid Vic for the pump and packed to leave for Minot. Vic couldn't find the pump. He could see the money going and looked frantically around the place, at the dump. It took a day, but he recovered it. At Ardmore the next spring, I told Cov that I had the pump:

"What did you buy that thing for, John, you know the leathers weren't any good."

The entry for '82 was not much more than the year before, but the report tells the story:

"For the third time in its sixteen years, a Pointer that won the National Championship over the Ames Plantation in Tennessee won the Saskatchewan Championship over the Queen's prairie land at Mortlach. Starkly different.

"Michael's Express Babe twice found coveys of Hungarian partridge on the first hour course of Leon Covington's running grounds, relocating the first with wisdom and tact. She hunted the hay and farmland forward and far. She succeeded where other down-south champions have failed.

"She is six years old, orange marked and ran on the last morning of the 37-entry stake, guided by 28-year-old Andy Daugherty, who also handled the first and second placed winners in the half-hour Open All-Age that started the trial, and the season, August 30. Babe was second.

"The strapping young man from Inola, Okla., was in charge of the training camp at Jansen this season, and this was his first trial as head of his own enterprise. His noted handler-father, Bud Daugherty, retired from the major circuit in the spring and moved to his Missouri farm.

"Babe was Andy's 'first dog', though owned by Michael Faller of Springfield, Ill.

"By contrast, Marshall Loftin, the Louisianan, the sage who started handling bird dogs 37 years ago at age 12, guided the runner-up. She was the lofty, quick Sweet Fever, liver marked and female. Twice she whirled and pointed prairie chickens. She was gone early, hunted in view awhile, and finished with strength. She is owned by a trio of Louisianans – Bill Heard, Byron Vernon and Gerald Roberts of Baton Rouge.

"Both females were competent, industrious, desirable winners though they were not in the mold of some prairie champions that have challenged the grounds and their handlers and scouts. Both were without flaw around the game they found. They were separated by details, not great accomplishments. They withstood the challenge of three others that thwarted their own bids for the title with errors fatal to their cause.

"It was Country Express Doc in the Open All-Age that displayed the range, speed, style and desire that was truly the equal of the unequalled grounds. He was staunch, high and correct on his one find of chickens, and, at the end, it took strong horse and knowledgeable man to produce him. He is owned by Faller Kennels.

"Babe drew the first course in the All-Age, and she hunted the bluffs wisely, missing none ahead. She pointed at the end just beyond pickup corner, clocked by the dog wagon driver who saw her stop with but a minute to go in her 30 minutes.

"Whippoorwill's Rebel, liver-marked three-year-old, moves with ease. He is stylish and so pointed his one find for handler Tommy Davis and owner S. R. (Tate) Cline of McArthur, Ohio, to be third. Rebel was also earning himself championship position in the later stake when he had two finds, but failed to remain in place on the third contact.

"Davis, also 28, is the epitome of a young man who knows his craft. He has the talent, the sense of dog and horse, that extra understanding that allows him to develop a performer, not merely handle it. In the 22-entry Derby he showed the judges littermates which were placed first and third. Both Canaan and Power Scan are owned by Dr. Jack D. Huffman of Memphis, Tenn., the man who has supported Davis since he started his own business.

"Canaan was forward, stylish and used the country fully. He pointed well ahead, high, intent, and Davis spurred his horse to caution him, but just as he arrived the Derby took the chickens across the field. Power Scan was not seen around game, but his ground heat was superb.

"Between the two was Nugent's Daisy Duke, owned by Mike Nugent of Evansville, Ind., and handled by Freddie Epp. The black-marked female had a slow beginning, warming to her hunt and finishing strong. She was found pointing at a considerable distance; a covey of chickens scattered on the prairie in front of her and she moved a horse-length at flush."

There was a pretty female we overlooked, Pure Delight, orange-marked, future champion. She didn't have bird work in the Derby, but her pattern for the time was special, returning time again, all out front.

We did not overlook one of the landmark dogs of the period, Whippoorwill Rebel. He was beautiful moving, with grand style, light of foot. That beauty was forgot in his later years of competition, injured by two dogs that tried to pull him apart on a stake-out chain, and a back problem which required surgery.

Canaan later sired National Champion Dunn's Fearless Bud.

R. L. (Bob) Duncan of Blanchard, Oklahoma, was Andy's scout, mounted on a Canadian horse. Duncan proved his immense talent with a bird dog through those he bred, started, finished. The winner of this stake was a Duncan-bred, and he was given credit for her early days. His Warhoop Express Doc was the best example of a Duncan at its prime. The dog was his, in every sense. He won a creditable all-age stake when very young, a dog with style and drive and sense. Lee Cruse of Springfield, Missouri, bought half of him and the dog was put, as were most of Duncan's products, with the Daughertys. He became ill of speargrass, and, unfortunately was treated by vets who knew not what they had, or what to do with it. He was operated on, taken North, and by Mortlach was deathly ill. He did not live long, and only in his second all-age year.

"It was a Canadian trial in every respect, save one. It had no rancor, none of the summer bickering that has blighted some northern stakes. If ever a group of handlers performed as professionals – keen of competition, courteous to bracemate and judge – it was at Mortlach in 1982.

"The trial itself moved with uncommon smoothness. The squire, the veteran of near 50 summers on the prairie and 75 summers of life, Leon Covington, was there with a story and the collection list.

" . . . The lure of Mortlach is the landscape. It is Canada. Time was when large galleries rode, when the Midland and the Caronport Motels overflowed owners and handlers into Moose Jaw. The economy and a range of other reasons have reduced that.

"But they have not changed the land that lies around the farm which Vic Eastmond's dad homesteaded at the turn of the century. It is there, as it has been, with distant bluffs calling to ranging bird dogs, chickens and Huns feeding on the prairie alfalfa in the morning cool, loafing in the shade from an afternoon sun."

Cov had stopped drinking liquor. As he told it, he just decided he didn't "want any more. Didn't say I quit. Might have one any time." But during the summer he had only a couple of beers one warm afternoon standing under the shade at Vic's after the day's running. He came on to the house, but didn't want any more.

"You know we stopped somewhere down there in Nebraska on the way up here. Lois wanted a drink. I went over and got her a half pint. Mixed her a drink. Mixed me one.

"I took a drink of it, and didn't taste good at all. I asked myself, 'that the stuff I've thought was so good all these years?' "

Don Ryan was there, as he had been for every trial. Warren Palmer and his wife, Mickey, spent the summer in Mortlach, and it was Palmer's truck that became the dog wagon when a helper wrecked Appleton's. Joe Davis of Alabama was there to visit with Ryan as they drove the courses.

We did not realize it would be a last. The last for Joe and Warren and Cov, for they did not live out the year ahead. The last for the Saskatchewan at Mortlach for a few seasons.

Mortlach, Sask., August 30, 1982
Judges: Bill Burris and John Criswell
Open All-Age — 38 starters

1st — Country Express Doc 33353, pointer male, by Warhoop Express Doc — Gwinn's Little Jan. Faller Kennel, owner; Andy Daugherty, handler.

2nd — Michael's Express Babe 32952, pointer female, by Warhoop Express Pete — Gwinn's Little Jan. Michael Faller, owner; Andy Daugherty, handler.

3rd — Whippoorwill's Rebel 141926, pointer male by Hawk's Rex — High JV. S. R. Cline, owner; Tommy Davis, handler.

Open Derby — 22 starters

1st — Power Scan 180551, pointer male by High Octane — J H Cotton. Dr. J. D. Huffman, owner; Tommy Davis, handler.

2nd – Nugent's Daisy Duke 158771, pointer female by Merryway's Blackbelt – Berryhill Happy Hanna. Mike T. Nugent, owner; Freddie Epp, handler.

3rd – Canaan 180503, pointer male, by High Octane – J H Cotton. Dr. J. D. Huffman, owner; Tommy Davis, handler.

Saskatchewan Open Championship – 32 pointers, 4 setters

Winner – Michael's Express Babe, 59153, pointer female, by Warhoop Express Pete – Gwinn's Little Jan. Michael Faller, owner; Andy Daugherty, handler.

Runner-up – Sweet Fever 32952, pointer female, by The Texas Heir – Frierson's Little Dixie. W. L. Heard, Jr., Byron Vernon, Bill Heard & Gerald Roberts, owners; Marshall Loftin, handler.

Open Shooting Dog – 7 pointers 1 setter 2 Brittanies

1st – Tall Oaks Bandolero 23101, Brittany male, by Ban Dee – Princess deSandra. John McConnell, owner; Marc Appleton, handler.

2nd – Warhoop's Trouble Doc 71380, pointer male, by Wahoo's Trouble Jack – Dolly's Lady Warhoop. L. D. & Lou Ann Hayes, owners; L. D. Hayes, handler.

3rd – Miss Discard 154844, pointer female, by Bill's Discard – Clardy's Lou. Keith McLean, owner and handler.

Chapter 18

Leaving Saskatchewan

DURING THE WINTER of '82, Cov was hospitalized and operations were done in Fort Smith on his legs to improve the circulation. He was not accustomed to hospitals, or doctors that didn't own bird dogs, like Dr. Gordon and Dr. Calame. He suffered from a heart condition which medication seemed to regulate.

As spring came around, his heart problems increased and he was again in the hospital. In early May he was told that the condition was quite serious. It was a few days before the Oklahoma Field Trial Clubs Assn. held its annual meeting. In '83 it was to be at Ardmore.

He called and I suggested he come over for the dinner on Saturday night and stay through the Sunday program. He "believed he would."

He drove the green station wagon from Booneville and was at the lake for the cookout, full of stories, renewing friendships, but ready to go to the Lodge early. I drove him, and he wanted to talk about the next summer. He wasn't sure about the trial. Actually it hadn't turned a profit in two or three years. He had thought about judges.

And he wanted to talk about "if I can't go back." I tried to end that, but he said he wanted me to help Lois with it "if she wants to mess with it. I think she's tired of going up there. She likes to see Florence." He had depended on Appleton the last couple of summers, and during the winter word got to him that Marc had trouble with the law. Cov was totally exercised about it, but not so much as Lois.

Cov was certain "those Canadians won't let Marc cross that border. They might even put him jail from what I've heard — if his Dad don't get him out of it."

His information was second-hand. The records in Montague County, Texas, reflect the incident.

"The grand jurors, for the County of Montague, State of Texas, duly selected, empaneled, sworn, charged, and organized as such at the December Term AD 1982 of the 97th Judicial District Court for said County, upon their oaths present in and to said court at said term that Meridith Mark Appleton hereinafter styled Defendant, on or about the 23rd day of November, A.D. 1982, did then and there intentionally and knowingly appropriate by acquiring and otherwise exercising control over property, to-wit: 12 head of cattle of the value of $200.00 or more, but less than $10,000.00 from the owner Kent Henry and F. T. Fenoglio without the effective consent of the owner and with intent to deprive the owner of said property." It was signed by the Foreman of the Grand Jury.

That was the legal language. What Cov knew was that Appleton had been charged with stealing cattle off the Running High Ranch where he had been working dogs near Stoneberg. The ranch had been the site of the Texas Championship the season before.

On Feb. 28, Appleton appeared in the Montague County District Court and entered a guilty plea. Judge Frank J. Douthitt placed him on probation for a term of five years. Cov understood that anyone in such a situation was not eligible to enter Canada. Even more vehement were his intentions that "he's damn sure not going around my place."

Next morning Cov was in the restaurant early, entertaining the early risers. Andy Daugherty and I were to be a panel of two. We shortly expanded it to three. Cov was never better.

At the break, he said he was going to go on home, and I suggested he stay through lunch. "No. I don't want to be after dark getting to Booneville. Got lost coming over here."

He had in mind another stop or two he didn't mention, at Caddo and Hugo. He saw his friends that ran the corner filling station on Highway 69, and drove to Stub Poynor's. Four days later he went to his old grounds to look around and see if it would be possible for Perry Mikles to start a trial there, that was the excuse he used. He drove over Henscratch mountain,

220

and, coming down, the station wagon swerved into a ditch. He was found a few hours later slumped over the steering wheel.

Lois knew something was wrong when he didn't get home to see Judge Wapner preside at his evening TV program. A deputy sheriff came with the news.

Shortly she called to tell me what had happened. Her next sentence was about the trial. "You plan to run it, and Cov wants you to have the grounds."

The funeral was attended by a number of Cov's friends — Raymond Rucker and Fred Oliver. Appleton was there. Bud Epperson. Dr. Gordon.

The short of the long proceedings that followed is that the grounds were assigned by the bureaucracy of the Department of Parks and Renewable Resources to David Gates of Regina, with the understanding that Appleton would be his "assistant trainer."

The rules of the Canadian government as they concern bird dog trainers have never been clear, and apparently operate at the whim of bureaucrats, principal among them a man named Grant Fladager. He was asked, if the grounds could not be transferred to me, that a number of days in late August be set aside for the Saskatchewan Championship program. But after much correspondence, he said, "no."

Since the early '70s there has been a resurgence of interest in field trials among Canadians. Tim Twomey is the leader of a group of Alberta enthusiasts who have held trials and established a shooting dog championship of their own. They are a group of fun-loving sportsmen who enjoy the game to the hilt. They had access to a beautiful ranch near Nanton.

In Saskatchewan, William D. Preston and Doug Vaughan of Saskatoon, were prime-movers of a Saskatchewan Amateur club which had established itself at Ardath. Of course, Ken McLean had been The Canadian field trialer, operating the All America and Dominion trials in Manitoba, since the days of John S. Gates. The Legion at Stoughton operated the Border International with the advise and counsel of John Gardner.

Preston and Vaughan apparently thought at the outset that the Saskatchewan title stake attached to the land, Preston, an attorney, called Lois, and she asked me to return his call. I did, assuring him that our first interest was to run at Mortlach — but under our supervision. If that wasn't possible, it would be moved.

221

In 1982, Appleton, sensing that Cov wouldn't be coming back many summers, became close friends with Gates and Vaughan, and encouraged them — against Cov's usual attitude toward amateurs on his grounds — to hold a trial there.

She received a letter and sent it on to me with this hand-written note:

"I am enclosing a letter from this Canadian lawyer in Canada. He is the one that called me last week wanting to take over the trial & offering me 15% of the net take of the trial. I told him that wasn't good enough & that you were going to run it if possible. I think (according to him) that Vic is trying to pull a fast one on us. Anyway, maybe you can answer him. Oh, by the way, he was going to try to get Marc Appleton to end up with it."

As it worked out, Ken McLean and his friends were tired of their trials and ready, when approached, to let the new group in Saskatchewan move the All-America and Dominion to Mortlach.

The Saskatchewan was homeless for a few weeks, until Dennis Jeffrey of Minot, helped get the land of the Leach Ranch near Towner.

The Monday before Labor Day, 1983, the Saskatchewan opened at its new home.

Chapter 19

1983:
Towner, North Dakota

I HAD NO IDEA what to expect. Dennis Jeffrey said the grounds were good, and there was enough of them. When Arlin Nolen and I arrived at Towner, North Dakota, it was a warm afternoon. Jeffrey was in Minot an hour away, and I only knew how to get John Ray Kimbrell on the phone.

He said "come on," and, despite a full house, made room for the horses. We strung a stake chain across the edge of his camp house yard. It was a couple of days before Jeffrey came out and we got a tour of the Leach Ranch, some 15 miles to the south and east of Kimbrell's grounds, which were made up mostly of farm land.

We went past the house where Jeff and Mary Dosch, the foreman and his wife, lived, and crossed the Moose River into the hay fields that lay beyond. There was obviously ground aplenty. But few objectives. Then, with Dosch at the wheel, we drove to the Cow Camp, or, East Division of the Ranch, 5,000-plus acres of native prairie about four miles from the headquarters.

Ideal. Bluffs for objectives. Prairie that had never felt a plow. Sandy country. And we saw chickens in the bluffs as Dosch drove past, game that had likely never seen man. We came to the working pens. There was no question that the trial would have a home, and a good one.

Only four days were left before the start, and none of the group had really ridden all of the East Division, save Dosch, and he didn't know what was needed for courses. The second afternoon, Nolen saddled a horse and didn't come back until dark. He had an idea of the lay of the land, and generally how the fences cut it into pastures. He had an idea of how we could get three hours. Next morning, we tried it. We found chickens as we went, and felt that the lot of the trial could actually be improved, especially considering there would be no Canadian government to contend with. That included the border requirements, absurd as to horses, and an impossible vet on the American side at Peace Garden.

In doing research on another matter, I ran across the information that Towner was really the first center of field trials in the north, save the Manitoba. The All-America Open Chicken Championship program had been run nearby in 1912.

Albert Hochwalt wrote about the Towner trial, where John Proctor won his first championship in '13, "the dog which unfurled the banner of the short-hairs on its highest pinnacle . . . another son of Fishel's Frank, and 'the noblest Roman of them all.'"

John Proctor came back to North Dakota in 1915 and won the All America title a second time, this running at Denbigh, just a few miles west. Said Hochwalt of this:

"On this occasion it was at Denbigh, N.D., in a field that was considered the best ever gotten together in an event of that nature, for competing in this race were two National champions, three chicken champions, and thirteen other well-known setters and pointers, nearly all of which were frequent winners on the regular circuit."

John Proctor, a Texas product, won all three of the championships on the 1915-16 schedule and during his career he placed 23 times. It caused Hochwalt to write:

"This record may be equalled some day, but this is a matter for the future to decide."

In his book, Makers of Bird Dog History, Hochwalt wrote about "Peerless Mary" Montrose, winner of three National Championships (one while a Derby), two Chicken Championships and one Derby Championship. She made her debut at Denbigh in 1917 in the All-America Derby.

"There was something especially attractive in the way she went out and hunted her country, being a large, nearly all white pointer she loomed up on the horizon like a piece of moving statuary and it seemed that she possessed an almost human knowledge that she was playing to the galleries, for many of her finds were made far out on a long cast and there she posed perfectly intense until her audience came up," Hochwalt wrote.

Fred M. Stephenson trained the 1915 National Champion "on the prairies of North Dakota" where he spent several weeks of the chicken season.

The history of bird dogs and North Dakota goes on. Of Comanche Frank, Hochwalt wrote:

"In 1912 Comanche Frank was placed in the hands of J. M. Avent and he began the season of 1912 and '13 by winning a place in the Manitoba All-Age; then, coming down to Towner, N.D., he won second to Momoney in the All-America All-Age."

A major championship had returned — some 70 years later.

The Canadians had caused it, but Jeffrey, Foreman Dosch and two young men from Minot — Doug Jess and Lee Diebert — made it possible.

I wrote about it for the FIELD at some length:

"In the summer of 1966, a gangling pup with liver spots spent a lot of time around the front door of the camp near Youngstown, Alberta, where Fred Arant, Jr., had trained since 1952.

"One morning Fred saw him standing on point not far from the house, his head high, taking in the full scent of prairie chickens, tail straight up. He went in the kennel, got a call name, Jack, and a chain of events had started which would profoundly influence the Pointer breed. For the August puppy, just a year old, would be registered as A Rambling Rebel. He had been whelped in Charleston, S.C., while Arant was in Canada, August 7, 1965.

"He would catch the public fancy, and, though lost in his breeding prime, his get and grand-get are a continuing family of winners, the Rebels.

"The genetic handiwork of the soft-spoken trainer from South Carolina reaches deep into the background of a majority of the winners of the 1983 renewal of the Saskatchewan Open Championship Club's prairie program, competed the week before Labor Day over the virgin lands of the Leach Ranch south of Towner, N.D.

"The new champion is double bred to A Rambling Rebel, the runner-up from one of his daughters, and two of the Derbies which placed were from a daughter and granddaughter.

225

"Thunderclap is archetypical of the Arant Rebels. He seems to float across the prairie, without regard for thorny cover or heat, points with arresting style and ranges to the extreme. His performance, in the next to last brace, was as deserving of a prairie title as any ever seen.

"Tony Terrell handled him with an all-purpose effort, riding out of sight to make the breakaway turn, and sat with confidence as he reached to distant bluffs at the end. Twice he handled game, once at a bluff, the second time on the prairie.

"His was one of three memorable hours. The other two were by Pete Hicks' Bisco Tat and Marshall Loftin's Anvil. Tat was thrilling. She was in the 100-degree heat of the first afternoon brace, and she was constantly ahead, as far as one could see, and for the entire hour never slacked the pace. She showed an endurance and inner toughness beyond belief. Anvil was just that tough, with a little better of the heat, he, too, went and went, and came back time and again when he did so only from instinct and training.

"Thunderclap is owned by David Suitts of Denver, Colorado, a sportsman who cut his field trial teeth on the prairie, and who planned the mating of Swing Along and Buckboard, which produced the champion.

"The runner-up was early in the stake, a one-find performance highlighted by a stunningly strong last half and a find on the breakaway, the head of Addition's Go Boy twisted toward the prairie chicken which were ridden up by handler, lifting to his rear, but in front of his nose. Go Boy is five years old, handled by Garland Priddy for owner Pete Frierson of Jackson, Miss.

"The 30-minute all age stake opened the program—all run in some of the greatest heat these northern lands have ever known. There is heavy cover on some of the courses. Add the two, with the expanses that allow great range, and you have quite a test of a bird dog.

"Marshall Loftin showed Sweet Fever to an impressive one-find performance. She was full of run, disregarded the elements and handled game perfectly. She is owned by Bill Heard and Gerald Roberts of Baton Rouge, La.

"Doug Sellers showed Hub City Rex as owner Doug Cooper watched. He, too, reached far and with speed, never hesitating in his search, though not as forward as the winner. He found a covey just at pickup and did that right.

"The third placement went to a black-marked female that jumped and hunted the country afar for Randy Downs. Craftsman's Delight is totally attractive. She had a stand where nothing was flushed.

"The Derby was a dandy, and the sun bore down as the young dogs ran. It was surprising under the conditions that the judges had such a group of impressive performances to pick among.

"There was no questioning of the results which put FJ's Blueberry Babe at the top of the list. She ranged as far, toward distant objectives, as anyone could want. She needed a good bit of help early, and some of that came from Hall of Fame handler Ed Mack Farrior, who has been in North Dakota at the camp of Kenny Robinson, handler of the orange-marked female for owner Jerry Racke.

"Second was Idol—making it two placements for Downs, whose summer grounds are some 150 miles to the west of Towner. Idol was on the same course as the winner, and his was a running performance of the highest order. The female which bested him had a more attractive jump and the edge on range.

"Essay, a rangy, black-marked male, was third. In his first field trial, he was handled by Tony Terrell. He made the bluffs, thorough heavy cover, and did it with high style in the afternoon heat. He is owned by Terry Flansberg, who bred him, of Colony, Okla., and Whileaway Kennel of Stigler, Okla."

That summed up the event, but there was more about the area's history:

"Where is Towner? And what's this North Dakota?

"The ranching community of 4,000 with its tree-lined streets is some 50 miles from the Canadian border. It is the 'Cattle Capitol' of the state. And it is surrounded by bird dog trainers in the summer.

"The landowners have generously made their hay lands, farm land and pastures available to a dozen trainers from the south.

"Why did the early handlers pass it by and go another 100 miles across the border? As Ed Mack Farrior remembers it, the state's laws of the late teens and 20s caused it.

" 'They had a law that prohibited hunting upland game with a dog, or even training on them.' The handlers who preceded his dad, Ed Farrior, set the pattern out of necessity. They came to Rugby on the train and then were switched to another train at Antler, where they were met by teams to be driven to their camps in southeast Saskatchewan and southwest Manitoba.

" 'I first came with Dad in '21. We shipped the dogs and the railroad employes were supposed to take care of them. I remember that Dad, Mack Pritchette and Ches Harris arranged for a baggage car. All the dogs were put in it and we went back to take care of our own dogs. For some reason, the station manager at Rugby took the car away from us, but it wasn't too far to Antler,' Farrior remembers.

"E. V. Humphries worked his dogs near Towner in the '40s and '50s and in '51 Arant worked with him and George Evans, of Quitman, Georgia, who was sharing the camp. Evans' string included Gerald Livingston's National Champion Shore's Brownie Doone."

Of the new grounds:

"It is difficult to describe land so those who have not seen it can get a feel of it, but to try . . .

"Imagine a long oval, formed with sandhill ridge across the east and west, opening into hay fields to the south and heavy bluffs on the north. It is more than three miles across one way and five the other.

"The headquarters is the Cow Camp calving pens, a set of working chutes and holding pens, a couple of small barns, well with electric pump, the water cold and tasty from a sandpoint only 10 feet down.

"This is on a rise with considerable tree cover and shade. The breakaway is at the red gate that marks entry to the property. That is two miles from the highway. The dogs are sent to the north with a sweeping right curve past a working windmill and the sandhills which are usually crossed at 15 minutes. They are narrow and from the top the prairie opens, a vista of bluffs for a dog to reach toward, the curve continuing toward the south into a pasture where the division's cows were held during trial.

"On south along the edge of the cow pasture ridge, turning for a long straight run through the smaller pond pasture with its relatively sparce cover into the valley of the lake pasture.

A fresh water lake, approved for human consumption is on the far end, and the course comes back northwest to a double gate. From here there is an expanse of pasture to the eastern sand ridge. Midway there is an opening, a valley that beckons to the eastern ranch border.

"The cover is heavy and a bend brings the course back to the prairie and into heavy bluff country for some 10 minutes, emptying into the north pasture with its big open horseshoe, the turn around an old wooden windmill, back south for another half hour of big country, far bluffs and the middle pasture's short cover.

"It is a place to test a bird dog. There is an abundance of running room. There were some turns used in the all age stakes which were straightened for the Derby and Championship. The Leach Ranch is Grade I.

"Game is where you find it, in high prairie grass, in swales of low brush, in or near bluffs. No one knew the hot spots, for the grounds had not been worked this year. Chickens could be anywhere, and were. There seemed a heavier concentration of chickens on the first hour, but during the stakes they were found in all sections. Experience teaches that when working on grounds 75% more game is found than during a field trial when a prescribed route must be followed . . .

"John Little of South Carolina, Dr. Robert Crockett and Leon Harris of Texas pitched in, and rode a great deal, as did Kevin Lyons of Chicago, Charles Taylor of Florida and Troy Newman of Missouri.

"Prairie trials have a reputation for sordid incidents, precipitated by the slips of paper judges hand to club officials. This was one time when there were none. The judges had, at the end of each stake, quality performances, and, in each case, they selected them in the order which would have clearly received majority approval. Charles Young came from Cassatt, North Carolina. His judging partner was John Ray Kimbrell, also a Carolinan, and a trainer whose camp is some few miles to the northwest. They applied the historic rules of the prairie. They did it with courtesy. They were in the positions to see, calm, cool about the job. They were first-rate in knowing what they would like to see and recognized it when they did."

Towner, N.D., August 28
Judges: John Ray Kimbrell, Charles Young
Open All Age—26 pointers 4 setters

1st—Sweet Fever 32592, pointer female, by The Texas Heir—Frierson's Little Dixie. William Heard and Gerald Roberts, owners; Marshall Loftin, handler.

2nd—Hub City Rex 97207, pointer male, by Tabasco Rex—Warhoop's Miss Sue. Doug Cooper, owner; Doug Sellers, handler.

3rd—Craftsman's Delight 183649, pointer female, by The Master Craftsman—Keemil's Bonny. G. G. Jefferson, owner; Randy Downs, handler.

Open Derby—23 pointers, 2 setters

1st—FJ's Blueberry Babe, unreg pointer male, by Traditional Bob—Twelve Gauge Sue. Jerry W. Racke, owner; Kenny Robinson, handler.

2nd—Idol 184400, pointer male by Himself's Flying Matt—Texas Gingersnap. Dr. K. L. Roux, owner; Randy Downs, handler.

3rd—Essay 191891, pointer male, by Evolution—Gallery Gossip. Terry Flansburg & John Criswell, owners; Tony Terrell, handler.

Saskatchewan Open Championship—37 starters

Winner—Thunderclap 184451, pointer male, by Buckboard—Swing Along. David Suitts, owner; Tony Terrell, handler.

Runner-up—Addition's Go Boy 121822, pointer male, by Builder's Addition—Nell's Rambling On. Pete Frierson, owner; Garland Priddy, handler.

Open Shooting Dog Classic—20 pointers 6 setters
Judges: John Criswell and Arlin Nolen

1st—Carolina Wildfire 88663, pointer male by Bonafide—Julie Warhoop. Dr. P. B. Kinman, owner; Thelmar Page, handler.

2nd—Brierpatch Little John 113005, pointer male, by Little John Boy—Hendricks Jewel. Odis Mason, owner; Wayne Elsberry, handler.

3rd—Rambling Yankee Man 143727, pointer male by A Rambling Yankee—Gordon's Spirited Pat. Silas Courtney, owner; John Ray Kimbrell, handler.

Chapter 20

1984:
A Come-Back Season

IT WAS THE SECOND year at Towner, and a come-back season so far as entry was concerned. Sixty-eight were in the championship, fifth largest number to compete in the stake.

A second all-age stake was added, one with the entries limited to those which had placed in a Derby stake the year before. It effectively gave owners with dogs in their first all-age season a chance to get a placement – an unlikely thing except for that rare dog that only occasionally appears. It was named for Cov and drew 25 starters. In the regular Saskatchewan Open All-age there were 42, and 47 Derbies.

The shooting dog stake had been run with the all-age program since the early '70s, and this was the inaugural running of the Saskatchewan Open Shooting Dog Championship.

I reported the trial, and excerpts tell the story:

"Whatever, those two are making it rough on poor boys at Towner, this year." Marshall Loftin was talking about Flatwood Bill and his kennelmate, Flatwood Hank. Between them they won the Saskatchewan Open Championship, the Saskatchewan Open All-age, and placed in the Leon Covington Open All-age. Pete Hicks handled them to the four placements for owner Frank Cox of Bennett, N.C. Joe Hicks, Pete's son, handled the winning Derby, Connecuh River Snoot, to keep five of the 11 placements in the family. Snoot is owned by A. J. Schorr and Bobby Gene Renfroe of Union Springs, Ala. The father and son accounted for $8,150 of the $12,259 distributed in purse.

"Flatwood Bill ran on the least favored course, a rollicking prairie race, needing help to keep the front, but never slacking his drive or willingness to go yonder. He pointed a large covey of prairie chickens at the end of a distant cast, the orange-marked, black-nosed pointer standing intent for flush and shot, turning his head to watch one bird that pitched just in front of him.

"The runner-up was quite a different type dog, the other extreme. Copper Rush, owned by Stephen Harwood of Houston, Texas, handled by Tony Terrell, hunted a handy, up-front pattern and pointed a large covey just off to the left of gallery and course some 75 yards at pickup. He was lofty and intent for the flush and shot.

"Though there seemed an abundance of game on the courses, it also seemed difficult for dogs to handle the birds, especially in the championship. Rush ran the last morning and moved Anvil off the list which had been posted the evening before.

"It was a big-entry year, the largest in several seasons. There were 42 in the half-hour Saskatchewan Open All-Age, won by Flatwood Bill with Flatwood Hank second. Third went to Plumcover Taco, owned by Edwin Brown of Troup, Texas, and handled by Andy Daugherty. Each had one find and races that suited the judges.

"Pecos Gal, owned and handled by Gary Pinalto of Broken Arrow, Okla., won the Leon Covington Open All-Age, a half-hour stake, with one find and a forward hunting pattern. Flatwood Hank was second with one find, and Mortlach, owned by Perry Mikles of Booneville, Ark., handled by Daugherty, was third on the basis of a strong ground heat.

"There were 25 starters in the Covington All-Age, which the club limited to those that had placed in Derby stakes last season. The Saskatchewan Derby brought out 47 contestants, an especially large number when compared with entries of recent seasons. Snoot won for Hicks. Doin Things, owned by David Suitts of Boulder, Colo., was second, handled by Terrell, and third went to Classic Plumcover, handled by Daugherty for Texan Edwin Brown. All three were placed on the basis of their ground efforts, though there were dogs in the stake with bird work.

"Ten days were required to complete the whole program. Large galleries watched during the first few days, more than 40 riders following on the first day and 30-35 during most of the first week. As Bud Daugherty, who made the prairie trials

232

for years before moving to his farm in Missouri a couple of seasons ago, put it:

" 'I haven't seen so many people in the gallery on the prairie since they moved the Border to John Gardner's place – and maybe not then.'

" . . . There was plenty of water on the course. Windmills are well spaced, and they bring clear, cold water from no more than 12 feet underground, sandpoints tapping the vast reservoir. They were not needed, obviously, for ranch cattle, but (Foreman Jeff) Dosch and crew started them for the field trial. It was a dry year, the hay crop off a third, and the spring-fed lake was down. Footing was good for the horses, sandy country with only one buffalo wallow and it was dry and not a problem.

"The ranch was put together by Tulsa oilman Tom Leach, who invested heavily and profitably in minerals in North Dakota and other northwest areas. After his death, with homes in Tulsa and New York, Mrs. Leach opted for the lodge on the Towner ranch as home. Upon her death, the ranch was left with other holdings in a trust which has decided now to sell the ranch the couple so enjoyed.

"It is not possible to have a complete list of those who attended, but with full knowledge of that shortcoming a few will be remembered and others in the running. Judge Lee R. West had been north for a week before and took time out for a judicial conference at Jackson Hole, returning with his wife, Mary Ann, for the early running. Leon Harris and Dr. R. M. Crockett of Tyler, Tex., left their horses before the trial and went to the Marion Gordon camp where Dr. Crockett suffered a heart problem and was flown home. John Rex Gates and Mrs. Gates spent an afternoon on the grounds, stayed over for dinner and the next morning. Gates was at his camp in Manitoba where Pete Thuman had the dogs of Stephen Harwood. Another veteran of the prairie competition, Bud Daugherty and Mrs. Daugherty went first to his old camp at Jansen, Sak., where his son, Andy trains, and then rode the trial through the Derby. He was the amiable, entertaining war horse enjoying taking it easy and coaching Tommy Alsop who helps Andy. With the Daughertys were the Down Powells and Jake Kirkland.

"Louisiana Senator B. B. Rayburn and Cecil R. Rester came with the Loftin group, which included Gerald Roberts . . . from the Kentucky country of handler Kenny Robinson there were

Tommy Hamilton, Earl Tucker, Jimmy Pendergest, Becky and Glen Hance . . . There were Gib Edwards of Oscaloosa, Iowa, and Arlin Nolen, of Stigler. Without their management of the dog wagon and many another chore – including inventing the water system that provided use of the 'big house' and horse water outside the pens – it just wouldn't have worked. Edwards came to Towner a couple of weeks before the trial, and Mrs. Edwards joined him. Don Hickman of Stigler, took time off to ride and to help and to watch his dog run. Lynn Bennett, who was with Terrell, and Squeaky (Dennis) Terrell and David Johnson, who came down from Broomhill with Thuman, could also be counted on."

John Ray Kimbrell, the South Carolina handler who has trained nearby for several seasons, judged the Derby and championship for the second time. Rush Campbell of Richland, Wash., who campaigned the remarkable winner and sire Ch. Elhew Copper Strike and his son Ch. Silver Strike, among others, joined him. Dan Clarke Jr. and Bud Williamson, both of North Carolina, chose winners in the two all-age stakes.

There were no great disagreements over placements in the first three stakes, though there were those who thought Hank and Pecos Gal might have been reversed. Pete Hicks, upon learning that the two North Carolinians were to judge the first two stakes, was concerned, and expressed it. But with the end of the trial he was all smiles.

There were those who thought that the champion was an obvious choice, but there was a question about the runner-up's range. Anvil got the nod for second in some books.

Towner, N.D., August 27, 1984
Judges: Dan Clarke Jr., Bud Williamson
Open All-age – 42 starters
1st – Flatwood Bill 174484, pointer male by Evolution – Garner's White Candy. Frank Cox, owner; Pete Hicks, handler.
2nd – Flatwood Hank 184390, pointer male, by Blackwater – Galway. Frank Cox, owner; Pete Hicks, handler.
3rd – Plumcover Taco 179981, pointer female, by Texas Squire's Hank – Flush's Melody. Edwin Brown, owner; Andy Daugherty, handler.

Leon Covington Open All-Age—25 Starters

1st—Pecos Gal 205036, pointer female, by Man's Flintrock—My Main Dot. G. L. Pinalto, owner and handler.

2nd—Flatwood Hank 184390, pointer male, by Blackwater—Galway. Frank Cox, owner; Pete Hicks, handler.

3rd—Mortlach 184416, pointer male, by Rebel Hawk—Greener Pastures. Perry Mikles, owner; Andy Daugherty, handler.

Open Derby—47 starters

Judges: John Ray Kimbrell, Rush Campbell

1st—Connecuh River Snoot unreg pointer female by Connecuh River Sport—Connecuh River Mona. A. J. Shore & B. G. Renfroe, owners; Joe Hicks, handler.

2nd—Doin Things 214613, pointer male, by Understatement—Doin My Number. David Suitts, owner; Tony Terrell, handler.

3rd—Classic Plumcover 226262, pointer female by J R—Flush's Melody. Edwin Brown, owner; Andy Daugherty, handler.

Saskatchewan Open Championship—68 starters

Winner—Flatwood Bill, 174484, pointer male, by Evolution—Garner's White Candy. Frank Cox, owner; Pete Hicks, handler.

Runner-up—Copper Rush 124595, pointer male, by Elhew Copper Strike—Sunday Sunshine. Stephen Harwood, owner; Tony Terrell, handler.

Chapter 21

1985:
When the Lady Sings

THE STORY OF THE Saskatchewan and Towner in '85 was to find the trial and the ranch moving along happily with a large entry and performances of merit.

It is best told by the report:

"A six-time champion, seven years old and obviously carrying a litter of pups, won the 27th renewal of the Saskatchewan — in the last brace, and on the course nobody wanted. For the second consecutive season, 68 were drawn in the largest title stake on the prairie, the program starting the major circuit season on the Monday before Labor Day.

"Robert (Robin) Gates, competing for the first time for a title which dogs handled by his older brother, John Rex, won four times, could see K's High Rise standing in the distance, and he was far ahead of the judges. He raised his hat and the long ride to the lemon-marked double winner of the National Free-For-All began. With the race she had already put down, it was obvious that if she finished well the title was hers.

"This was an independent prairie field trial find. She did not need the game she was to point at pickup. Her performance met the legendary standards. Young Gates' father, the late Cap'n John S., won more prairie championships than any other handler, 26 — his first the U. S. Chicken in 1941 with Mercer Mill Jake, and his last, the Dominion with Technique in 1964. John Rex is second leading prairie handler with 24, from 1965 to '80.

"It was also the first trial for Gates to handle High Rise. Jimmy Honea of Atlanta, bought her for a reported five-figure sum earlier in the summer from Ed Kuntz of O'Fallen, Missouri. Mississippi professional Roy Jines handled her in all of her previous title victories.

"At the end of the first full day of the championship, the judges posted two dogs, Thunderclap and Double Rebel Jack, sons of the same dam, both developed and handled by Tony Terrell of Canton, Texas. The title and runner-up were theirs until the final brace of the eight-day program.

"The judges were not asked to post in order, and it was the liver-marked Thunderclap, winner of the '83 Saskatchewan, who earned the second spot over his kennelmate. Thunderclap, or, Clyde, is owned by David Suitts of Boulder, Colorado, who bred him. He was riding to watch the performance.

"The dog was exceedingly fast, attractive, searching forward throughout the time, and he had one distant find on a covey. At the end, point was called, but nothing was put up.

"In the Saskatchewan open all-age, the champion and runner-up were also first and second, but in reverse order. Third went to Black Ebony, never really up to prairie standards on the ground. But he pointed a covey and was credited with two stops-to-flush. He, too, was handled by Gates for Honea.

"Thunderclap was a showman in this appearance, too, displaying his tremendous turn of speed, and he pointed in a far valley, watched from the Anderson hills, an area added this season, which offer an exceptional view of a ranging, hunting dog. High Rise hunted the country to the fullest, and had one find. At pickup, she was standing just a dot at the bottom of the sand-hills, but nothing was there.

"For the third season, the Saskatchewan program, four all-age stakes, were run over the same grounds, with additions and adjustments. It is the property which oilman Tom Leach put together and enjoyed during his life. His trust allowed the grounds to be used in '83 and '84. Earlier this year, Dennis Jeffrey of Minot, N. D., purchased the 10,000-acre ranch. He had trained on the grounds in previous years. He was the primary host for this renewal, with near an hour of the big-vie land of Harry and James Anderson added. A loop is also made on the Ken Booth ranch alfalfa field.

"Eight hours were run through the eight days, a grueling effort for man and horse. The half-hour stakes turned the working day into 12 and 14 hours.

"The weather could not have been better for a field trial. That is not true for the farmers, whose crops suffered from the cool days and cold nights. Jackets felt good every morning, at least until noon, and throughout the running some days.

"Pete Hicks, who took the measure of everyone in the Saskatchewan a season ago with Flatwood Bill and Flatwood Hank, was off to an impressive start. In the Leon Covington Open All-Age, which started the trial, every one of his entries pointed game, except one which was lost from judgment. He handled all three winners – Bisco Big Jack, first; Kashmir, second; Bisco Ranger, third. Jack is owned by Barry Carpenter of North Carolina; Kashmir by A. J. Canale of North Carolina, and Bill Wester, also of North Carolina, was there to see his Ranger. Each had one find.

"There were 17 in the Covington, a stake limited to Derby winners of the previous season. Forty competed in the all-age. There were 56 in the Derby, one short of the record set in '69. The championship's 68 exactly equaled the number drawn a year ago, that the fifth largest for the stake.

"A total of $12,209 was distributed in purses, $5,000 to the champion and $1,700 to the runner-up.

"The extraordinary Derby was won by an orange-marked male, Chief's Marshall, owned by James Ray of Tishomingo, Mississippi, and handled by Bill Humphreys. His was quite a show. Five times he was around game, handling the first large covey perfectly on relocation, with great maturity. On two other equally large coveys, his bracemate, which tended to like his company, helped him flush. Judges saw him with another covey going onto the Anderson Ranch, and Humphrey called point for him at pickup though the judges had seen him moving just before. He was strong and going on well at the end.

"Second went to Chief's Addition, handled by Peter Thuman for owner Stephen Harwood. He got two birds up as he worked in a swale, handler quite near calling him on. He stopped and was shot over. Third was Pardon My Dust, handled by Doug Sellers, a regular at the Saskatchewan at Towner, and owned by Jerry Reed and Harley Fancher. The Setter pointed with arresting style and perfect manners. Neither the second nor third placed dog hunted at the range usually demanded of Derbies on the prairie. However, they fit the criteria which the judges set."

The report pointed out that the judges made two lists for Derby placements, one which required bird work of some fashion, another that did not. They used the first, while the second would have been more in keeping with history and custom, but they believed bird work was a requirement.

Others mentioned: Sally for Colvin Davis and Sweet Ann for Joe Hicks, braced together, had multiple finds but little range. Their "other list" included Hamilton's Big O and Bisco Flame for Robinson and Pete Hicks, and the entry included Dunn's Fearless Bud, Newman's Royal Flush, Elhew Strike, Specialist, Whippoorwill's Rex.

The report went on:

"The present location of the Saskatchewan is rich in field trial history. It was September 10, 1912, that the All-America Championship was first contested over the land of the Alfalfa Valley Land Co. north of Towner. A $500 trophy, called the N. Rowe Cup, named for the Chicago sportsman who started the American Field, was offered, and Comanche Frank was the winner.

"In 1913, there was a repeat at Towner, the same grounds were used that cool September, with rain falling during much of the competition. The next year, the trial moved south – to Aberdeen, South Dakota. But in 1915 it was back to Towner. More specifically, Denbigh, a small community to the west. It was a civic event, complete with parade. The start was about a half mile from the center of town, and the courses ran some 10 miles across country to the ranch of J. J. Torey, who had field trial dogs. He was host and marshal. An arbor was set up for the lunch site which offered ice cream and sandwiches.

"Gustav Pabst, a bird dog enthusiast, had his Pabst Blue Ribbon beer especially labeled 'to my good friends at the All-America Chicken Championship.' William Corcoran of Pittsburgh, made a movie, and John Proctor won the purse of $300. More than 100 participated, the Field reported, most coming by train. Horses from local farms and ranches provided transportation for handlers, judges and gallery. The prairie was 'filled with chickens, 30 to 40 coveys raised during a half-day's running.'

"The hospitality of the '80s is equal to that of the teens. The club was host to a barbecue on Tuesday evening at the Lodge where Jeffrey and his family now reside. Many trainers work in the immediate area, and they and their land owners were among the 125 who attended what amounted to an open house at one of the area's points of interest. The Leach lodge was featured in Sports Illustrated when Tom Leach hosted a hunt that included notables of industry. Mrs. Leach was full-time resident the last few years of her life, preferring the rolling McHenry County land to her Manhattan apartment, or her home in Tulsa.

"The Towner business community, headed by Jim Williams, president of the State Bank of Towner, was host to a steak supper one evening. Williams and others of his group rode several days.

"Henry and Minnie Schmidt had hot lunches at the grounds from their mobile kitchen, and prepared the barbecue dinner.

"Without O. G. Edwards of Oscaloosa, Iowa, and Arlin Nolen of Stigler, Oklahoma, the trial could not have moved along. They were there the week before, when fences were to be let down, water system to be put together around the pens, and when horses needed to be saddled and fed, dog wagon to be superintended, and things to be put back together at the end. Mrs. Edwards joined Gib late in the week.

"Nolen also was judge for the Leon Covington and open all-age. He was joined by Dan Clarke, Jr., of Hickory, North Carolina, who was at the camp of John Ray and Mary Kimbrell for several weeks. Clarke is making duplicates of the Canadian trooper saddle, and offers several other items for field trialers.

"It is acknowledged that on the prairie judges don't get the care and tending they deserve. The stake managers usually have too much going to spend time with them, and they often are relegated to hunting transportation with handlers. Head-quarters for this trial was the Hamilton Motel at Rugby, some 25 miles from the grounds. It is a large, comfortable establishment, with indoor pool, hot tub, spacious rooms and good prices. The bar has legal gambling tables and the steak house is excellent.

"Frank Thompson teaches at Georgia College in Milledgeville. He is a Virginian by birth. He is a scholar. A meticulous man who keeps his counsel. He is devoted in many special ways to bird dogs and field trials. He has been coming to the prairie for more than a decade, first with his wife, Marietta, and they camped out in a tent near Vic Eastmond's old house. He is a breeder of bird dogs. He enjoys working with them from birth, and he enjoys knowing about their ancestry – not just from paper, but from having been on the prairie and at such places as George Moreland's to see how the paper figures translate to the field. Several years ago he felt the need to know more facts about the dogs he was breeding, more about what actually happened, what the numbers really were, rather than what was recollected or supposed. He set about the laborious job of keeping track of the dogs registered by selected sires. He also kept data of the wins of those sires' offspring by category. Thus, he has been able to figure the sort of job leading sires are – and aren't – doing. He has now published two Pointer Breeders' Almanacs. They're invaluable contributions. While the figures reveal the good, they also disclose those whose popularity with breeders is not supported by the success of their get.

"He approached judging the Derby and the championship with the same steady manner, his mind set with guidelines of what he hoped to see. Frank Thompson is the soul of integrity, and a large part of him is devoted to the speediest, most distant hunting field trial dogs.

"With the science education professor from Georgia was Darrell Privett, the Tennessee cotton farmer whose home is Frog Jump – but gets his mail at Halls. He is, likewise, no stranger to the north. Two seasons ago he came to Towner before the trial and stayed throughout the running. He has an earned reputation for fairness, and for making those around him enjoy life, too. He has trained and handled his own dogs, winning the Southwestern Open Championship with Black Creek Missy, which was also runner-up in the Texas Championship. He demonstrated his ability to preside with the attitude of 'we'll treat you as we would like to be treated.' Mrs. Privett drove north with him."

Something of the two dogs which were placed:

"When K's High Rise was a Derby, she won two thirds. That was not to happen again. She won first in the St. Louis Club's Walter Johnson Memorial all-age at an hour, and then seven championships, plus the Missouri Open All-Age. No runners-up. Hers are the International Pheasant Championship, the Missouri Championship, two Florida championships, two Free-for-Alls, and now the Saskatchewan. Her count is 11 placements. She is one of the remarkable, versatile field trial performers.

"Charles Hodum of Corinth, Mississippi, bred her, whelped March 9, 1978. She was first with Tommy Davis, but for virtually all of her public career in the charge of Rob Jines, who stands high on the all-time handlers' list with 21 championships. Her owner during the previous wins was Kuntz, who advertised her for sale earlier this year under a bid arrangement. The highest bid came from Jimmy Honea, who transferred her registration in July and put her with Gates. She was bred to Ch. Flatwood Hank, first said not be with pups, a diagnosis that became obviously wrong as she came to Towner, her flanks full and breasts dropping and filling.

"High Rise is not pretty in the sense that she is sleek, stands with high tail and has an effervescent personality. She is seven, the veteran of miles on a dog truck, and hours on strange fields. She has had to be all business. Her strength is unseen, true class which comes from within . . . the heart that drove her through thorny prairie roses as if they were not there . . . the intelligence that made her come across the distance front . . . and the training and desire that caused her to find prairie chickens far from any person, and to stand with them in front of her so long, so intently. She did not crack her tail every jump. It was not poker straight when she pointed. So what. Her exhibition was of character. Desire. Grit. It was a pity so few were riding, for they could have been thrilled by what the prairie is about.

"It was a disappointment for Terrell, but he understood what had taken place. For four days he had the winners, no small fete in a championship so filled with stars. He had gone the miles behind Double Rebel Jack and Thunderclap since they were puppies. He followed them on the Packsaddle of Western Oklahoma, across the quail fields of the King Ranch. He helped Jack as he won the National Derby Championship, the Texas twice, and watched as his owner, Dr. Mike Furcolow of Boulder, Colorado, won the Region 7 Amateur All-Age Championship with him. He rode after Thunderclap as he won this title two seasons ago, and sat back and watched him win the all-age this year.

"What was the difference between these two kennelmates? The judges thought Thunderclap was faster, more the showman, more the field trial performer, the eye-catcher. He demonstrated he wound go yonder and point game with manners and style.

Others might have chosen them in reverse – neither choice would be wrong, just the judges' honorable preference. That is what you ask for.

"The dogs are from the same dam, Swing Along, a daughter of Double Rebel Dan and Swingin Thru by Ch. Riggins' White knight and a daughter of Ch War Storm and Sugarplum."

"What was the competition? The likes of Master Charge, Mercer Mill Race, Jody Rebel, Bisco Big Jack, Flatwood Bill, Rhythm Maker, Cajun Special, Cumberland River Mark, Special Number, Classic Edition, Plumcover Taco, Flush's Reedy Rogue, Miller's Chief, Oliver's Warhoop Jane, Bye Bye Blackbird, Hawk's Nimrod, Flatwood Hank, Major Revolution, Paper Rosie, Pike Creek Mike, Pink Lightning, Black Ebony, El Sauz Doll, Pinehurst King, Chief's Bo, Giant, Sun Brown Honey.

At the end of the report there were some "Afterthoughts:"

"There are no prairie trials, few elsewhere, over which the specter of Flush's Country Squire does not hover.

" 'They were already talking about him when he got to Canada. The Cap'n didn't have to tell many folks about a dog until everyone was waiting to see him.

" 'The first time we turned him loose, five of us were horseback, and the Cap'n was in the truck. Every time he'd come by, the Cap'n would hollar, 'There he goes – he's my kinda dog.' That night we were talking about what to do with him, and Louis – we called him Mule – said, 'Let me try him.' The Cap'n did. Louis and Sport would leave in the morning, just the two of them, and we wouldn't see 'em until after noon. We didn't see either of them much that summer.'

"Colvin Davis was remembering other times at Broomhill, and Louis was Louis Fleming, who replaced Peck Kelly as the chief scout for the Gates operation. Colvin was much like John Rex to the Cap'n, hander of The Hurricane in the callback with Safari, a man who Robin says, 'Still does things just like daddy did.'

"Colvin is proud to be a disciple of the legendary breeder, developer, handler. And he and his wife, Mazie, made things more pleasant at Towner this summer, he with quiet reollections, she with a smile. Colvin trains dogs in Alabama, and at Broomhill at the camp where James Norris, John Moore and others have summered.

"Louis retired after heart problems and still lives near the Gates Kennel at Leesburg, Georgia. (Note: Louis died in 1990).

* * *

"Field trialers were sad to see Mary and Jeff Dosch leave the Leach Ranch. They moved from the place where he was foreman for 10 years, and was the person who gave approval for Jeffrey to work on the grounds and for the field trial to run there the past two years.

"Rick Hammon remains a part of the staff for Jeffrey, and he helped with such things as hauling hay to the horses and seeing the windmills were flowing.

"Doug Jess of Minot, took leave from his flying duties with the Air Force to be present during the trial, busy in the hay fields and with errands during the all-age stakes, and many projects during the shooting dog program.

* * *

"It's no secret that Pete Hicks is one of the exceptional bird dog developers and handlers. It is also no secret that occasionally he is satisfied more with his own judgment than that of the judges.

"It is a better kept secret that he has two sons like Joe. There is John, a Myrtle Beach realtor, who flew to Towner on vacation to be with his dad and brother during the trial. Pete had a couple of days when he ran a fever and let the sons handle some Derbies. John knows dogs, too, and likes them, but the business world pays better and more regularly. His is the personality of a guy who makes the gallery more fun – helpful, full of humor, enjoying life."

Towner, N. D., August 27, 1985
Judges: Dan Clarke, Jr., and Arlin Nolen
Leon Covington Open All-Age – 16 pointers, 1 setter
1st – Bisco Big Jack, 1214241, male, by Bronzini – Bisco Tat. Barry Carpenter, owner; Pete Hicks, handler.
2nd – Kashmir, particulars not given, Pete Hicks, handler.
3rd – Bisco Ranger, 1209729, male, by Bronzini – Bisco Tat. Bill Wester, owner; Pete Hicks, handler.

Open All-Age – 37 pointers, 3 setters
1st – Thunderclap, 1184451, male, by Buckboard – Swing Along. David Suitts, owner; Tony Terrell, handler.
2nd – K's High Rise, 1122727, female, by High Fidelity – Reed's Little Anne. Jimmy Honea, owner; Robert Gates, handler.
3rd – Black Ebony, 99460, male, by Colfax – Miss Wewa. Jimmy Honea, owner; Robin Gates, handler.

Judges: Darrell Privett and Frank Thompson
Open Derby – 53 pointers, 3 setters
1st – Miller's Marshall, unreg, male, by Miller's Chief – Tiara's Babe. James Ray, owner; Bill Humphries, handler.
2nd – Chief's Addition, 1322416, male, by Miller's Chief – Miss Addition's Lady. Stephen Harwood, owner; Peter Thuman, handler.
3rd – Pardon My Dust, 233302, setter, by Just A Swinging – Fury. Jerry Reed and Harley Fancher, owner; Doug Sellers, handler.

Saskatchewan Open Championship – 68 entries
Winner – K's High Rise, 1122727, female, by High Fidelity – reed's Little Anne. Jimmy Honea, owner; Robert Gates, handler.
Runner-up – Thunderclap, 1184451, male, by Buckboard – Swing Along. Davis Suitts, owner; Tony Terrell, handler.

Judges: John Criswell and Arln Nolen
Saskatchewan Open Shooting Dog Championship – 28 entries
Winner – Warhoop Express Liz, 1148530, female, by Warhoop Boy Express – Gwinn's Little Gal. L. C. Shepard, owner; Gordon Hazlewood, handler.
Runner-up – Carolina Bullet, 1183548, male, by Mississippi Rifle – Babe of Springhill. R. O. Woods, owner; John Ray Kimbrell, handler.

Open Derby – 14 entries
1st – American Made, 1233544, female, by Thunderclap – Rebel Woman. Stephen Harwood, owner; Peter Thuman, handler.
2nd – Elhew Strike, 1223787, male, by Hook's Bounty Hunter – Elhew Gimli. Alvin Nitchman and Robert Wehle, owners; Alvin Nitchman, handler.
3rd – Prairie View Jenny, 1241640, female, by Northland's Buckaroo – Reid's Rambling Gay. Rick Foresberg, owner; Dennis Jeffrey, handler.

Chapter 22

1986:
Keep On Livin'

THE LEAD OF the report of the Saskatchewan for 1986 in the FIELD pretty well told the story of the trial:

As the story goes, Wallace Sessions was asking Billy Taylor about one of those perplexities which has no answer, no explanation. He thought a second or two, and replied:

'Just keep on livin'.'

There was a lot of that during the 28th running of the Saskatchewan Open Championship and program which started August 25 over the East Division of the Prairie View Ranch and Shooting Preserve south of Towner, North Dakota. It ended 10 days later.

Pete Hicks first came up with the story just after a Derby, standing like a statue during the flush of a large covey, went down as he walked back to him. The judges applied the homespun philosophy for days as the heat and wind seemed to conspire against excellence.

By field trial terms, a good deal of money – $14,787 – was paid out in purses for the four stakes, the $9,100 for the champion and runner-up likely a new record for the prairie. Ten percent of the 70% of entry fees was designated for the owners. There were 161 entries.

History repeated.

Last Fall, a champion female pointer was drawn as a bye. She was handled by Robin Gates. Twice she pointed game, hunted a full-blown prairie race and won the championship. This Fall, a champion female pointer was drawn late in the stake.

She was handled by Robin Gates. Twice she pointed game, hunted a full-blown prairie race and won the championship. A year ago it was K's High Rise. This year it was Ronco Lucky Siete, bred and nurtured in the west, and owned by Stephen Walker of Novato, California, whose holdings are the most extensive on the circuit — and growing.

Another westerner, 6-year-old Concerto Ace High, was runner-up, for an owner Dr. Bruce McCarthy, and a handler, Doug Sellers, both from Hattiesburg, Mississippi. He found game one time and pointed it with arresting style, hunted a forward, reaching pattern through most of the hour, waning a bit toward the end. A few days later he was third in the Saskatchewan Amateur All-Age Classic.

The historic running order of all-age, Derby and championship, was readjusted this year to accommodate those who wanted to go into Canada to other title stakes. First came the Derby, then the championship, followed by the Leon Covington Open All-Age (for first-year dogs) and the Saskatchewan Open All-Age at an hour.

Just as Ace High placed in the amateur stakes, so did the winning Derby, A Windfall, which was first in both. He was handled by Arlin Nolen of Stigler, Oklahoma, with a prairie race and a stop on a single chicken. Second and third, Dottie and Redemption's Man, were both placed on the way they hunted the prairie, and were handled by Freddie Rayl. Dottie is a stylish, liver-marked female owned by Phil Moser of North Carolina. Man is a black-marked male owned by T. Jack Robinson of Dayton, Tennessee, who was riding to watch. There were 45 entries.

The Rayl contingent was again dominant in the Leon Covington, winning first with Lady Addition and third with Sandspur, littermates owned by Larry Voorhies and Steve Matonis of Orlando, Florida. Lady was given credit for a stop-to-flush. Both had strong hunting heats. Second was Newman's Royal Flush, handled for owners Troy Newman of Columbia, Missouri, and Roger Austin of Marshfield, North Carolina, by Randy Patterson. This season's National Derby Champion had a limited race and one game contact. Twenty started.

Randy Downs kept in touch with the orange-marked Master Charge as he scoured the countryside and was credited with one find on a large covey to win the Saskatchewan all-age hour.

He is owned by Dr. Roux, of Meterie, Louisiana. Second and third were from Geraldine Livingston's famed Dixie Plantation, Kilsyth Jack and Kilsyth Judy. They proved themselves stylish, mannerly bird-finders, if not prairie running dogs. Jack pointed prairie chickens three times, Judy twice for their developer, Pete Hicks of Bisco, North Carolina.

With the winners told . . .

The offering of the Prairie Chefs — better known as Minnie and Henry Schmidt — put strength in 150 and more handlers, owners, helpers, landowners and their families one evening during each Saskatchewan at Towner. The produce of the Longhorn Bar from the icy watering troughs on Dennis Jeffrey's lawn, made them lighter of foot, freer of speech and quicker of wit.

The evening event, which the championship club hosts, is a good deal more than the noontime offering from the Chefs' mobile kitchen, though the lunch-on-the-grounds makes it possible to keep the trial moving. Trips to town and the wait at the Dairy Cup would mean a half-day's running, for no one would be back for the 2 o'clock start.

The business community of Towner, through the Commercial Club, invited the visiting crowd to the Golf Club on the second Monday evening for steaks and cocktails, an indication of the welcome being extended to the 'dog people.'

A season ago Jeffrey bought the Leach Ranch property, and it is under his hospitality that the trial continues at Towner. The custom of putting the east division cattle in the Albright pasture where the courses don't go, was followed. Windmills are started. The cold, clear water springs through sand points from a reservoir no more than 10 to 15 feet below the surface. It's one of the chores which the landowner and his associates — Rick Foresberg and Johnny Rognlien — undertake.

This chunk of land over which dogs hunt in late August is pure prairie. Only a few acres — less than 200 — are hay land, and there are no crops. The floor of this fragile place . . . sand and silt blown together to make an oval of hills with a hollow of ground that dips and sways, cupped with sand sculptured swales . . . glows green with water, turns brown and brittle with days of sun. On a morning damp with dew, it can be a postcard of wild flowers, those intricate, color-splashed blossoms that are the seed of native cover . . . the purple thistle with a bright yellow finch having breakfast, a bee harvesting a purple flower you never saw before. Even the thorny prairie rose which earlier had four-peteled flowers of pink and red where, in late August, bright red hips ready to make vitamin C.

The sandhills have large bluffs, and there are those of the middle pasture which are especially so. It is a landscape which in an hour demands that a dog hunt through obstacles like the prairie rose gnawing at its underside as do the briars at Quitman. He may find cactus scattered where the land is weather-scarred. There are open expanses where he has the opportunity to become but a dot, only to be required to make a turn or go between heavier growth.

Sharptails were found during the 17 days that trials ran this year at virtually all the spots where they have been the past few seasons. However, the coveys were half to a third their usual size, and the concentration that claimed the first 30 minutes in '83 and '84, have moved, many of them to the neighboring 'Raymond's Refuge,' as Raymond Jaeger's farm is called. He leaves them alfalfa and plants corn and oats and wheat on his place, just across the west ranch fence.

Why was the crop short? There are a hundred theories, but nature is required to tell no secrets. Perhaps it will deepen the mystery another year by repopulation.

More from the report:

These have been the facts of the matter. It is the color and feel of the years . . . the images and memories which times and dogs and people revive . . . as many, as varied as the loyal, thin legion of purists who come the week before Labor Day to see what the summer's training has wrought. Theirs are the stores of the questioned and the questioners, the grumbles, and, ah, the sportsmanship of nature's sharptails and treachery of her Huns . . . the long reach to the north bluffs at Mortlach and the sweep off Anderson hill at Towner . . . the Sports, Rexs, Spurs and Jacks . . . her badger holes and the horses that dodged them.

It is no incidental fact that John Ray Kimbrell is listed among those who have three times helped choose the champions. In field trialing today there is no man with valid claim to better eyes with which to see handler and dog and bird. None could be more consistent in applying the historic standards of game handling. He is blessed with friends, for he is one. He can watch any man's dog without mental pressure to give or take, for his judgments are even-handed, understanding that, at the heart, it is, indeed, a sport. Words of handlers with their prejudices and prejudicing are lost on him. He knows what he is about — from the position of a handler who wins championships, a trainer who feels the sting of others' judgments, and the pleasures of it. When it comes to applying the subjective views on range and hunting patterns, he has his yardstick earned by seeing what can be.

The Fort Mill, South Carolina, handler has been coming to the Towner area for many seasons, to the land owned in great part by the Green families. Mary attends the old house, and it has at times been a prairie hotel to family, owners and guests and the occasional handler coming through. Their teen-age son, George, gave up the north this season for a job at home.

Judging with Kimbrell this year was a fellow South Carolinian, John Little of Chester, far from a stranger to this part of the field trial world. He has been at the trials since they came to Towner in '83, and last year was judge for the shooting dog championship. He brings integrity and conveys a feeling that he is treating others as he would want to be treated, judging as he would be judged. The two men are friends and that is a factor which can give strength to a judiciary where on some occasions differences between judges who are but acquaintances can be exploited by those who enjoy such.

Dan Clarke of Hickory, North Carolina, has judged the all-age stakes for the past four seasons. He is the same Carolinian who was chief of staff at the Kimbrell camp this year, and ambassador to the community. And he is the same one whose name can be seen on small plaques screwed on the underside of Canadian saddles, either those which he has expertly and identically reproduced, or those which he has restored to their former condition. He also turned scout for Kimbrell during the shooting dog stakes, and, with Rick Foresberg of the ranch, chose six winners after watching them closely. Foresberg, a Williamston native who spent several years in Hawaii, has been at the ranch since Jeffrey became owner, a man whose abilities cover a wide area. He keeps the harvest equipment moving, and mounts sharptails, Huns, ducks, and a peacock, with artistry. Several of his mounts were taken home with trialers, and another year the community may award them to the championship owners.

For years the same judges watched all of the dogs, and the championship was last. By the time they got to the title stakes, the judges were worn threadbare. Two teams solves that.

Towner, North Dakota, August 25, 1986
Judges: John Ray Kimbrell and John Little
Saskatchewan Open Championship—65 entries
Winner—Ronco's Lucky Siete, 1181750, female, by ronco Traveler—Blackbelt's Jenny. Stephen Walker, owner; Robin Gates, handler.
Runner-up—Concerto Ace High, , male, by Sailin Sam—Gem Strike. Bruce McCarthy, owner; Doug Sellers, handler.

Open Derby—45 entries
1st—A Windfall, 1250749, male, by Understatement—Wine List. Arlin Nolen, owner and handler.
2nd—Exotic Dancer, 126068, female, by Reedy Fork Flush—Arcanum's Zephyr. Phil Moser, owner; Freddie Rayl, handler.
3rd—Redemption's Man, 1259080, male, by Redemption—Evolution's Kitty. T. Jack Robinson, owner; Freddie Rayl, handler.

Judges: Dan Clarke, Jr., Rick Foresberg
Saskatchewan Open All-Age—[One-hour heats] 31 entries
1st—Master Charge, 1137194, male, by the Master Craftsman—Execution. Dr. K. L. Roux, owner, Randy Downs, handler.
2nd—Kilsyth Jack, 1225791 , male, by Evolution—Rollins White Wind. Geraldine Livingston, owner; Pete Hicks, handler.
3rd—Kilsyth Judy, 1225902, female, by Evolution—Chicaroo. Geraldine Livingston, owner; Pete Hicks, handler.

Leon Covington Open All-Age—20 entries
1st—Lady Addition, 1243024, female, by Builder's Free Boy—Builder's Scarlet. B. W. Switzer, owner; Freddie Rayl, handler.
2nd—Newman's Royal Flush, 1243750, by Flush's Red Ranger—Galway. Newman & Austin, owners; Randy Patterson, handler.
3rd—Sandspur, 1228745, male, by Builder's Free Boy—Builder's Scarlet. Voorhies & Matonis, owners; Freddie Rayl, handler.

Judges: Don Hickman and John Criswell Saskatchewan Open Shooting Dog Championship – 39 entries
Winner – Honor Roll, 1157644, male, by Pork rol – Carolina Bonfire. Charles Jackson, owner; John Daugherty, handler.
Runner-up – Warhoop Express Jill, 1201249, female, by Warhoop Boy Express – Nicker Bushglider. Brad Calkins, owner; Gordon Hazlewood, handler.

The Trip Home

When you look back across four years of trials over a particular set of grounds, and realize that you have ridden every brace that has been run, the mind naturally moves to the best of the performances – and some of the more memorable, or, regrettable, incidents.

In making these many rounds, you're riding for the good and bad. It is regrettable that the prairie trials are so far from the centers of field trial population, and that so few who would like to enjoy all-age performances simply can not. There are those who have come year after year, the judges who have seen it all, and others who had the chance at one summer. They are the fortunate minority.

Thus, a relatively small number of fans have witnessed even a single exceptional hunting hour in the north. Even for those who are lucky enough to go north, few have the good fortune to be riding when the truly outstanding ground heat unfolds. They are so far between; often playing out when least expected.

Take Towner as an example. There have been remarkable ones – Thunderclap that first season, Anvil and Bisco Tat. Flatwood Bill the second year. K's High Rise and Thunderclap. Chinquapin's Addition, Fiddler's Pride and Ronco's Lucky Siete. Some of them had no game. Most did. They can be used as yardsticks for what's possible in terms of desire, range, purpose.

Until you have seen such a ground heat and quality chicken handling, you lack the real sense of those possibilities. It's customary to ride a few braces, see nothing and retire to the cranny of belief that 'they're nothing more than our shooting dogs.'

My yardsticks go back to Mortlach in the 60s when Freddie James stood on his horse, barely a dot in the distance, and when we got to him, the dog was another half mile, standing perfectly, not a step did he take nor a caution did he need. Game in front of him. The long-bodied, short, straight-legged Flush's Country Squire was broke out of sight, and hunted out of sight. A Rambling Rebel was doing the same in those days, Texas Silver Spur and Homerun Johnny and Texas Fight.

But back to North Dakota and the cup of sandhills south of Towner. When K's High Rise won the championship a season ago, there were no more than four riding; maybe another, judges included, when Siete went her last half hour this year. Bisco Tat had a good-sized gallery in '83, as did Anvil, despite the heat. Chinquapin's Addition may have had the smartest, driving ground pattern of them all this year, and five watching would be a generous count.

When the name dogs are on the ground, the gallery fills. Just human nature. Whatever, the name dogs, like all others, have their bad days, and when you're looking to see the prairie performance it's poor odds to limit yourself to those few. It's worth the ride, the long days, the heat, the sore spots, to see a Freddie James and Sport, or to thrill at Chinquapin's Addition going around the most distant bluff, down more than an hour, oblivious to the noontime heat that made so many 'get birdie.'

When someone answers, 'You'll know what an all-age dog is when you see one,' it's likely the words are from a man who has kept riding, and based his repeating the old adage on some private high from the performance of a Sport or Tat or Rob.

* * *

It doesn't take a great number of people to make a field trial function, if those who help are willing to do about anything.

Such is the case with three of the Saskatchewan directors: O. G. (Gib) Edwards of Oscaloosa, Iowa, and Don Hickman and Arlin Nolen of Stigler.

If a dog wagon isn't vital, try to get along without one. If the guy who drives it doesn't understand what the needs are, try to make it answering all the questions he gets. Gib, a retired contractor who has campaigned dogs for years, has been at Towner the past three seasons, in charge of the strange conveyance pulled by a tractor or truck. He is also the entry fee collector, who knows what else. He trains on Raymond's

Refuge, the only compensation other than being north with friends.

Nolen and Hickman are pressed into whatever slot needs filling.

* * *

We all get questions about this dog or that, about which dog should be a good one to use as a sire. Some have used the prairie as the benchmark for the decision.

What did the Towner trial say this summer? Naturally it would be different to different folks. Each to his thoughts. One: The courage to hunt the hour in heat and briars at acceptable range is on the wane. Style seemed aplenty. Some sire prospects emerged through their own performances, or through those of their offspring – the best test – and appeared to offer a helping of stamina and hunting talent.

Chinquapin's Addition. He won a championship on the prairie in '81. He is a strong bird-finder on his home grounds in Florida, as well as on chickens. His hour in the championship here was a demonstration of absolute endurance; he was hunting bluff-to-bluff in conditions that caused others to shorten or quit. He is the maternal grandsire of some successful Derbies of last season and sire of an impressive Derby which Sessions runs this year.

Redemption. He has demonstrated his own desire and strength, and had three impressive Derbies, all among the leaders.

Miller's Chief has had more opportunities than most dogs get in a lifetime, and information on his percentages aren't at hand. It is obvious he is siring a good deal of quality.

Understatement. He carries a heavy concentration of Red Water Rex blood, was a bold-going individual from that sort of family. Two of his Derbies, A Windfall and Viscount, gave good accounts of themselves.

Ronco Traveler. He's alive and well and at the west coast kennel of Ron Bader. Because of his geographic location he has not had the opportunities with name females, but that has not kept him from consistently siring quality, including Siete.

These are singled out because of their demonstrated ability to transmit desire and purpose in at least some of their off-spring, beauty not the first priority, though that is not foreign to most of their get. It is also with the full knowledge that there is another set of young dogs competing in other trials also demonstrating the abilities of other sires and dams.

Something to talk about.

* * *

Gregory Robinson is the number two son of the Kenny Robinson family. He has started school the past two seasons at Towner, and missed week days of the trial. But that doesn't mean he wasn't a cog in the summer training wheel.

Greg's really something of an independent operator, with his personal equipment, and he wound up the summer dealing with Dan Clarke to expand his holdings by a pair of saddlebags.

* * *

The June issue of National Geographic has a special section on smells. There is a page pictures showing a pheasant's path and the hunting pattern of a lab trying to get him located.

The article doesn't go into the wiles of upland game, but dwells a good bit on hounds tracking men. A few lines, however, might have some application, as least as to ground scent:

'Heat and sun quickly dissipate a human track. Frost helps preserve it, and cool, moist conditions are ideal for tracking."

(NOTE: The Trip Home appeared with the report of the Saskatchewan in the American Field.)

Chapter 23

1987:
Callbacks Get A Bad Name

"AS THE CHAMPIONSHIP ground on, seven hours each day, it became painfully obvious that not much was happening."

That opening of the section in the FIELD about the running of the title stake pretty well summed the fifth renewal of the Saskatchewan Championship over the Towner ranchlands, and it would be the last. The report:

"When Double Rebel Jack was posed for his portrait as the winner of the 29th Saskatchewan Open Championship, it was the 6th time he had done so for a title. He became the second prairie champion for his dam, Swing Along, and the fourth placement in this championship for his handler, Tony Terrell of Canton, Texas.

"He continued to be a dog with good fortune smiling on him, for his performance — and that of the other 73 in the championship — was not that of fondest memory. His point of sharptail grouse scattered in the alfalfa, 24 of them rising in pairs, threes and fours in front of him, was pretty to see. His early hunting pattern was relatively near, though out front, with a prairie cast near the end. Jack is owned by Dr. Mike Furcolow of Boulder, Colorado, who was riding.

"The runner-up, Cumberland River Mark, was handled by Randy Downs of Reinzi, Mississippi, for Kentuckian Vernon R. Vance. His ground performance was one of extremes — close early, lining out late. He pointed a pair of sharptails, but they were not flushed, and he moved to them on relocation precisely and stopped before they rose near the dugout on the usual first hour course.

"At the end of the hour heats, Judges John Ray Kimbrell of Fort Mill, South Carolina, and Arlin Nolen of Stigler, Oklahoma, conferred for quite a time, considering the option of naming three dogs and withholding the championship title. Finally they announced they would give the pair an opportunity to separate themselves on the ground the next morning, and that one would be champion, the other runner-up; that they had bested the others.

"The result was, at the end of 50 minutes, the same as it was in most books the afternoon before. At a half hour Jack had the best of Mark on the ground, but they were left down another 20 minutes, most of which Mark was gone, and Jack, unheeding the whistle, was close in front, stopping once as a chicken rose. The callback ended with Mark gone.

"That is the basic story of the winners of the championship, though far from the story of the trial. The all-age program began August 25 over the east division of the Prairie View Ranch and Hunting Preserve of Mr. and Mrs. Dennis Jeffrey, a mile off Highway 14 south of Towner. It ended 10 days later with 176 dogs having been run in a four-stake program.

"The championship returned $10,360. The three open stakes in the all-age section of the trial returned $14,700. But the competition didn't end there, the shooting dogs arrived and by the time it was all over at the Prairie View Ranch 17 days had been consumed, hunting season had started by one day, and 277 dogs had been run over the sandy virgin prairie country.

"The weather was ideal, consistently cool mornings, and some days an outer garment felt good through the afternoon. Nights were so cool heaters came on before dawn, and twice there were heavy frosts.

"Game was found all around the courses. The second hour would be the least popular, but the runner-up was on it, as was one of the Covington winners. A season ago the population was down, drastically. The come-back placed it along with the 1984 crop. It seemed few birds were on the second half of the first hour during the all-age stakes, but were all over it in the shooting dog. The alfalfa was often full of game, sometimes 50 or more seen during the 30-minute swing. An accounting might show that there was more trouble handling game than finding it.

257

"The Anderson Ranch which adjoins on the southeast was used in part, and the Eideman acreage was crossed. The pasture with the high ridge and grand view was not available. The alfalfa land to the east is part of the Booth land, now leased and two ranchers allowed the loop to be made where chickens were concentrated.

"Judges are a constant subject, and, with the occasional flair of disagreement, interest becomes more focused. the prairies have a history as a place where judges can have a tough time — both from handlers and horses. Not so this season at Towner. While there might have been those in disagreement with this point or that, it was kept to themselves."

Actually there were some strong feelings about the championship, though none who thought highly of their dogs had a legitimate claim, for in the first round they either erred or simply did too little.

Trainer Dave LaChance teamed with Dr. Furcolow; John Ray Kimbrell, for the fourth time, chose Derby and championship dogs with Arlin Nolen. Lynn Bennett of Arnett, Oklahoma and Keith Martin of Georgia, picked amateur winners.

Of them, I wrote:

"Six men - totally able, good horsemen, interested in what they were doing, energetic, courteous — gave time and ability. they were accorded the same courtesy by those who competed, and there was no legitimate basis for complaints about the decisions they came to."

Of the championship:

"The dogs that ran well had no game, or messed up when they found them. There was the smattering of dogs which had hours where their hunting patterns were suspect by prairie standards, but had acceptable or good bird work.

"The usual field trial question lingered and grew: What are they going to do?

"The question grew with the judges, too, and at the end they were not presented with either an array of choices or the performance which was obviously outstanding. They said they considered naming the dogs in numerical order, withholding the title. This had never been done in the Saskatchewan, and only one time on the prairie. In 1953 the Border International title was withheld from Betty Heelfly.

"They may have considered two others, Jedi Pilot and Craftsman's Delight. Pilot pointed game three times, but was behind, virtually never to the front. Delight pointed game once, but had a race of less range and purpose than the two named.

"Randy Patterson asked the judges about Mill Worker, and was assured he was never considered, though he handled game correctly and found them impressively. His last half was so close that he was often between handler and the judges. Patterson's white Pointer, Dunn's Fearless Bud, had an impressive hour on the ground.

"Kenny Robinson's Scraps hunted the country, the judges believed, for 55 minutes just as he should, ranging far and forward, showing wear those last few minutes, and without game.

"The veteran handler Bud Daugherty has been off the circuit for several seasons, but was back training in the Towner area this summer. But for misjudgment on his part of where a covey of birds came from, he might have been in the money with Black Crude, a stylish Pointer owned by Pat Morgan of Oklahoma City.

"At one point, the judges pointed out that seven of the last eight dogs they had seen were taken up because of errors on game handling."

Among those in the championship: Kreole, Chickasaw Deke, Fred Warrior, Black Moon Rising, Pike Creek Mike, High Country Mo, Molesworth John, Bisco Big Jack, The Hitch Hiker, Fiddlin, Special Number, Hi Volt, Bozeann's Rawhide, George Rambler, Texas Hummer, A Windfall, Lady Addition, Fiddler's Pride, Mercer Mill Race, Jody Rebel, Burlington Man, Bozeann's Mosley, Hamilton's Big O, Mill Worker, West O'Mississippi, Sandspur, A Fool's Gold.

On the evening news the day Prizzi's Honor became winner of the Leon Covington, there was the report of the death of the legendary John Huston, who was responsible for the movie for which the dog was named. Honor was described, "an orange-marked dog of attractive carriage and plenty of range, went to the bluffs in the north section of the alfalfa, to those near the gate and on to those in the northeast corner, an impressive distance. He was found pointing. He was found pointing. He was looking toward the bluff, and the bird was flushed just on the prairie to his side. Sent on, he pointed a covey not far away, and continued strong.

The alfalfa was kind to Loftin. when he came through the course with Kahlua, the pretty white female went well ahead, and, early, in the foot-high green cover, she pointed and birds were in front of her. Chickasaw Doll had the loop onto the Anderson-Eidman land, and she pointed a bird for Brady Porter, her deputized handler when Mike Furney, her owner, lost his voice.

The stake had Limelight, which found a covey and went with a straggler, A Striker with two finds, but didn't like the wind, Black Moon Rising, good on the ground, but an unproductive.

The blue of the Derby was to Redemption's Battle Kat with Sandy Wyatt helping handler Sellers, a daughter of the remarkable sire, Redemption, which Cecil Rester owned and developed. Hall's Main Addition was a free-wheeling young dog, touring the Booth, a product, basically, of Jack Harper breeding, raised by George Smith of south Mississippi and owned with Dr. Emmett Hall, the Caruthersville, Missouri, surgeon. Ch. Miller's Chief was bred to Ch. Miss Ten to produce the third placed Lane's Plain Jane, owned by Bobby Lane and handled by Loftin.

At the announcement, Richard Boteler pointed out that it had been a Mississippi sweep, to which Freddie Rayl reminded the winner was bred by a Tennesseean – T. Jack Robinson – and whelped in Georgia.

Towner, N. D., August 25, 1987
Judges Dr. Mike Furcolow and Dave LaChance
Leon Covington Open All-Age – 34 Pointers, 3 Setters
1st – Pritzi's Honor, 1245527, female, by High Country Mo – Fiddler's Peach. Charles Posey, owner; Robin Gates, handler.
2nd – Kahlua, 1261106, female, by Miller's Chief – Breakthru's Ginger. Barry Saunders and John Seawright, owners; Marshall Loftin, handler.
3rd – Chickasaw Doll,1259685, female, by Redemption – Addition's Lonnie. Mike Furney, owner; Brady Porter, handler.

Judges: John Ray Kimbrell, Dr. Mike Furcolow
Open Derby – 50 Pointers, 3 setters
1st – Redemption's Battle Kat, 1271607, female, by Redemption – Addition's Lonnie. Cecil Rester, owner; Doug Sellers, handler.

2nd – Hall's Main Addition, 12258470, male, The Linwood Ranger – Buckboard's Princess Di. Dr. Emmett Hall and George Smith, owners; Randy Downs, handler.

3rd – Lane's Plain Jane, 1259430, female, by Miller's Chief – Miss Ten. Bobby Lane, owner; Marshall Loftin, handler.

Judges: Keith Martin and Lynn Bennett
Amateur All-Age Classic – [One-hour heats] 12 Pointers
1st – Allegiance, 1266707, male, by Krug – Take A Bow. Don Hickman, owner and handler.

2nd – Jolly Rancher, 1201469, male, by Barshoe Buzzsaw – Michael's Express Lou. Kevin Lyons, owner; Dan Clarke, Jr., handler.

3rd – Scraps, 1240152, male, by Finale – Glendale's Amazing Grace. James Fornear, owner and handler.

Saskatchewan Open Championship – 74 entries
Winner – Double Rebel Jack, 1176374, male, by Jumper Jim – Swing Along. Dr. Mike Furcolow, owner; Tony Terrell, handler.

Runner-up – Cumberland River Mark, 1179202, male, by Cedric Birdwell – Faye's Candidate. Vernon Vance, owner; Randy Downs, handler.

Chapter 24

1988:
Gone South

THE WEAR OF going north had set in the season before, and the Mid-America Championship had been run over the Packsaddle Ranch of Western Oklahoma for four years. Most of those involved with operating the Saskatchewan were involved with running the Oklahoma trial.

Jeffrey had been a gracious host, but he realistically could be expected to want a trial on his land where he would be the moving force, and there were indications of that during the '87 trial.

So, the Saskatchewan moved to the southern prairie for a year.

The semantics were a bit awkward, the Saskatchewan in Oklahoma, Contacts with David Gates of Regina, were made and for a time it was thought the Saskatchewan would go back to Mortlach in exchange for the All-America, which would go to Oklahoma. But the agreement fell through when the Canadian board met.

Thus, on October 19, a two-championship program started over The Packsaddle Ranch of Larry and Sparky Dawson. Of it, the report said:

"Nobody should ever say the Packsaddle is easy. It isn't. It's a real test. One can expect tough wind conditions on any prairie field trial grounds, and this is certainly no exception. The shinnery, which Marshall Loftin describes as 'little oak bushes' covers much of the land—about shin high. It has no thorns, but, like all oak, it's hard. Quail, prairie chickens and pheasants (one pointed) stay sometimes in the 'open' and at other times in the motts (bluffs in the north) obviously their only two choices. There is no hay land or alfalfa or plowed ground to run across. There is no easy sledding.

"Those who like it, love it. And there are those who find it too different from what they're accustomed to in farm lands.

"The Dawsons presented an unique trophy buckle to the owner of the dog which accumulated the most points in the two championships. The ranch's five-spot brand was formed by turquoise dots. The Packsaddle has become an institution to trainers and bird dog people who come to this area of Oklahoma, hard on the Texas Panhandle border. Tony Terrell is senior among the handlers, and is still at his same camp on the hillside overlooking the Cedar Pens which Dawson turns over to the field trial to hold walking horses in lieu of steers and cow horses.

"They are gracious hosts, and chief among the 'without whoms' the event could not be held. Leon Harris of Tyler, Texas, drove the dog wagon, that with the special knowledge of the grounds only experience can bring, on the money every time at the end of a heat. Dr. Mike Furcolow provided the dog wagon, and it is his trailer at the camp that is the place where Gayle Bennett had lunch courtesy of the club. Her husband, Lynn, started training at Arnett this season after several years on the King Ranch with Terrell and traveling with him to trials. He is also the guy who does the things others don't care to, or can't.

"Mona D. Johnson opened the Longhorn Bar 'annex' for a cookout. The popular watering hole was burned the week before the trial and the event was in a large building on her farm north of Arnett. Buck Cadwell was chief chef. Mr. and Mrs. O. G. Edwards were at the trial, Gib a director, along with Arlin Nolen and Don Hickman. Joe Loewenhardt of Hawaii, was horseback a couple of days."

The winner and runner-up were brother and sister, from different litters. Barshoe Czar, but a Derby, the champion; Barshoe Vintage, the runner-up.

"Andy Daugherty strode over and asked the judges, 'Why?' Fred Dileo took a swipe at the ground with his boot."

Vintage had won the Mid-America over the same area a season before.

It was a first open title win for handler Lee West, and the first amateur to win the Saskatchewan. Czar had won the Region 8 Amateur All-Age Championship, another first for West and Czar, over the same course some two weeks before. I was co-owner of the winner, and bred both dogs.

Czar found four coveys of Quail in his hour, the third brace, and he handled the first three correctly. The judges decided the last was a stop-to-flush, a question that might have been answered otherwise by other judges. He got every benefit of the doubt. His race was at moderate range, though forward, hunting to the cover he knew so well.

Vintage, on the same course, pointed game twice, found on the first deep in a large mott. The judges thought she was lateral, perhaps her strength husbanded when out of sight to the side.

"The winner and runner-up have much in common," the report said. Czar was whelped January 27, 1987; Vintage, March 13, 1985, in the same red shed near Cass Hill in Oklahoma. Their sire is Understatement by My Main Man out of Gwinn's Redwater Pat by Ch. Red Water Rex, and their dam is Wine List by Ch. Palariel Stormy Clown out of Fashion Show by My Main Man. The combination has produced four champions with 12 championship placements.

"The Vintage litter included Ch. A Windfall, which was Oklahoma Derby of the Year, winner of the Region 8 Amateur All-Age title over the Packsaddle, and runner-up in the George and Continental Derbys and the Border International; Limelight, winner of two dog-of-the-year awards and 12 placements; winners LeCourier and Grand Cru. Vintage won the Mid-America last season and was runner-up in the Oklahoma Championship. During October she won the Kansas Classic and was runner-up in the Mid-America which followed the Saskatchewan.

"The young litter that included Czar, which became the third brother to win the Region 8 Amateur All-Age in as many seasons, also has Wine Steward, a dog-of-the-year winner; Barshoe Sayonara, which recently died after being placed eight times; Sweet Dreams, Five Star, Sovereign and Anna, all placed.

"They have Don Hickman and Arlin Nolen in common, for they have done the earliest walking of the Wine List pups since her first litter.

"And they have Lee West in common . . . The Barshoe prefix is attached to all which pass his kennel gate—and that first gate was on West's Barshoe Ranch near Ada, in central Oklahoma.

"He has always worked his own dogs, very early and late, from the first days when the late Harve Butler had Twiggie for a time. His personal views are readily available, and they expound the handier dog, and extoll what his memory of history says were the considerable negatives of the likes of Texas Fight.

"About the three obvious leaders:

"Czar's first find was on a covey to the right front at 10, and he stood with grand style and intensity on the birds scattered out before him. His manners were ideal. It was basically the same with the next two coveys, the dog with tail and head up, and the game accurately located. The second was at 30, and the third before the Davis water tank.

"He made some casts early that were ambitious, forward and this remained into the South SA pasture. Returning along the west rise from the Tip Davis water tank, he was not going on in prairie fashion, and not encouraged to do so.

"As the entire party was on the rise, the dog came down another just ahead, whirled into a covey with speed and stopped after they had flown. He was taken on with no negative word from the judges, and completed a better cast than the last period of time to a mott across the red road, and was coming back to the front at pickup.

"Vintage had the same course. she made early casts to the first pasture and was shown well ahead, pointing her first covey at 15, but from the water tank blowout she was not seen until after the gate, and she came under a fence near where scout was seen. She hunted to near the water tank, and was found, remarkably, by Daugherty deep in a big mott, hardly visible. Birds were flushed from it. Coming along the rise toward the north, she was out of view, handler riding much of the time further to the right. More land was needed from the red road gate and the course looped to the right as it did in such circumstances. She was not shown to the front, but when the loop was completed toward the dog wagon she was shown far in the front, as was her bracemate, Quillin's Ramona Rex, fading away.

"Chacoan Warrior was on the rough third course, though getting some of the second course ground. He was shown on casts to the distant front, and was found pointing at about 20 minutes, an extraordinary find in terms of prairie range. He was standing at a mott, and relocation was required to one nearby, the dog going to them on his own. He was to the far left of the course when found, but had logically gone there before it turned. The judges were unable to see him on one cast when the regular route was missed for a time, but at the end he was in the good going of the New Well pasture, and disappeared to the front. He was worked on the grounds as a young dog, and showed he had some understanding of the cover and sand.

"As one of the judge explained, they were required to 'consider a lot of negatives,' in evaluating the performances given them – the winner's game incident, and the shorter period in his race, the runner-up's range and absence from the front, and what they thought was an irregular pattern of Warrior.

"Dale Gummersall of Brighton, Colorado, a breeder and on good terms with the shinnery country, judged with Paul Haas of Stony Point, Texas, who chose to work dogs on the West grounds as the stake went along and to keep his dogs there, a situation which gave some pause, a trialer and officer of clubs in his state and eventual AFTCA Trustee.

"Quillen's Ramona Rex was gone from the breakaway virtually all of the allowable time, and had one find to which the judge rode back a considerable distance. His pattern was that of a fast, strong dog, just not in view much."

Bill West was working a female, called Women's Lib, for an Arizona owner, and sent her to the trial with Chuck Quillen, who, with the help of scout Lynn Bennett, promptly won the Derby with the strong race and one find that will usually accomplish that goal. Flatwood Bobo, in Robin Gates string, but brought west by Dileo in search of points for the Prairie Derby Award, was second. He had a find, high of head and tail and intent, and hunted a wealth of country. A Texas Rifle was third, based on his ground pattern, and no game.

Quillen bought Women's Lib, changed her name. But they never got on well, and she was shot and killed at a trial in Washington.

Quillen arrived in western Oklahoma with stories about how he had been mis-put at those trials he had just attended, and left much the same.

* * *

During the winter, the Canadian field trial club contacted me and an arrangement was made to have the 1989 Saskatchewan run at its old home near Moose Jaw, in exchange for the All-America Prairie Championship, which had a history of changes in location through a very long period of existence.

Arnett, Oklahoma, October 19, 1988
Judges: Dale Gummersall and Paul Haas
Saskatchewan Open Championship – 27 Entries
Winner – Barshoe Czar, 1280177, male, by Understatement – Wine List. Lee West and Whileaway Kennel, owners; Lee West, handler.
Runner-up – Barshoe Vintage, 1250945, female, by Understatement – Wine List. Faller Kennel, owners; Andy Daugherty, handler.

Open Derby – 15 Pointers
1st – Women's Lib, unreg female. Betty Kenley, owner; Chuck Quillen, handler.
2nd – Berrong's Flatwood Bobo, 289615, male, by Flatwood Hank – Berrong's Little Sis. Nick Berrong, owner; Fred Dileo, handler.
3rd – A Texas Rifle, 296545, male, by Understatement – Take A Bow. G. W. Reid, owner; Gary Pinalto, handler.

Chapter 25

Cov's Puppy Classic

AMONG COV'S INVENTIONS was the Oklahoma Puppy Classic. He had recently moved back to Oklahoma from Alabama and the Dixie Puppy Classic was quite an event thereabouts.

A similar stake for his place at Caddo seemed the thing to start. He trained on the Stuart Ranch at the edge of Caddo, extending several miles to the east on each side of an all-weather dirt road.

He and Lois lived in a neat, white frame house in view of Caddo, just off the blacktop road. Behind the house lay a sweeping piece of prairie. It rolled away down a hill into a neighbor's place at the west edge of the Stuart Ranch.

Cov arranged to go through the wire gate and across the pasture, sending his course to the creek, turning to the right, and making a loop back toward the starting point. The finish was up the hill, a hill that was to dash many hopes.

It took a full 30 minutes to make the route. It was ideal. A pup could run as much as he would want, but he had to make the turn across the creek — and he had to have enough engine to finish going up Cov's hill.

It was not the pine woods, like those used for the Dixie. At Cov's the "courses" were absolutely equal — just one. In other continuous-course puppy stakes it isn't possible for the courses to be equal. It is up to the marshal to say which of the identical pine trees is the turning point.

It is said that the determination of when to turn was governed by whose dog it was.

Not so at Cov's. It was all there for everyone to watch. Actually, there was a high point at the start from which most of the course could be seen.

It was a success from the start.

In the spring of 1969 he ran a small ad in the American Field and there was a full day's running. It was contested at the end of the regular field trial season — in late March or early April.

The first running attracted Bud Epperson and the two liver-marked pups he was working for Claremore physician Dr. M. E. Gordon. They were called Crossmatch and Mossbond. He also drew Delbert Clancy who had two daughters of Spaceglider, Monte Bello Peggy and Flying Dottie. W. C. Kirk came and brought a setter owned by H. P. Sheely, unregistered and called Dan. It was third.

When the shouting of the day was over, the winners were obvious to everyone: the Epperson pups. They were close, but judge Wayne Cornelius and his partner settled on Mack, or, Crossmatch. The years supported their action as he won the Continental and National Championships.

He was an exceptional performer, one which never got his due credit, unless one would consider standing in front of the Museum at Grand Junction his just due. Epperson developed him and Gordon ran him in amateur stakes, winning the Oklahoma Amateur's Derby two seasons. No dog was more of a pleasure for his owner. He was strong, full of desire — too strong, some faint hearts would argue — and always a bird-finder.

His dam was a black-marked bitch, heavily ticked, and an all-day gun dog. She had been bred to Dr. Stormy Mack, a head-strong dog from the Stormy Mike line.

Crossmatch won 27 placements during his career. Epperson was getting along, and not up to following the dog that was becoming bolder, if possible, with age. He and Gordon agreed to put him with Bud Daugherty. That was 1974. When the Daughertys went south, there was not a great deal of optimism about Mack.

He was worked with John Rex Gates on Blue Springs Plantation before the Continental. He had just come through a season when he was lost often, though the year before Epperson had an exceptionally good season, the dog coming around on his own, pointing a lot of game.

At Blue Springs he go it back together and won the Continental at Dixie Plantation. Just a few weeks later he won the National Championship at Grand Junction.

He had not been bred, save once, until his National win. And then he was not patronized heavily. It was a regrettable decision that he was to be run after the National, for Mack had lost a good deal in style and the wear and tear of the endurance stakes had left him with less in drive and heart.

Even so, his few offspring included winners of the American Field Quail Futurity, the United States Shooting Dog Futurity, the Quail Championship Invitational. He sired two champions, 37 winners with 220 placements.

1970

The second year brought another big entry. Cov was working an orange-headed pointer for A. E. Simmons. He was a handsome dog with an easy, fast gait. He was sired by Gwinn Williams' littermate to Wrapup, Gwinn's White Knight. The dog was to become an important contributor to the breed and Thunderbird Jack was to be his first prominent winner.

Cov won the stake with Jack and left second for K. L. Keesee with his Oklahoma Sister, from the same cross that got Ch. Oklahoma Flush. It was the mating of Paladin's Royal Flush and Baconrind's Sandy. Don Bodiford had the third-placed dog for owner Jackie Brosch, Speed Limit's Beau.

Thunderbird Jack was eventually bought by Jack Fiveash and earned 12 placements, most of them all age wins.

1971

Bud Keesee, K. L.'s son, had "turned pro," as they say. He had his eye on the puppy classic with justification. He had a string of young dogs which had won most of the amateur puppy stakes in the region.

Swingin Thru was a bright white, orange-headed female with no end of endurance. She was slight of build and could carry herself with the greatest of ease, and would, to distant places. I had purchased her as a pup from Hoyle Eaton, who had bred Ch. Riggins White Knight to Sugarbeet (Ch. War Storm ex Sugarplum) to get her.

When she crossed the creek and went away east, she was a diamond sparkling across a field of bright green grain a few inches high. She went out of sight, returning far ahead, just a speck, to finish.

Swingin Thru, or, Liz, won 12 placements. But it is her production that is more important. She was the dam of American Field Quail Futurity winner Paramount Squire (by Ch. Flush's Country Squire), all age champion Cementer, winner Harvest Moon and producer Exact from the same litter.

She had Special Event, by My Main Man, which won the Florida Puppy and Derby Classics for Hugh Branch, to be lost the next year en route to Canada.

Swingin Thru was bred to Double Rebel Dan and produced winner-producers Wolf Creek Knight and Swing Along, which became the dam of champions Thunderclap, Double Rebel Jack and Rebel Wrangler.

Second to Liz was another of the Keesee-bred pointers, a brother to Ch. The Texas Squire, Oklahoma Squire. He was owned by Lee West and me, and Bud Keesee handled him too, as he did the third placed Jacobs W. Knight, also an orange-headed pointer owned by Lefty Jacobs of Holdenville, Oklahoma.

Oklahoma Squire was to win the Alabama Shooting Dog Championship in the ownership of Hoyt Henley and Tobe Stallings of Montgomery.

1972

The dog which would eventually win a championship from the three winners was Call N Raise, named second. He was the second son of Ch. Flush's Country Squire to be second in the classic in as many years.

He was purchased from T. R. Miller of Sadorus, Ill., by the West-Criswell partnership, out of Miller's Red Water Rex female, Red Water Sugar. Sugar, like Swingin Thru, was out of a daughter of the War Storm-Sugarplum cross, Sweet Sugar. Miller was a respected breeder and developer of young dogs, Ch. War Storm, as an example.

Call 'N Raise later won the Saskatchewan Championship for owner Brad Calkins and handler Bud Daugherty, the handler's first prairie title.

First was Pine Ridge Tammy, and it was one of the placements that regulars at the trial didn't completely understand. The grounds usually made winners quite clear to the judges, but this one raised some questions as to whether Tammy actually reached more, and in as logical a hunting pattern as did Call 'N Raise.

1973

My Main Man was quite a "talk dog." He had run loose on West's Barshoe Ranch for some time and earned a reputation for range, stamina—and an uncanny ability to stay in front.

He had not been entered in any of the usual amateur puppy stakes. He had been worked on foot, showing his unusually strong front-handling ability. Tommy Long came west to work for me, and we went to Caddo early—the day before the Classic. We were going to see how Man looked and decide whether to run him.

West drove up as he was about to be turned loose, and the race was perfect. Tommy volunteered to come up with the entry fee if there was any doubt. He repeated next day with the same sort of performance, was first in one of his five placements of six starts. I was the only one to ever run him in a trial, though Tommy broke him the next summer.

West helped Henry Oldham handle Sharp Tail to win second with a strong race, consistently ahead and making the turn, not as wide and just not as strong at the end as Man.

The third-placed entry was also a West-Criswell. He was a son of Ch. Riggins White Knight that had got all the spots in the otherwise white litter out of Whileaway Royal Ann, a sister to Ch. Oklahoma Flush. West handled Knight Edition, and he was later sold to Dr. Knight of Houston, Eaton won the All-American Derby championship at Carbondale, showing him on game five times.

1974

Based on their performances through the regular season, I thought two females which Bud Keesee had worked would likely win. They were Harvest Moon, by Ch. Flush's Country Squire out of Swingin Thru, and Call Me Madam, by Ch. Riggins White Knight out of a sister to Country Squire.

Jake Waller, a big, rangy pup which Cov had for Bob Stewart—not the ranch owner—had not been taken into account. He was the clear winner.

Keesee got mad and quit the morning of the stake and Terry Terrell was there with his brother, Tony. Terry became the scout, quickly when I offered half the winnings, and speculated that we should win first and second. I helped Cov with Jake, and Terry was not a happy man when I brought him back on the turn after he had gone under the fence and it was obvious our two good performances had been beaten. Our two females, which were second and third.

Harvest Moon and Jake Waller went on to win all age stakes.

1975

The classic had a comeback. There were 32 entries and great interest. The hill top was crowded with horses and trailers.

Ashley Edwards was living on West's Barshoe Ranch and had a number of pups running loose. One was a small, orange-headed female by My Main Man out of Chorus Line, a daughter of Ch. Red Water Rex and Ranger's Atakapa Lady, the dam of Ch. Ormond Smart Alec. She made up in grit for what she lacked in size.

The Edwards dogs were named with the prefix "Special", this one registered as Special Duty. When the very long day was over, she was named winner.

Bill Hunt handled Duncan Express Dot for H. G. Barber, and she, too, had shown range and stamina, to be second. Third was Tulsa Light, owned by Bud Daugherty and handled by John (Buzzy) Daugherty, and Light ran a very great deal.

One of the strongest challenges of the day came from a pointer, the pride then of Edwin Brown, who handled him with his son, Wayne, scouting.

Special Duty was sent to John Rex Gates and was sold to Keith Gardner of Michigan, who bought her just after she won the Georgia Derby Championship. She won the North American Sportsman's Derby and its big purse, and was second in the open all age that followed. At Albany, in the Masters Championship, she had 5 finds and "jumped at a bird and stopped," to be thrown out. "Chigger" was owned through most of her career by R. A. Weber. For him, she won the Quail Championship Invitational and the Suwanee Open All-Age the year before it became the Florida Open Championship. Twice she was runner-up in the Oklahoma Championship. In all she had 17 placements.

1976

It was to be the last classic over the Covington Course at Caddo. With the loss of the grounds went the measuring stick,

273

and subsequent renewals at Wagoner and Ardmore failed to provide the consistent quality in the winners that had come from the first eight years.

In the final Caddo classic, Bill Risinger, with Tommy Long helping him, handled the first and second placed dogs – C'm On and Special Agent. Both were sons of My Main Man, which I owned. Bud Frechin won third with G. H. Shaw's The Country Count, a son of Ch. Flush's Country Squire.

Cov moved from Caddo before the '77 running, and it was held near Wagoner. He found some land near Fort Gibson Lake, not open enough and the date was late, the weather hot.

There were a couple of years off, '78 and '79, and the stake moved to Ardmore in '80.

There it was first run over continuous courses – the regular Lake Murray layout. They are uneven and don't offer a fair advantage to pups which are to be judged on race and seeming hunting desire. But there seemed to be no land at Lake Murray to make a one-course layout that would be as desirable as Cov's at Caddo. In 1988 one was figured out, going toward the bear-trap woods, skirting them back along the west edge.

But there has been no equal to Cov's course. It was totally fair, and demanding. The record of the dogs which were placed there was testimony that one puppy stake could, indeed, be a measuring stick.

Appendix I

Cov's Championships

Leon Covington campaigned on the major circuit during a time when championships were few. This listing includes titles only, no runners-up, or placements in all-age stakes so popular then.

1948	Texas Open	Lone Survivor
	Dr. E. R. Calame, owner	
1950	All-America Open Chicken	Marvelous Jack
	C. L. Little	
1952	Border International	Betty Heelfly
	W. V. Garnier	
1953	Texas Open	Lone Survivor
1954	Border International	Lone Survivor
	National Free-For-All	Lone Survivor
1955	National Championship	Lone Survivor
1956	Southern Open	Wholesaler
	Dick Dumas and Ned Wilfong, owners	
1960	All-America Open Chicken	Notus
	B. M. Hogan, owner	

Appendix II

Saskatchewan Statistics

SASKATCHEWAN CHAMPIONSHIP
THE JUDGES

Year	Name	Judges
1934	Fort's Dixie Proctor	Frank Walsh, W. A. Wilson, C. T. Chaney
1935	Doctor Blue Willing	Frank Walsh, W. A. Wilson, J. M. Miller
1936	Air Pilot's Sam	T. Benton King, J. M. Miller
1937	Highland Bipkins	Henry P. Davis, J. M. Miller
1938	Uncas Flying Devil	Nash Buckingham, W. T. Windsor
1939	Spunky Creek Coin	Harry Decker, Paul Hatch
1940	Young's Billie	T. Benton King, T. Dean Coridan
1941	Young's Billie	T. Dean Coridan, James C. Griffin
1967	Flaming Star	Delmar Smith, J. H. Criswell
1968	Red Water Rex	Wm. J. Jarrett, W. K. Young
1969	Homerun Jim	Wayne Cornelius, Marshall Loftin
1970	Fugitive	Lee R. West, Dempsey Williams
1971	The Texas Squire	Casey Black, Clifton R. Scarborough
1972	Oklahoma Flush	Wayne Cornelius, Henry Havens
1973	Call 'N Raise	Raymond R. Rucker, John Criswell
1974	Mission	Raymond R. Rucker, E. B. Epperson
1975	The Nimrod	U. L. Hudson, Marvin Reid
1976	Strongman	U. L. Hudson, Ed Butler
1977	Flush's Wrangler	L. D. Hayes, W. C. Kirk
1978	Barshoe Ingenue	E. B. Epperson, Don Powell
1979	Texas Silver Spur	Bill Burris, Jim Cohen

1980	Buckboard	Marc Appleton, Bill Burris
1981	High Fidelity	Ed Butler, W. C. Kirk
1982	Michael's Express Babe	John Criswell, Bill Burris
1983	Thunderclap	J. R. Kimbrell, Charles Young
1984	Flatwood Bill	Rush Campbell, J. R. Kimbrell
1985	K's High Rise	Frank Thompson, Darrell Privett
1986	Ronco Lucky Siete	John Ray Kimbrell, John Little
1987	Double Rebel Jack	John Ray Kimbrell, Arlin Nolen
1988	Barshoe Czar	Paul Haass, Dale Gumemrsall
1989	Classic Editions	Wayne Lineback, David Gates
1990	American Way	Wayne Lineback, Doug Vaughn
1991	Rebel Wrangler	Butch Friis, David Taylor
1992	Quicksilver Pink	David Gates, John Thompson
1993	Bear Creek Bess	Bob Blyth, Freddie Epp

SASKATCHEWAN CHAMPIONSHIP
THE CHAMPIONS

Year	Name	Breed	Sex	Color
1934	Fort's Dixie Proctor	P	M	
1935	Doctor Blue Willing	P	M	LV
1936	Air Pilot's Same	P	M	LV
1937	Highland Bipkins	P	M	
1938	Uncas Flying Devil	P	M	
1939	Spunky Creek Coin	P	M	LV
1940	Young's Billie	P	M	
1941	Young's Billie	P	M	
1967	Flaming Star	S	M	O
1968	Red Water Rex	P	M	LV
1969	Homerun Jim	P	M	LV
1970	Fugitive	P	M	LV
1971	The Texas Squire	P	M	O
1972	Oklahoma Flush	P	M	O
1973	Call 'N Raise	P	M	O
1974	Mission	P	M	LV
1975	The Nimrod	P	M	O
1976	Strongman	P	M	BL
1977	Flush's Wrangler	P	M	O
1978	Barshoe Ingenue	P	F	O
1979	Texas Silver Spur	P	M	O
1980	Buckboard	P	M	LV
1981	High Fidelity	P	M	O
1982	Michael's Express Babe	P	F	O
1983	Thunderclap	P	M	LV
1984	Flatwood Bill	P	M	LE
1985	K's High Rise	P	F	O
1986	Ronco Lucky Siete	P	F	O
1987	Double Rebel Jack	P	M	O
1988	Barshoe Czar	P	M	LV
1989	Classic Editions	P	M	LV
1990	American Way	P	F	LV
1991	Rebel Wrangler	P	M	O
1992	Quicksilver Pink	P	F	O
1993	Bear Creek Bess	P	F	LV

SASKATCHEWAN CHAMPIONSHIP
SIRES, DAMS, BREEDERS OF CHAMPIONS

Sire	Name	Dam	Breeder
A Rambling Rebel	Fort's Dixie Proctor		Fort, J. H.
Admiral Rex	Buckboard	Barshoe Cuz	Criswell & West
Air Pilot	High Fidelity	Paladin's Royal Cheryl	Huffman, J.D.
Buckboard	Air Pilot's Sam	Nancy F	Farrior, Ed
Doctor Norman	Thunderclap	Swing Along	Suitts, David
Evolution	Doctor Blue Willing	Miss Willing	Scarborough, J. E.
Flush's Country Squire	Flatwood Bill	Garner's White Candy	Garner, W. T.
	Call 'N Raise	Red Water Sugar	Keesee, K. L.
	The Texas Squire	Flush's Royal Sally	Miller, T. R.
Go Boy's Shadow	Bear Creek Bess	Henrick's First Lady	House, Joe Don
Guard Rail	Classic Editions	Autumn Chase	Hanley, R. J.
Haw Branch Sport	Uncas Flying Devil	Beauty Uncas	Shenk, W. R.
High Fidelity	K's High Rise	Reed's Lil Annie	Hodum, Charles
Homerun Johnny	Homerun Jim	Homerun Sis	Phelps, Claudia L.
Jim Peters	Young's Billie	Frost's White Boos	Carroll, Ira
		Frost's White Boots	Carroll,
Jumper Jim	Double Rebel Jack	Swing Along	Harwood, Stephen
	Rebel Wrangler	Swing Along	Suitts, David
Lem Ripcord	Strongman	Sam's Stylish Ginger	Berryhill, R. O.
Miller's Chief	American Way	Patsy Rebel	Ray, James
Mr. Perfection	Barshoe Ingenue	Gunsmoke's Elhew Dancer	Harwood, Stephen

279

New Money	Highland Bipkins	Spicer's Bipkins Girl	Spicer, R. W.
Oklahoma Flush	Flush's Wrangler	Susan of Arkansas	Harper, F. W.
Paladin's Royal Flush	Oklahoma Flush	Baconrind's Sandy	Keesee, K. L.
Ronco Traveler	Ronco Lucky Siete	Blackbelt's Jenny	Casciaro, Jim
The Texas Squire	Texas Silver Spur	Pinewood Gussie	Elliott, J. R.
Tiny Wahoo	Red Water Rex	Sea Island Gale	Alexander, E. B.
Turnto's Hightone Pete	Flaming Star	Miss Boo's Loch	Williamson, R. J.
Understatement	Barshoe Czar	Wine List	Criswell, John
Vendetta's Jake	Mission	Jeannie Mae Go	Godwin, J. W.
Village Boy	Spunky Creek Coin	Spunky Creek Amazon	Billingslea, Nina
Volcanic's Nimrod	The Nimrod	Oklahoma Nimrod	Greenwood, A. J.
Warhoop Express Pete	Michael's Express Babe	Gwinn's Little Jan	Duncan, R. L.
Wayriel Allegheny Sport	Fugitive	The Druggist's Pat	Cox, Pat
Whippoorwill Rebel	Quicksilver Pink	Whippoorwill's High Ann	Cline, Tate

SASKATCHEWAN CHAMPIONSHIP HANDLERS OF CHAMPIONS

Handler	Name	Year	Owner	Entry
Arant, Buddy	Mission	1974	Bennett, J. M.	57
Arant, Fred	Homerun Jim	1969	Burgess & Fagan	85
Daugherty, Andy	Bear Creek Bess	1993	Calkins, B. H.	36
	Michael's Express Babe	1982	Faller, Michael	37
Daugherty, Bud	Barshoe Ingenue	1978	Calkins, B. H.	41
	Buckboard	1980	Hawthorne, D. E.	65
	Call 'N Raise	1973	Calkins, B. H.	54
Davis, Colvin	Quicksilver Pink	1992	Stallings, Tobe	59
Davis, Tommy	High Fidelity	1981	Huffman, J. D.	34
Eaton, D. Hoyle	Red Water Rex	1968	Alexander & Pruitt	82
English, W. D.	Highland Bipkins	1937	Crumpler, L. O.	32
	Uncas Flying Devil	1938	Eyster, H. E.	33
Farrior, Ed	Air Pilot's Sam	1936	Johnson, L. D.	27
	Doctor Blue Willing	1935	Johnson, L. D.	14
Gates, John Rex	Flush's Wrangler	1977	Deal, D. R.	59
	Oklahoma Flush	1972	Vredenburgh, S. H.	61
	Texas Silver Spur	1979	Nishimura, Haruo	64
	The Texas Squire	1971	Brown, Edwin	76
Gates, Robin	K's High Rise	1985	Honea, Jimmy	68
	Ronco Lucky Siete	1986	Walker, Stephen	65
Hicks, Pete	Flatwood Bill	1984	Cox, Frank	68

Owner	Horse	Year	Breeder	No.
Humphreys, V. E.	Spunky Creek Coin	1939	Shaffer, E. J.	24
	Young's Billie	1940	Yoakum, H. J.	15
		1941	Yoakum, H. J.	
Hunt, Bill	American Way	1990	Walker, Stephen	70
	Classic Editions	1989	Walker, Stephen	72
	Rebel Wrangler	1991	Walker, Stephen	62
Poynor, G. W.	Fugitive	1970	Denton, W. S.	67
	The Nimrod	1975	Pinalto, Gary	71
Pritchette, Pete	Fort's Dixie Proctor	1934	Shartel, Kent	12
Rayl, Freddie	Stongman	1976	Moses, D. C.	71
Smith, Herman	Flaming Star	1967	Jordan, G. G.	76
Terrell, Tony	Double Rebel Jack	1987	Furcolow, Mike	74
	Thunderclap	1983	Suitts, David	37
West, Lee	Barshoe Czar	1988	Criswell & West	27

SASKATCHEWAN CHAMPIONSHIP
THE RUNNERS-UP

Year	Name	Breed	Sex	Color
1936	Tenbroek's Bonnet			
1937	Bess Blue Willing			
1938	Amazon's Village Girl	P	F	LV
1939	Amazon's Village Girl	P	F	LV
1941	Spunky Creek Coin	P	M	LV
1967	Homerun Johnny	P	M	LV
1968	Hangman	P	M	
1969	Texas Allegheny Pete	P	M	BL
1970	Red Water Rex	P	M	LV
1971	Sweet Bippie	P	F	
1972	Tradition II	P	M	O
1973	Oklahoma Flush	P	M	O
1974	The Texas Heir	P	M	LV
1975	The Texas Heir	P	M	LV
1976	Forty Grand	P	M	O
1977	County Seat	P	M	O
1978	Man's Knighted Squire	P	M	O
1979	Blackbelt	P	M	BL
1980	Mardi Gras	P	M	LV
1981	Snake Creek Warrior	P	M	
1982	Sweet Fever	P	F	LV
1983	Addition's Go Boy	P	M	LV
1984	Copper Rush	P	M	O
1985	Thunderclap	P	M	LV
1986	Concerto Ace High	P	M	O
1987	Cumberland River Mark	P	M	LV
1988	Barshoe Vintage	P	F	LV
1989	Quicksilver Pink	P	F	O
1990	Mac's Reelfoot Chief	P	M	LV
1991	Go Boy's Shadow	P	M	LV
1992	Barshoe Barbarian	P	M	LV
1993	Mega Dancer	P	F	LV

SASKATCHEWAN CHAMPIONSHIP
SIRES, DAMS, BREEDERS OF RUNNERS-UP

Sire	Name	Dam	Breeder
Addition's Go Boy	Bess Blue Willing	Fiddler's Gal	Hankins, Floyd
	Tenbroek's Bonnet		
	Go Boy's Shadow		
Barshoe Brute	Barshoe Barbarian	Barshoe Fly	West, Lee
Buckboard	Thunderclap	Swing Along	Suitts, David
Builder's Addition	Addition's Go Boy	Nell's Rambling On	Rayl, W. F.
Cedric Birdwell	Cumberland River Mark	Faye's Candidate	Helm & Antle
Elhew Copper Strike	Copper Rush	Sunday Sunshine	Campbell, Rush
Flush's Country Squire	Blackbelt	Quailwoods Sally	Lang, Billy
Miller's Chief	Mac's Reelfoot Chief	Miller's Lady Bird	Miller, Ferrel
Montana Rod	Mardi Gras	Rebel Fantastic	Capps, Ross
My Main Man	Man's Knighted Squire	Sunday Clothes	Criswell, John
Paladin Heir	Forty Grand	Rex's Tiny Red	Lamb, Bob
Paladin's Royal Flush	Oklahoma Flush	Baconrind's Sandy	Keesee, K. L.
Rail Dancer	Mega Dancer	White Plains Tiny	Maxwell, W. G.
Rambling Rebel Dan	Homerun Johnny	Homerun Bet	Phelps, Claudia L.
Red Warrior	Snake Creek Warrior	Second Creek Lou	Traweck, L. B.
Royal Heir's John	The Texas Heir	Palariel Wahoo Kate	Royal, C. H.
		Palariel Wahoo Kate	Royal, C.
Sailin Sam	Concerto Ace High	Gem Strike	Kelley, E. L. Jr.
Texas Allegheny Sport	Texas Allegheny Pete	Home Again Lou	Chandler Kennel

Texas Fight	County Seat	The Matador's Patador	Hunt, Bill
The Hipster	Sweet Bippie	Paladin's Royal Missy	Huffman, J. D.
The Texas Heir	Sweet Fever	Frierson's Little Dixie	Spears, C. C.
Tiny Wahoo	Red Water Rex	Sea Island Gale	Alexander, E. B.
Tradition	Tradition II	Lemon Drop Survivor	Rokish, Nick
Understatement	Barshoe Vintage	Wine List	Criswell, John
Village Boy	Amazon's Village Girl	Spunky Creek Amazon	Billingslea, Nina
		Spunky Creek Amazon	Billingsle
	Spunky Creek Coin	Spunky Creek Amazon	Billingsle
Wahoo's Arkansas Ranger	Hangman	Sharp Steppin	Schmeltz, D. C.
Whippoorwill's Rebel	Quicksilver Pink	Whippoorwill's High Ann	Cline, Tate

SASKATCHEWAN CHAMPIONSHIP
HANDLERS OF RUNNERS-UP

Handler	Name	Year	Owner	Entry
Anderson, Clyde	Tenbroek's Bonnet	1936	Phelps, Claudia L.	27
Arant, Fred	Homerun Johnny	1967	Park Farm Kennel	76
Crawford, Jett	Bess Blue Willing	1937		32
Daugherty, Andy	Barshoe Barbarian	1992	Faller, Tom	59
	Barshoe Vintage	1988	Faller Kennel	27
Daugherty, Bud	Man's Knighted Squire	1978	Schooley, T. M.	41
Davis, Colvin	Quicksilver Pink	1989	Stallings, J. F.	72
Downs, Randy	Cumberland River Mark	1987	Vance, Vernon	74
Eaton, D. Hoyle	Red Water Rex	1970	Alexander & Pruitt	67
Epp, Freddie	Blackbelt	1979	Dr. W. O. Pardue	64
Gates, John Rex	Forty Grand	1976	Curtis, Arthur S.	71
	Oklahoma Flush	1973	Vredenburg, S. H.	54
	Texas Allegheny Pete	1969	Morrow, Don	85
Humphreys, V. E.	Spunky Creek Coin	1941	Shafer, E. J.	
Hunt, Bill	County Seat	1977	Sallee, Frank	59
Kirk, Howard	Amazon's Village Girl	1938	Mcgonigal, H. E.	33
		1939	Mcgonigal, H. E.	24
Loftin, Marshal	Mardi Gras	1980	Diefendorf, D. C.	47
	Sweet Fever	1982	Heard, Vernon & Roberts	37
	Tradition II	1972	Woodside, T. M. Sr.	61
Poynor, G. W.	Sweet Bippie	1971	Huffman, J. D.	76

Author	Title		Year	
Priddy, Garland	Addition's Go Boy	Frierson, Pete	1983	37
	Go Boy's Shadow	Frierson, Pete	1991	62
	Mac's Reelfoot Chief	Frierson, Pete	1990	70
	Snake Creek Warrior	Frierson, Pete	1981	34
	The Texas Heir	Frierson, Pete	1974	57
		Frierson, Pete	1975	71
Rayl, W. F.	Hangman	Silvers, Virginia M.	1968	82
Sellers, Doug	Concerto Ace High	McCarthy, Bruce	1986	65
Smith, Collier	Mega Dancer	Craig, Kuykendall, Sayre	1993	36
Terrell, Tony	Copper Rush	Harwood, Stephen	1984	68
	Thunderclap	Suitts, David	1985	68

Appendix III

The Oklahoma Open Puppy Classic

1969
1st—Crossmatch*, Dr. M. E. Gordon, owner Bud Epperson, handler.

2nd—Mossbond, Dr. M. E. Gordon, owner; Bud Epperson, handler.

3rd—Dan (unreg), H. P. Sheely, owner; W. C. Kirk, handler.

1970
1st—Thunderbird Jack, A. E. Simmons, owner; Leon Covington, handler.

2nd—Oklahoma Sister, K. L. Keessee, owner and handler.

3rd—Speed Limit's Beau, Jackie Brosch, owner; Don Bodiford, handler.

1971
1st—Swingin Thru*, John Criswell, owner; Bud Keesee, handler.

2nd—Oklahoma Squire*, Lee West and John Criswell, owners; Bud Keesee, handler.

3rd—Jacobs W Knight, Lefty Jacobs, owner; Bud Keesee, handler.

1972
1st—Pine Ridge Tammy, S. W. Palmer, owner; Jack Bruner, handler.

2nd—Call 'n Raise*, Lee West and John Criswell, owners; Lee West, handler.

3rd—Crockett's Elite, R. R. Webster, owner; Harve Butler, handler.

1973
1st — My Main Man*, Whileaway Kennel, owner; John Criswell, handler.

2nd — Sharptail, Henry Oldham, owner and handler.

3rd — Knight Edition*, Lee West and John Criswell, owners; Lee West, handler.

1974
1st — Jake Waller, Bob Stewart, owner; Leon Covington, handler.

2nd — Harvest Moon, Whileaway Kennel, owner; John Criswell, handler.

3rd — Call Me Madam, Whileaway Kennel, owner; John Criswell, handler.

1975
1st — Special Duty*, Ashley Edwards and John Criswell, owners; Ashley Edwards, handler.

2nd — Duncan Express Dot, H. G. Harber, owner; Bill Hunt, handler.

3rd — Tulsa Light, Bud Daugherty, owner, John Daugherty, handler.

1976
1st — C'm On, Whileaway Kennel, owner; Bill Risinger, handler.

2nd — Special Agent, Whileaway Kennel, owner; Bill Risinger, handler.

3rd — The Country Count, G. H. Shaw, owner; Bud Frechin, handler.

1977 (Wagoner)
1st — Barshoe Overtime, Robert L. Duncan, owner and handler.

2nd — Pure Prairie, David Suits, owner; Walter Harper, handler.

3rd — Pat Fling, R. C. Surdam, owner; Thom Brower, handler.

1978-79 Not Held

1980 (Ardmore)
1st – Eloquent, Whileaway Kennel, owner; John Criswell, handler.

2nd – In Man's Image, Dr. R. L. Sifferman, owner; John Criswell, handler.

3rd – Patty Peppermint, Del Hollingsworth, owner; Bobby Robbins, handler.

1981
1st – Mountain Man, C. W. Moore, owner and handler.

2nd – Goin Places, Dr. R. L. Sifferman and Tommy Long, owners; Tommy Long, handler.

3rd – Man, unreg, Jerry Foster, owner; John Criswell, handler.

1982
1st – Fiddle Tune, Whileaway Kennel, owner; Arlin Nolen, handler.

2nd – Special Wish, Ashley Edwards and Whileaway Kennel, owners; John Criswell, handler.

3rd – Plumcover Brownie, Edwin Brown, owner; Tony Terrell, handler.

1983
1st – Bite the Bullet, Faye Throneberry, owner and handler.

2nd – Krug*, Don Hickman, owner; Arln Nolen, handler.

3rd – River Street, Arlin Nolen, owner and handler.

1984
1st – A Rebel Cause*, Stephen Harwood, owner; Peter Thuman, handler.

2nd – Silver Debutante, Barry Saunders, owner; Faye Throneberry, handler.

3rd – Phi Slamma Jamma, George W. Evans, owner and handler.

1985
1st – Elkco Go Boy*, Red Crupper,owner; Bill Trabue,handler.

2nd – Bullet Buckle, Wayne Avent, owner; Faye Throneberry, handler.

3rd – Fade Out, Dave Myers, owner; Andy Daugherty, handler.

1986
Judges: Jerry Fugitt, Leon Wilcox

1st – Jumpin Alive, Bill Crawford, owner; Gary Pinalto, handler.

2nd – Doublecross Belle, Bill Trabue, owner and handler.

3rd – Lawson, John Criswell, owner and handler.

1987
Judges: Ed Butler, Bill Bannister

1st – Morning Line, Gary Landrum and Harold J. Smith, owners; Gary Pinalto, handler.

2nd – Allegiance, Don Hickman, owner and handler.

3rd – Plumcover Sunrise, Edwin Brown, owner; Tony Terrell, handler.

1988
Judges: Lynn Bennett, Bill Bannister

1st – Last Word, Arlin Nolen, owner and handler.

2nd – Barshoe Czar*, Lee West and John Criswell, owners; Lee West, handler.

3rd – Matlock, Forest Roberts, owner; Gary Pinalto, handler.

1989
Judges: Lynn Bennett, Arlin Nolen

1st – Tailormade, Margaret Dunbar, owner; Gary Pinalto, handler.

2nd – Past Master, Randy Anderson, owner and handler.

3rd – Barshoe Barracuda, Lee R. West, owner and handler.

1990
Judges: Lynn Bennett, Ed Skinner

1st – Brute's Debutante, Dr. M. E. Gordon and Randy Anderson, owners; Randy Anderson, handler.

2nd – Million Dollar Babe, Max Kammerlocher, owner and handler.

3rd – Van Ripple, Don Hickman, owner; Arlin Nolen, handler.

1991
Judges: Lynn Bennett, John Criswell

1st – Annihilator, Bill Compton, owner; Butch Gerke, handler.

2nd – Whippoorwill's Jerry, Gilmore Flautt III, owner; Butch Winter, handler.

3rd—Leavin Town Hank, Red Baugh, owner; Marion Gordon, handler

1992
Judges: Lynn Bennett, Arlin Nolen (12)
1st—Jack's Dolly Scout. Jack Grammar, owner; Butch Winter, handler.
2nd—Fair Hooker. Creek Scott, owner; Lou Gleber, handler.
3rd—Eucha Jill. Gene Dooley and Rodney Aldridge, owners; Aldridge, handler.

1993
Judges: Lynn Bennett, John Criswell (21)
1st—Dixie. Mike Faherty, owner; Dale Bush, handler.
2nd—Whistlin. Arlin Nolen, owner and handler.
3rd—Babe. Scoot Terrell, agent and handler.

* Champion or champion producer

Lone Survivor

1948 2nd   Border International OAA
     1st   Central Texas OAA, 1 hr
     Wnr   Texas Open Ch, 1 1/2 hr
1950 1st   Muscle Shoals OAA, 1 hr
     2nd   Sportsman's Club of SW Missouri OAA, 1 hr
     2nd   Sunflower OAA, 1 hr
     1st   Fort Worth OAA, 1 hr
1951 1st   Pelican State OAA, 1 hr
     R-up Southwest Ch, 1 hr qualif, 2 hr finals
     1st   Fort Worth OAA, 1 hr
     2nd   Texas Open Ch, 1 1/2 hr
1952 2nd   Pelican State OAA, 1 hr
     1st   Oklahoma Amateur Assn OAA, 1 hr
     2nd   Border International OAA
1953 3rd   U.S. OAA, 1 hr
     R-up Border International Ck Ch, 1 hr
     3rd   Arkansas Assn OAA, 1 hr
     3rd   Fort Worth OAA, 1 hr
     Wnr   Texas Open Ch, 1 1/2 hr
1954 Wnr   National Free-For-All Ch, 1 hr qualif, 3 hr
          finals
     2nd   Oklahoma Amateur Assn OAA, 1 hr
     Wnr   Border International Ck Ch, 1 hr
     3rd   Fort Worth OAA, 1 hr
1955 National Field Trial Ch Assn., 3 hr

Ch. Lone Survivor
422955

Whelped: March 23, 1946
Breeder-owner: Dr. E. R. Calame of Jonesboro, Arkansas

Doctor Norman
Ch. Doctor Blue Willing
Miss Willing

Ch. Luminary

The Hottentot
Lullaby
Milligan's Jane

Ch. Lone Survivor

Ch. Spunky Creek Boy
Ch. Titan
Ch. Spunky Creek Joann

Titanette

Village Commissioner
Brenda Breeze
Marfak

Sports Afield October, 1950

How Bird Dog Champions Are Made
*Once a year, on the Canadian prairies,
the finest American dog trainers, and the most
promising canines, come together, to lay the groundwork
for
future field trial miracles –*
by Henry P. Davis and Evelyn M. Shafer

Each summer some 150 American professional dog trainers assemble on the Canadian prairies to work their canine pupils on the ample game bird supplies of southern Saskatchewan and Manitoba. Out of this inspired schooling will come the future bird dog champions.

I watched the tutoring of these dogs at Leon Covington's training camp, while Evelyn Shafer took her pictures. The training goes on from dawn to dusk – a fascinating example of both human and canine minds working together. Patience is the power that works the miracles, especially when the handler's long, piercing whistle falls on stubborn canine ears. Covington says, "A dog trainer's got to know what to do and how to do it – but also when to stop doing it." And when one of the older dogs suddenly goes sour on obeying commands, Covington's remedy is simple: he promptly returns the dog to yard training again – the elementary puppy lessons of walking at heel, coming when called, standing motionless at command and changing direction at whistle. When a pupil does well, he receives a petting and tidbit. When a too-eager pupil flushes a covey of some 15 prairie chickens and then high-tails it after them, Covington's method is both solemn, and, to the spectator, comical.

"Look here, dog," he drawls to the offender. "You aren't going to win any field trials by knocking game birds all over the landscape. You've got plenty of heels, mister, a good nose and some brains. But you've got to learn how to use 'em."

Many of the trainers here are shooting-dog men exclusively. Covington, however, is among the number who specialize in field trial dogs and depend upon cash prizes won in the money events of the major field trial circuit for extra dividends on their season's labors. The bird dog trainer has to solve many, and often perplexing problems. And to do it, he must have access to plenty of native game. Within the invisible boundaries of the some 8,200 square miles of gently rolling prairie land in southern Saskatchewan and Manitoba, is found the greatest concentration of upland game birds on the North American continent. All of the materials are here. Southern Saskatchewan and Manitoba have the two prairie grouse, the sharptail and the pinnated – and they call both the prairie chicken.

To see how bird dog champions are made, now study the picture on the following pages.

* * *

Six pages of photographs featured Cov and his Canadian training.

* * *

The January, 1951, Sports Afield had another feature by Davis and Shafer. It was six pages of photographs of yard work on a pointer called Judy, including check cording in a prairie bluff with grouse flying away.

In Memoriam

A lengthy obituary recounting some of the stories retold in this book appeared in the June 11, 1983, FIELD. Excerpts:

He started in life on St. Patrick's Day near the Red River at Denison, and his first ambition was to be a baseball star. He made it part of the way, catching for the McAllen Club of the old Texas League, there was a dispute over a friend, and the loan of the black-headed young man to another club, and he walked off.

... He worked his first dogs on the McAlester watershed area where trials are still held near the growing city, and he left on the train from the McAlester depot with Little June to compete in his first National Championship. He and Bud Epperson teamed up for the trip.

"We had to road the dogs out from the little old town to the Ames plantation. Put a rope on their collar. Nobody heard of a roading harness yet.

"Style? not so much then. Mr. Ames said what the style was, and he liked 'em level tailed, or just a little above. He didn't want a dog with his tail in the air like they do now."

" ... There's no place like that (Canada) for a young dog. I've tried 'em all. Bud Epperson and I took puppies to western Oklahoma years ago — but it was before time to go to Canada. Worked pretty good for that. But there's no equal to what you can get done in Canada.

Friday, May 27, he went to Mikles' kennel with a friend, and kidded him a lot about needing a .12-guage to shoot birds. "I can outshoot you with a .410." That was all he ever shot — or needed.

He seldom missed with a .410, or a golf club ... Later in the aftrnoon he drove out past the hospital, and on the roa down Henscratch Mountain. His station wagon weaved, and went into a ditch.

The man driving behind him watched. When Noble Rogers opened the door, he found Cov dead, victim of a heart that had pumped a full life for 76 years, and finally failed.

Rogers worked for Cov as a teenager when dogs were plentiful.

Lois arranged the graveside service with eulogy, and picked the plaid shirt and khaki pants for him to rest in ...

* * *

Also in the 11th edition, there was this note:

"Cov and I were planning to go to Canada in a few weeks, just like we have for years. He had been sick with some problems with his heart, and this winter he was operated on to improve circulation in his legs. He had a good time at Ardmore the weekend before he died, and I want to thank all of those who have come by and wrote and called. John Criswell will run the trial at Mortlach just as we have for all these years. I will miss being there, but Booneville is home now.

Booneville, Ark. Lois Covington

* * *

A year later, June 9, 1994, an obituary for Lois appeared in the Field:

Lois Consuelo Elizondo was a beautiful senior at McAlester High School in 1926, a member of the honor society. She had moved to Oklahoma with her family from Puerto Rico where her father served as the Mexican consul.

She became secretary to a Federal bankruptcy judge, and in the early 1930s met a black-haired young man who aspired to be a professional baseball player. He worked part-time for a poultry company and once came calling in a truck loaded with turkeys.

Shortly, they became Mr. and Mrs. Leon Covington, and he soon quit baseball for bird dogs.

Bird dogs and field trials were the center of their lives for the next 50 years.

Cov trained at McAlester, then moved to Booneville, Ark., where he worked on the grounds that were home to the Southwestern Championship. They became fast friends of their neighbors, Hope and Army Evans, he a local attorney. The friendship endured.

The Covingtons made the major circuit of those days and eventually moved to Alabama, not far from Sedgefields where Clyde and Sybil Morton lived. The two ladies were best friends, and were among the very first to judge a field trial.

As Cov remembered the story, it was a Derby, "you know Derbies qualified dogs to run at the National and when it was over they didn't name a single dog. They said they weren't going to be responsible for anyone having to ride around up there three hours and watch what they'd seen.

"Lois rode lots in those days. I bought her a spotted stallion."

From Alabama it was back to Oklahoma and they were on the Stuart Ranch near Caddo for several years. Cov started the Oklahoma Puppy Classic, and the Bryan County Field Trial Club, Lois, as always, in charge of the book work.

In 1967, the Covingtons were instrumental in re-starting the Saskatchewan Open Championship at Mortlach, Saskatchewan, where Leon trained in the summer.

The pair had made the trip north more than 40 summers. They went for the last time in '82.

Lois was in charge of the drawings at the Mortlach City Building, and it could be one of the most interesting events on the program.

She and Cov lived in a house on Vic Eastmond's ranch which was used only in the summer. It had long been otherwise abandoned. She cooked in a shed-like room for whatever help they had – and it was considerable in the early years after they moved from Ailsbury. Water came from the well just off the front porch; a hand pump that invariably needed priming.

Two years ago, the Covingtons moved back "home" – to Booneville where they could be near the Evanses. Both Cov and Lois were in failing health, and, in May, 1983, Cov was found dead on the grounds where he had won so many field trial placements.

Lois had a difficult year without him. She already had health problems and they grew worse. In February she fell and suffered a broken hip. There was a long hospitalization and convalescence.

She needed all of the attention the Evanses could spare, and her ailing hip would often fail.

In a drawer at the end of the couch were three copies of Field & Stream. In a 1950 edition there was a long illustrated feature on Cov training dogs, a major how-to article. In a '51 edition there was another on the Covington Canada camp—the illustrations the best anyone would want to see. And a May, 1954, edition reported the National Championship, a half-page picture of Leon Covington and Ed Mack Farrior just ahead of the gallery starting Lone Survivor and Warhoop Jake in the callback that lasted nearly two hours.

There was a yellowed newspaper report of Cov's dogs winning all the places in the Hogan All-Age.

She was buried beside Cov, a simple graveside service with an eloquent eulogy by Kathy Matlock for the eight who sat in the metal funeral parlor chairs and thought of Lois—and Cov.

There were no survivors, save the memories of those who met them along the way.